Praise for *Deep Adaptation*

'The authors of this book have courage to recognise the reality of our time and face the uncomfortable facts of climate calamity. The theme of this book is indeed scary. But it's full of bright ideas for how to transmute both fear and difficulty into kind and wise ways of living and working. The thinkers, academics and activists who have contributed to this book embody the wisdom to adapt to this unprecedented catastrophe. They also show the practical ways and means to live and act with the imagination and resilience. Not everyone would agree to these radical ideas but everyone needs to know about them. So, I recommend this book to all.'

Satish Kumar, Editor Emeritus for *Resurgence & Ecologist*
and Founder of Schumacher College

'Collapse followed by transformation is a common way that complex systems evolve. Perhaps collapse of our high consumption, climate-destabilising society can lead to transformation towards a brighter human future. The Deep Adaptation framework outlined in this book is a helpful way to seek that transformation.'

Professor Will Steffen, Australian National University
Climate Change Institute

DEEP ADAPTATION

DEEP ADAPTATION

Navigating the Realities of Climate Chaos

Edited by Jem Bendell and Rupert Read

polity

First published in 2021 by Polity Press

Polity Press
65 Bridge Street
Cambridge CB2 1UR, UK

Polity Press
101 Station Landing
Suite 300
Medford, MA 02155, USA

ISBN-13: 978-1-5095-4683-1
ISBN-13: 978-1-5095-4684-8 (pb)

A catalogue record for this book is available from the British Library.

Names: Bendell, Jem, editor. | Read, Rupert J., 1966- editor.¬†
Title: Deep adaptation : navigating the realities of climate chaos / edited
    by Jem Bendell & Rupert Read.¬†
Description: Cambridge, UK ; Medford, MA : Polity Press, 2021. | Includes
    bibliographical references. | Summary: "A new agenda for how we can
    prepare for societal collapse in an age of climate chaos"-- Provided by
    publisher.¬†
Identifiers: LCCN 2020052406 (print) | LCCN 2020052407 (ebook) | ISBN
    9781509546831 (hardback) | ISBN 9781509546848 (paperback) | ISBN
    9781509546855 (epub)¬†
Subjects: LCSH: Climatic changes--Social aspects. | Climate change
    mitigation--Social aspects. | Climate change mitigation--Social aspects.
Classification: LCC QC903 .D443 2021¬† (print) | LCC QC903¬† (ebook) | DDC
    304.2/5--dc23
LC record available at https://lccn.loc.gov/2020052406
LC ebook record available at https://lccn.loc.gov/2020052407

Typeset in 10pt on 12pt Janson by
Servis Filmsetting Limited, Stockport, Cheshire
Printed and bound in the UK by TJ International Ltd

The publisher has used its best endeavours to ensure that the URLs for external websites referred to in this book are correct and active at the time of going to press. However, the publisher has no responsibility for the websites and can make no guarantee that a site will remain live or that the content is or will remain appropriate.

Every effort has been made to trace all copyright holders, but if any have been overlooked the publisher will be pleased to include any necessary credits in any subsequent reprint or edition.

For further information on Polity, visit our website:
politybooks.com

Contents

Acknowledgements

The editors thank Katie Carr for providing editorial support for this book and the Griffith Centre for Sustainable Enterprise (Griffith University, Australia), with its director Dr Rob Hales, for helping to finance that support. We also thank Atus Mariqueo-Russell for editorial help and each chapter contributor for responding courageously to our call to apply their hearts and minds to this difficult topic.

We also thank the Club of Rome for their enthusiasm for this book, which joins the vital and vast conversation they began in 1972 when they warned of societal collapse. Jorgen Randers helped us in the earliest stages of the planning. We hope that our focus in this book about preparing to soften the impact and harm of any and all such collapses will be a useful, though unfortunate and stressful, addition to their ongoing dialogue and policy initiatives.

Jem Bendell: I thank the many volunteers in the Deep Adaptation Forum around the world, most of whom I have never met in person and yet feel admiration and affection for. Your decision to step up and help people come together in new ways for new initiatives at this difficult time has felt like a balm for my soul. I also thank the people who have been important to my intellectual journey in recent years, including Katie Carr, Richard Little, Matthew Slater, Zori Tomova, Vanessa Andreotti and all the authors cited in chapter 5.

Rupert Read: I thank many colleagues in and beyond Extinction Rebellion: the journey of transformative and deep adaptations will be a defining one of the 2020s; thanks to the post-XR 'TrAd' group for helping me pathfind (especially Oona, April, Simon, Skeena). And I thank my academic colleagues (and next-door neighbours) Jo Clarke and Nick Brooks for invaluable discussions on the same topics: what starts in Merton Road doesn't stay in Merton Road. Thanks finally to the AHRC for grant support that helped provide some time and resources for me for this book.

About the Contributors

Jem Bendell, PhD, is a University of Cumbria professor and founder of the Deep Adaptation Forum (deepadaptation.info). As a researcher, educator and advisor, he specializes in leadership, communication, facilitation and currency innovation for deep adaptation to climate chaos. He authored the viral 'Deep Adaptation' paper, downloaded around a million times. He has worked for over 25 years on social and organizational change, in more than twenty countries, with business, voluntary organizations and political parties. With 100-plus publications, including five for the United Nations, and involvement in developing multistakeholder initiatives, he was recognized as a Young Global Leader by the World Economic Forum.

Tereza Čajkova has been working in the field of education for sustainable development, focusing on questions related to what kind of learning and skills we need to face unprecedented global challenges together. She is currently working towards a PhD at the University of British Columbia. Her research is oriented on extending theories of social innovation beyond prevalent paradigms to support more socially and ecologically accountable innovation practices.

Katie Carr, MA, is a facilitator of collaborative learning with seventeen years' experience within formal education, with communities and within organizations. Her practice focuses on bringing conscious, loving awareness to the relational space between people where we can explore what it means to be human and alive together. As Senior Facilitator for the Deep Adaptation Forum (DAF), Katie has led the development of a community of practice for facilitators. Katie teaches leadership at Masters level and also acts as a guide and coach to senior leaders in the voluntary, private and public sectors who are working on the climate crisis.

Gauthier Chapelle is a Belgian author, lecturer and in-Terre-dependent researcher in biomimicry and collapsology, as well as a father, naturalist, agricultural engineer and doctor in polar biology. He was one of the pioneers of biomimicry in Europe (2003) and of the Work that Reconnects, inspired by Joanna Macy (2010), which he still offers with Terr'Eveille. Since 2015, he encourages organizational and 'low-tech' biomimicry in anticipation of the civilization collapse, alongside his friends and co-authors Pablo Servigne ('Mutual aid, the other law of the jungle') and Raphaël Stevens ('Another end of the world is possible', with Pablo Servigne).

Jonathan Gosling is Emeritus Professor of Leadership at Exeter University. He is now an independent academic with roles in the Forward Institute, promoting responsible leadership in government, NGOs and business; and supporting the frontline leadership of HIV and malaria control programs in Africa. He represented UK universities at the Rio+20 UN Sustainability summit and contributes to the 'greening' of management education, e.g. as co-author of the textbook *Sustainable Business: A One Planet Approach* and co-founder of One Planet Education Networks (OPEN). He worked for many years as a community mediator, co-founded Coachingourselves.com and is a keen sailor.

Sean Kelly, PhD, is Professor of Philosophy, Cosmology and Consciousness at the California Institute of Integral Studies (CIIS). He is the author of *Becoming Gaia: On the Threshold of Planetary Initiation*; *Coming Home: The Birth and Transformation of the Planetary Era*; co-editor of *The Variety of Integral Ecologies: Nature, Culture, and Knowledge in the Planetary Era*; and co-translator of Edgar Morin's *Homeland Earth: A Manifesto for the New Millennium*. Along with his academic work, Sean teaches Taiji and is a facilitator of the group process the Work that Reconnects.

Joanna Macy, PhD, is a scholar of Buddhism, deep ecology and general systems theory and a respected voice in the movements for peace, justice and ecology. She is the root teacher of the Work that Reconnects and author of many articles and books, including *Coming Back to Life*; *World as Lover, World as Self*; *Active Hope* (with Chris Johnstone); *Mutual Causality in Buddhism and*

General Systems Theory; *Widening Circles: A Memoir*; and *In Praise of Mortality: Selections from Rainer Maria Rilke's Duino Elegies and Sonnets to Orpheus* (with Anita Barrows).

Vanessa de Oliveira Andreotti holds a Canada Research Chair in Race, Inequalities and Global Change at the Department of Educational Studies, University of British Columbia in Vancouver, Canada. Drawing on different critiques of colonialism and human exceptionalism, her research examines the interface between historical, systemic and ongoing forms of violence, and the material and existential dimensions of unsustainability within modernity. She is one of the founding members of the Gesturing Decolonial Futures Collective (decolonialfutures.net) and one of the initiators of the In Earth's Care Network of indigenous communities in Latin America.

Rupert Read is a professor of philosophy at the University of East Anglia. He is author of eleven books, including *This Civilisation is Finished* (2019) and *A Film-Philosophy of Ecology and Enlightenment* (2018). He is a former chair of Green House think tank, and a former Green Party of England and Wales councillor, spokesperson, European parliamentary candidate and national parliamentary candidate. He has written for the *Guardian*, the *Independent*, the *Ecologist* and a range of other newspapers and websites.

Skeena Rathor, a Sufi Kashmiri, helped by her three daughters, the family, the community of Stroud and the woodlands, spends time dancing between outward commitments. She works as a district councillor, co-founder of the Compassionate Stroud Project and co-founder of Extinction Rebellion, including the Co-Liberation and Power-fullness Project. Skeena has been teaching body-brain and heart-brain restoration work for 20 years, with a specialist focus on birth, mothering health, child development, breath, trauma and love – possessing thirteen certifications. Grief resulting from relationship losses has led Skeena to be a campaigner, activist and activator since the age of fifteen.

Daniel Rodary, an ecologist, initially studied emperor penguins and worked in the management of international scientific projects (International Council of Science, the Cousteau Society in Sudan) and as a guide-lecturer in polar regions (Antarctica,

Spitzbergen, Greenland). Since 2010, he has been a coordinator of reforestation projects with local farmers in Haïti, India and Mexico, as well as an organic farmer in France and then South India. Since 2010, he has given lectures on climate change, planetary boundaries and biomimicry, co-founded Deep Adaptation Auroville in South India and is now involved in Deep Adaptation France (*Adaptation radicale*).

Pablo Servigne is an agricultural engineer with a PhD in biology (Belgium). He quit the academic world in 2008 to become an author and lecturer. He is the author of many articles and books about collapse, transition, resilience, agroecology and mutual aid, and is now editor-in-chief of the French magazine *Yggdrasil*. With Raphaël Stevens, he coined the word 'collapsology' in 2015 for the transdisciplinary study of the collapse of our civilization and the biosphere.

Charlotte Simpson is in the final stage of an MSc in sustainable food and natural resources. Her current research focuses on sustainable diets, the significance of social and cultural influences on behaviour change, long-term maintenance of behaviour change and the role of education for social transformation in the face of climate breakdown.

Dino Siwek is an independent researcher from Brazil with a background in anthropology and social communication. His work focuses on the interactions between ecological crises and systemic violences and on experimental and counter-intuitive ways of learning that involve embodied practices as a way of finding deeper possibilities of being in and with the world. He is co-founder of the Terra Adentro project.

Matthew Slater builds and runs open-source software for community currencies. His activism touches on various other topics, ranging from researching monetary theory to community building to the politics of software. He co-authored the Money & Society MOOC with Jem Bendell and has contributed to a handful of academic papers.

Sharon Stein is an assistant professor in the Department of Educational Studies at the University of British Columbia. Her research brings critical and decolonial perspectives to the study and practice of internationalization, decolonization, and sustainability in higher education. Through this work, she engages the challenges, complexities and possibilities of addressing the interrelated ecological, cognitive, affective, relational, political and economic dimensions of local and global (in)justice.

Raphaël Stevens is an independent researcher, author and lecturer. He studied business and environmental management before taking an MSc in holistic science at the Schumacher College and Plymouth University. In 2006, he co-founded Greenloop, a consultancy offering support and guidance in circular economy. Associate researcher at the Momentum Institute (FR) since 2011, he is co-author of several books, including *Comment tout peut s'effondrer* (Seuil, 2015, with P. Servigne), translated into six languages (published by Polity in 2020 as *How Everything Can Collapse*) and *Another End of the World is Possible* (Polity, 2021, with P. Servigne and G. Chapelle).

Rene Suša is a postdoctoral researcher in the Department of Educational Studies at the University of British Columbia. His research focuses on critiques of modernity and the modern subject based on postcolonial, decolonial and psychoanalytical thought. More specifically, he is interested in the educational challenges of generatively engaging with the unconscious modern/colonial desires, projections and affective investments that prevent us from expanding our imaginative, cognitive and relational capacities.

Adrian Tait worked for 26 years as a psychoanalytic psychotherapist, also teaching and supervising MRCPsych trainees in Devon. In 2009, he undertook a visiting fellowship at the University of the West of England to help develop and coordinate a global psycho-social response to the climate crisis. This led to the formation in 2013 of the Climate Psychology Alliance (CPA). Adrian has written extensively for the CPA and is active in bringing climate psychology perspectives to a wider audience.

Charlotte von Bülow, PhD, is a senior lecturer in leadership at the Bristol Business School, University of the West of England. She is the Founder of the Crossfields Institute Group (UK) – a state-recognized awarding organization for integrative education, a higher education institute and a consultancy. Charlotte has worked as an educator all her adult life; as a social entrepreneur, consultant and executive coach, she has served individuals, organizations and communities the world over. Her research and publications focus on integrative approaches to education, leadership in uncertainty and complex times and attentional ethics.

Introduction

What Next, Now That the Limits Have Been Breached?

Jem Bendell and Rupert Read

Are you confused and concerned about what seems like the disruption or even breakdown of normal life? Do you worry about becoming stuck, not knowing what to do? Do you want to explore with others how to respond creatively at this difficult time? If so, then you share that intention with the contributors to this book. Until recently, most people in modern societies have not had much reason or opportunity to explore what an anticipation of greater societal disruption – or even collapse – might mean for their life choices. It has been a taboo subject, policed by the argument that to even discuss it would be unhelpful to individuals and society. To have any level of anticipation of societal breakdown or collapse, whether from a range of environmental, economic, political or technological factors, has been labelled as pessimism, alarmism, doomism, fatalism or defeatism. Such negative dismissals can discourage us from engaging in this topic any further. Unfortunately, such avoidance could lose us all precious time to explore what can be done and learned at this difficult moment, especially if our aim is to reduce harm while saving more of society and the natural world. It might mean we postpone the opportunity to rethink what is most important to us and align the rest of our lives with that. Therefore, we consider it would be defeatist to not even begin exploring what we can do to help in the face of massive societal disruption.

That is why we believe it is time for a book that discusses various implications of anticipating societal collapse. *Deep Adaptation* is an agenda and framework for responding to the potential, probable or inevitable collapse of industrial consumer societies, due to the direct and indirect impacts of human-caused climate change and environmental degradation. With the term 'societal collapse', we mean an uneven ending of industrial consumer modes of sustenance, shelter, health, security, pleasure, identity and meaning. Rather than an environmental, economic or political collapse, the word 'societal' is important as these uneven endings pervade society and challenge our place within it. The term 'collapse' does not necessarily mean that suddenness is likely but rather implies a form of breakdown in systems that is comprehensive and cannot be reversed to what it was before. The word 'deep' is intended to contrast the agenda with mainstream approaches to adaptation to climate impacts (Klein et al. 2015) by going deeper into the causes and potential responses within ourselves, our organizations and societies. People who engage in dialogue and initiative for deep adaptation believe that societal collapse in most or all countries of the world is likely, inevitable or already unfolding. Typically, such people believe that they will experience this disruption themselves or have already begun to do so, while recognizing that the disruptions may be first and worst in the global South. Deep adaptation describes the inner and outer, personal and collective, responses to either the anticipation or experience of societal collapse, worsened by the direct or indirect impacts of climate change.

The vulnerability of our normal ways of life was highlighted in 2020 when a virus triggered a series of cascading effects beyond its initial health impacts. To begin with, there were shortages of medicines, protective gear and food, then a slowdown of economic activity, domestic political upheavals, diplomatic and geopolitical conflicts, and the creation of large amounts of national debt to reduce, or postpone, economic shock. The sprouting of volunteer-led mutual aid in many locations is an indicator of the capacity of people to respond positively. While Covid-19 has posed a stress test for the globalized economy, it is also a stark reminder of what deeply matters in our daily lives and is a real-time dress rehearsal for future disasters and psychological unease (Read 2020: ch. 26; Gray 2020). When some people consider societal collapse to be an abstract and theoretical matter, it is worth noting that the United Nations has warned us that outbreaks of coronaviruses, including potentially ones more serious than Covid-19, are more likely because of both environmental destruction and climate change (United Nations 2020). That analysis means that disruptions from the indirect impacts of climate change are already being felt by most societies around the world.

To assess the probability and processes of societal collapse is a complex endeavour, as described by expert 'collapsologists' in chapter 3 of this book. Such assessments can draw on many disciplines of scholarship, including sociology, economics, politics, psychology, philosophy and agronomy, as well as composite fields such as climate science, environmental studies, futures studies, catastrophic risks, emergency management and disaster reduction (Servigne and Stevens 2020). This complexity therefore means that any commentary on the likelihood of societal collapse will derive from the specialism, mentality, identity and lived experience of the scholar. Most scholars are not experiencing the climate-worsened hunger and displacement that hundreds of millions of people are at the time of our writing (FAO 2018). Despite the inevitable bias towards normality within the many fields of scholarship that could give us an assessment of the likelihood of societal collapse, in recent years more experts have come forward with warnings. One of the fields where such warnings are now coming from is climate science (Moses 2020).

In November 2019, seven leading climate scientists published a review in the journal *Nature* which said that a collapse of society may be inevitable because nine of the fifteen known global climate tipping points that regulate the state of the planet may have already been activated (Lenton et al. 2019). Soon after, an opinion from five scientists on our climate situation was published in the journal *Biosciences* and signed by more than 11,000 scientists worldwide as a warning to humanity: 'The climate crisis has arrived and is accelerating faster than most scientists expected . . . It is more severe than anticipated, threatening natural ecosystems and the fate of humanity . . .' (Ripple et al. 2019). The reasons why climate change is so dangerous to humanity are described in chapter 2, and the reasons why climate scientists have been conservative in their statement of that risk are explained in chapter 1.

In 2020, two hundred scientists warned of 'global systemic collapse' becoming likely due to the way different climate and environmental stressors can interact and amplify each other. They explained that the true situation is not being understood or communicated well enough because 'many scientists and policy-makers are embedded in institutions that are used to thinking and acting on isolated risks, one at a time' (Future Earth 2020). Research analysts that are experienced in integrating multiple forms of information on multiple risks are to be found in the financial sector. An internal report by analysts from the largest bank in the United States, JP Morgan, is therefore relevant to the question of whether humanity will make the changes to avoid disaster. They assessed that

> to meet the Paris 2°C objective on the global temperature ... would require the immediate elimination of 34% of the global coal-fired production capacity. The cost would involve not only the premature scrapping of these coal-fired power stations but also the increased investment in renewables. The end result could be energy shortages and higher electricity prices for consumers. It isn't going to happen. (*Guardian* 2020)

Although we can and must increase efforts for significant reductions in carbon emissions and effective natural drawdown of carbon from the atmosphere, the recent science and analysis should not be ignored because it is too painful to consider. Unfortunately, new climate models are predicting much greater climate change than past models did (Johnson 2019). Already we are witnessing temperature changes in air and ocean that are at the extreme end of previous predictions, and with impacts on ecosystems that are in advance of what was anticipated (Nisbet et al. 2019). For instance, in May 2020 the previous 12 months were 1.3 degrees warmer than pre-industrial temperatures.[1] Such rapid climate change is a massive stress on ecological and human systems and is not something that humans can stop entirely. We must try to slow it down, but our efforts might not be very successful. Dangerous climate change is therefore in one important sense an unsolvable predicament which in our view will probably, or inevitably, lead to the collapse of industrial consumer societies.

---

[1] https://climate.copernicus.eu/surface-air-temperature-may-2020

It is for this reason that we consider it useful in the title of this book to describe the instability we are creating as 'climate chaos' and that we will need to learn to 'navigate' varying levels of that chaos, rather than being able to 'solve' the 'problem' outright. For this is more than a problem, more even than a 'wicked' one. It is a tragedy and an ongoing series of disasters that provide *a new condition for humankind* along with the rest of life on earth (Foster 2015).

Some communities are already experiencing breakdowns due to direct or indirect impacts of climate change, as well as issues relating to epidemics, the failures of capitalism, and racial inequality, to name but a few stressors on societies (Future Earth 2020). More research is being done on assessing when and where societal breakdowns may occur, though that is very difficult to predict and such work could become a distraction from inquiry into the root causes and into rapid meaningful action. With this book, we wish to contribute to the field of inquiry and action that starts from an anticipation of societal collapse. In other words: what if we were actually to look the very real prospect of such collapse in the face, rather than always shying away from it or only attempting to prevent it? What might happen? What might we feel? What might shift? How might our plans and struggles – including perhaps those intended to mitigate the chaos – be transformed or energized?

We know first-hand how it is psychologically challenging to reach the conclusion that there will be massive disruption, or even collapse, of societies around the world, including the ones we live in. Not only is it difficult to allow this outlook into one's awareness, it is difficult to live with it because to anticipate societal collapse means we feel personally vulnerable as well as afraid for the future of people dear to us. That psychological distress occurs even before we experience specific disruptions from the direct and indirect impacts of a degrading environment and growing public anxieties. The matter of emotional well-being is important within the deep adaptation agenda, as explored in chapter 4 on insights from psychology, as well as in chapter 8 on some of the psycho-spiritual implications. There are particular concerns about children and young people. We are acutely aware of how young people are growing up into a climate-disturbed future. For us, real solidarity with them must include efforts at practical and psychological adaptation to that future, rather than suppressing this difficult agenda. Some of the initial implications for education and schools are discussed in chapter 10.

The concept of deep adaptation and an associated framework for dialogue was created by the transdisciplinary sociologist and co-editor of this book, Professor Jem Bendell. It became popular in a paper released by the University of Cumbria in the United Kingdom (Bendell 2018). That paper was downloaded around a million times within a couple of years and influenced many people to join and lead climate activist groups (Green 2019). To support this movement, the Deep Adaptation Forum was launched in April 2019 to freely connect people who believe that deep adaptation provides a useful framework for them to respond to this predicament.[2] The Forum explains an intention to embody and enable loving responses to our predicament where we can help each other prepare in ways that may reduce harm, especially by reducing conflict and trauma. It is founded on a collective leadership philosophy, where generative dialogue is both a key modality and aim (Bendell, Sutherland and Little 2017). To help with that, Deep Adaptation involves a framework of four questions, providing people with a way of exploring those potential changes together. Outlined in chapter 2, they are called the 4Rs. What do we most value that we want to keep and how? That is a question of resilience. What could we let go of so as not to make matters worse? That is a question of relinquishment. What could we bring back to help us in these difficult times? That is a question of restoration. With what and with whom shall we make peace as we awaken to our common mortality? That is a question of reconciliation.

We continue to meet people who believe an anticipation of societal collapse is a credible perspective but who think it is unhelpful to articulate that or work from that basis. Our experience has been the opposite. After concluding that collapse is likely or inevitable, many people become very engaged in social and political action to slow dangerous climate change, reduce impacts, help each other and reverse injustices (Bendell and Cave 2020). Additionally, the more time we have to try to adapt, the

[2] See www.deepadaptation.info

more likely we can hold societies together to keep one another safe while cutting and drawing down carbon emissions (Read 2020a, 2020b; Foster et al. 2019).

Some of the resistance to deep adaptation may arise because it represents a fundamental break with the international policy paradigm of the past 30 years. Adopted at the UN in 1987, the concept of sustainable development suggests that it is possible to maintain capitalism while integrating concerns about the environment and society (Foster 2019). The deep adaptation perspective sees the pace and scale of dangerous levels of climate change and ecological degradation to be so fast that neither a reform of capitalism nor of modern society is realistic. Therefore, deep adaptation is a form of 'post-sustainability' thinking (ibid.). However, the concept does not equate societal collapse with 'the end of the world' or with near-term human extinction. It does not imply lessening our efforts at carbon cuts (mitigation) and drawdown (natural sequestration) but implies that efforts on those aims within the current system must pragmatically be considered likely to continue to fail to significantly reduce atmospheric levels of greenhouse gases; so now we must prepare for societal breakdown and ultimate collapse. If we fail to prepare for such failure, then we are preparing to fail ourselves and our children even more.

By inviting attention to whether an assumption of the continuation of modern society is tenable, a deep adaptation perspective suggests rethinking mainstream approaches to climate change adaptation (CCA). The most resonance with mainstream climate adaptation is in the field of ideas and practices becoming known as 'transformative adaptation'. Such approaches anticipate the need for systemic change in modes of production, trade and lifestyle to both reduce carbon and be less reliant on the stability of existing ecosystems (Coulter, Serrao-Neumann and Coiacetto 2019). In future, we anticipate a coming together of transformative and deep adaptation as a complement to bolder attempts at carbon cuts and drawdown.

In any future dialogue between people working with different analyses of the predicament we are in, it will be important to recognize how 'collapse anticipation' produces a distinctly original paradigm for reflection, learning and action. So much of what people have hitherto taken for granted can be questioned.

Therefore, the chapters in this book are merely illustrative of an agenda which offers no simple answers but hopefully provides ways of reaching meaningful answers for your own context. In Part I, the predicament of facing societal collapse is presented in three chapters. We explain in chapter 1 how, for decades, the field of climate science has been conservative in its assessment of the risks facing humanity. The situation is now far worse than tends to be reported in individual climate studies or by the Intergovernmental Panel on Climate Change (IPCC). In chapter 2, a revised version of the original deep adaptation paper by Dr Jem Bendell presents the case for human-triggered climate change having become unavoidably dangerous and explains why the contemporary environmental movement and profession have remained in denial of that reality. The original paper was intended for people researching, educating and practising within the corporate sustainability field, and the chapter retains the original focus and style. In chapter 3, Dr Pablo Servigne and a group of scholars who focus on the science of societal collapse, or 'collapsology', provide an overview of the state of knowledge to make the case that collapse anticipation is a credible starting point for both research and policy development.

In Part II, the 'shifts in being' that can occur – and be supported – as we anticipate societal collapse are explored in five chapters. In chapter 4, psychologist and co-founder of the Climate Psychology Alliance Dr Adrian Tait describes the ways in which the psychotherapy profession must – and is beginning to – change in response to growing public eco-distress. In chapter 5, Jem Bendell tackles the subject of how we can avoid making our bad situation worse by sharing insights on the ideology that he believes is at the root of our predicament. He explains how this destructive ideology has been mainstreamed and maintained by the monetary system. A similar theme is developed further in chapter 6 by Rene Suša and her colleagues, who work on developing and articulating their analysis of indigenous persons in the global predicament. They argue that people have become addicted to patterns of thought which will hamper our abilities to respond to collapse, and they offer some ideas to help break those addictions. How to apply these critiques in new ways of organizing interactions on deep adaptation is important. Therefore, in chapter 7, the senior facilitator of the Deep Adaptation Forum joins Jem Bendell to explain the rationale and some modalities for facilitating connection and conversation about our predicament. This part of the book is completed in chapter 8 by environmental philosopher Joanna Macy and her colleague Professor Sean Kelly. In a more informal and heartfelt discussion of the topic, they draw on ancient wisdom to provide some reflections on how we might discover strength during the difficult times ahead.

In Part III, some of the 'shifts in doing' that occur when people anticipate societal collapse are explored in four chapters. In chapter 9, renowned leadership scholar Professor Jonathan Gosling explores possible ways of leading in response to increasing turbulence in society. He explains how traditional understandings and enactments of leadership will be unhelpful. Instead, leadership of adaptation is diverse and sometimes hardly recognizable as leadership. One of its key effects, he argues, is enabling equanimity in anxiety-provoking circumstances. In chapter 10, education specialist Dr Charlotte von Bülow explores new approaches to schooling and education that are necessary in the face of the climate emergency. In chapter 11, by drawing on his experience as a spokesperson and political advisor with the activist group Extinction Rebellion, as well as his work as a political philosopher, Professor Rupert Read shares his ideas on the future of politics and activism in the face of societal collapse. He explains how the systemic economic and political drivers of the ecological and climate crisis mean that a radical and transformative political agenda is essential for the future of deep adaptation. In chapter 12, community currency expert Matthew Slater and Extinction Rebellion founder member Skeena Rathor explain why and how 'relocalization' of economies and societies is an important part of the response to climate chaos. They describe how future relocalization efforts could benefit from incorporating a co-liberation philosophy and supporting international action for policies that enable localization and climate justice.

As a first edited collection on this huge topic, we realize that the coverage of issues and the diversity of voices will be insufficient. We are particularly aware that at the time of writing, like most readers of this book, we are not involved in high-intensity situations of societal disruption and collapse. Over time, we intend to both hear and support more diverse voices and participate in more practical solidarity for people who are suffering the consequences of societal disruption and collapse. Therefore, in the concluding chapter, we discuss a range of live issues within the emerging field of deep adaptation.

As you read this book, it is likely you will be witnessing situations where lifestyles, livelihoods and outlooks are being disrupted. Those disruptions will probably be reported in most mass media without foregrounding our degrading environment. Looking behind the headlines, there is credible evidence that all manner of disruptions, including rising prices, coronaviruses, financial instability, mental illness, displaced persons and xenophobia, are being made worse by the declining health and stability of our natural world. Unfortunately, the Club of Rome was right. In 1972, their bestselling report on the *Limits to Growth* predicted that humanity would be experiencing difficulties now due to our impact on the natural world (Meadows et al. 1972). Unless more people today make the connections between the many difficulties faced and ask questions about how modern humans have generated them, societies will lose the opportunity to learn and change. We intend this book to help you make fuller sense of the many disruptions around you so you can invite your friends, colleagues and community members to join you in reconsidering the fundamentals of our societies and our relationship with the natural world. Whatever happens, the opportunity to learn from this unfolding global disaster is still ours to seize.

References

Bendell, J. (2018) 'Deep Adaptation: A Map for Navigating Climate Tragedy'. IFLAS Occasional Paper 2. Available at: http://www.lifeworth.com/deepadaptation.pdf

Bendell, J. (2019) 'Doom and Bloom? Adapting Deeply to Likely Collapse', in C. Farrell, A. Green, S. Knights and W. Skeaping (eds), *This is Not a Drill: Extinction Rebellion Handbook*, 1st edn. London: Penguin Random House.

Bendell, J. and Cave, D. (2020) 'Does Anticipating Societal Collapse Motivate Pro-Social Behaviours?' IFLAS website. Available at: http://iflas.blogspot.com/2020/06/does-anticipating-societal-collapse.html

Bendell, J., Sutherland, N. and Little, R. (2017) 'Beyond Unsustainable Leadership: Critical Social Theory for Sustainable Leadership'. *Sustainability Accounting, Management and Policy Journal* 8(4): 418–44.

Coulter, L., Serrao-Neumann, S. and Coiacetto, E. (2019) 'Climate Change Adaptation Narratives: Linking Climate Knowledge and Future Thinking'. *Futures* 111: 57–70.

FAO (Food and Agriculture Organization) (2018) *Disasters Causing Billions in Agricultural Losses, with Drought Leading the Way*. Press release, 15 March.

Foster, J. (2015) *After Sustainability*. Abingdon: Earthscan/Routledge.

Foster, J. (ed.) (2019) *Post-Sustainability: Tragedy and Transformation*. London: Routledge.

Foster, J. et al. (2019) *Facing Up to Climate Reality*. London: London Publishing Partnership/Green House.

Future Earth (2020) 'Our Future on Earth 2020'. Available at: www.futureearth.org/publications/our-future-on-earth

Gray, J. (2020 'Why This Crisis is a Turning Point in History'. Available at: https://www.newstatesman.com/international/2020/04/why-crisis-turning-point-history

Green, M. (2019) 'Extinction Rebellion: Inside the New Climate Resistance'. *Financial Times Magazine*. Available at: https://www.ft.com/content/9bcb1bf8-5b20-11e9-9dde-7aedca0a081a

Guardian (2020) 'JP Morgan Economists Warn Climate Crisis is Threat to Human Race'. Available at: https://www.theguardian.com/environment/2020/feb/21/jp-morgan-economists-warn-climate-crisis-threat-human-race

Johnson, J. (2019) '"Terrifying" New Climate Models Warn of 6–7°C of Warming by 2100 if Emissions Not Slashed'. Common Dreams. Available at: https://www.commondreams.org/news/2019/09/17/terrifying-new-climate-models-warn-6-7degc-warming-2100-if-emissions-not-slashed

Klein, R. J. T. et al. (2015) 'Adaptation Opportunities, Constraints, and Limits', in C. B. Field (ed.), *Climate Change 2014: Impacts, Adaptation and Vulnerability: Part A: Global and Sectoral Aspects*, 1st edn. New York: Cambridge University Press.

Lenton, T. M. et al. (2019) 'Climate Tipping Points – Too Risky to Bet Against: The Growing Threat of Abrupt and Irreversible Climate Changes Must Compel Political and Economic Action on Emissions'. *Nature* 575: 592–5.

Meadows, D. H., Meadows, D. L., Randers, J. and Behrens, W. W. (1972) *The Limits to Growth*. New York: Universe Books.

Moses, A. (2020) '"Collapse of Civilisation is the Most Likely Outcome": Top Climate Scientists'. Voice of Action. Available at: https://voiceofaction.org/collapse-of-civilisation-is-the-most-likely-outcome-top-climate-scientists/

Nisbet, E. G. et al. (2019) 'Very Strong Atmospheric Methane Growth in the Four Years 2014–2017: Implications for the Paris Agreement'. *Global Biogeochemical Cycles* 33(3): 318–42. Available at: https://doi. org/10.1029/2018GB006009

Read, R. (2020a) 'Theses on the Coronavirus Crisis', in Samuel Alexander (ed.), *Extinction Rebellion: Insights from the Inside*. Melbourne: Simplicity Institute Publishing. Available at: https://249897.e-junkie. com/product/1668648

Read, R. (2020b) 'The Coronavirus Gives Humanity One Last Chance – but for What Exactly?' Compass online. Available at: https://www. compassonline.org.uk/the-coronavirus-gives-humanity-one-last-chan ce-but-for-what-exactly/

Ripple, W. J., Wolf, C., Newsome, T. M., et al. (2019) 'World Scientists' Warning of a Climate Emergency'. *BioScience* 70(1): 8–12. Available at: https://doi.org/10.1093/biosci/biz088

Servigne, P. and Stevens, R. (2020) *How Everything Can Collapse*. Cambridge: Polity Press.

United Nations (2020) 'Unite Human, Animal and Environmental Health to Prevent the Next Pandemic – UN Report'. Press release, 6 July. Available at: https://www.unenvironment.org/news-and-stories/ press-release/unite-human-animal-and-environmental-health-prevent -next-pandemic-un

Part I

The Predicament

1

What Climate Science Can and Cannot Tell Us About Our Predicament

Jem Bendell and Rupert Read

Where we are after 125 years of climate science

Climate science was probably born in 1896 with the first, and still valid, calculation of how much the earth would warm if atmospheric CO_2 content were to double from pre-industrial values (Arrhenius 2009 [1896]). Given the means of the day, without the use of electronic computers, the Swedish physicist Svante Arrhenius, famous for his contributions to thermodynamics and the understanding of chemical reactions, calculated that the earth would warm by about 4°C. His value still lies within the range of modern estimates, produced by hugely complicated computer models (Slingo 2017). Arrhenius even calculated that regions near the poles would warm much more than those near the equator, something that is still seen as a major finding of climate science.

Awareness of humanity's vulnerability to changes in climate was high at the close of the nineteenth century. Arrhenius's native Scandinavia and much of northern Europe had only recently come out of the Little Ice Age, a cold period that had led to frequent crop failure and starvation (Lee 2009). His hope was therefore that increasing amounts of 'carbonic acid' in the air – atmospheric carbon dioxide – would bring about better weather and increased crop yields for the colder regions of the earth.

Fast forward one and a quarter centuries, and the predicted climate heating has become obvious to almost everyone (WMO

2019). Even if we did not have the benefits of modern climate science, we would still be able to recognize that we are in a situation never seen by humanity since modern civilization started with the onset of agriculture. Essentially nineteenth-century technologies such as thermometers, the collection of data on emissions of carbon-containing fuels, in combination with Arrhenius's science, already tell us a complete story: while rates of carbon dioxide emissions from human activities have been rising more or less exponentially (Global Carbon Project 2020), with no signs that this will change any time soon (Betts et al. 2020; Le Quéré et al. 2020), the earth is warming at an accelerating rate (NOAA 2020a). The climate system seems to be out of control, and human activity is the cause.

Human interest in understanding the geological past has created a different branch of climate science a long time ago, now called paleo-climatology. On its own, paleo-climatology can already tell us a compelling story of where we are and further help us understand the scale of our calamity. By drilling deep holes into Antarctic ice and analysing the composition of tiny bubbles found in them, researchers have been able to construct a continuous record of atmospheric carbon dioxide going back 800,000 years (Masson-Delmotte et al. 2010). The data show that CO_2 levels have fluctuated between around 180 parts per million (ppm) during ice ages and 280 ppm during warm periods. Only once did they briefly increase slightly above 300 ppm. At the time of writing, the last estimate of global mean CO_2 stood at 415 ppm, with an annual growth rate of almost 3 ppm over the last five years (NOAA 2020b). The last time atmospheric CO_2 was about as high as now was around three million years ago, during the Middle Pliocene (Lunt et al. 2008). Even that was only a temporary excursion, and we have to go back a staggering 25 million years to find values exceeding 500 ppm (Pagani et al. 2005), a value that at current trends we will reach in about 30 years.

When a kettle is switched on, the water in it does not heat up instantaneously, but there is a delay. The same happens with the earth's climate: according to the International Panel on Climate Change (IPCC 2019a), 90 per cent of the heat from the enhanced greenhouse effect is absorbed by the oceans' water. This means that the warming we have seen so far lags behind the steep rise in atmospheric carbon dioxide levels, and that even if we suddenly managed to stop the rise, warming will continue (Huntingford, Williamson and Nijsse 2020). Earth's surface is now over 1°C warmer than during the late nineteenth century (NOAA 2020a), which is comparable to or slightly warmer than during the last geological warm period between 10,000 and 5,000 years ago (Marcott et al. 2013). But during that time the warming was caused by changes in the way the earth circles and wobbles around the sun, with the result that tropical lands were slightly cooler than today. Nowadays, the (over)heating effect is seen universally across the globe, and as such differs decidedly from any climate fluctuations since the end of the last ice age more than 10,000 years ago (Barbuzano 2019; Neukom et al. 2019).

Currently the enhanced greenhouse effect is created only to about two-thirds by CO_2 and one third by other gases, of which about half by methane.[1] Countering this warming to a certain extent are several other human-caused effects, notably from atmospheric pollution through aerosols, which cause some cooling (Myhre et al. 2013). These cooling effects probably approximately cancel out the warming effect of the non-CO_2 greenhouse gases. CO_2, however, is by far the most important greenhouse gas because its lifetime vastly exceeds almost all of the other greenhouse gases or aerosols. A question of substantial theoretical value is what would happen if we not only prevented a further rise of CO_2 but stopped all emissions of CO_2 and other greenhouse gases tomorrow. Because the oceans and land tend to take up more than half of human-made CO_2 emissions (Global Carbon Project 2020), such an instantaneous net-zero balance of man-made carbon fluxes would lead to some drawdown of CO_2 by natural sinks, and a lowering of atmospheric CO_2 levels. The extent of the drawdown, however, is by no means understood and could easily be overestimated. Forests are responsible for a large part of that sink (Global Carbon Project 2020), but are increasingly being fragmented and damaged (Grantham et al. 2020). Some recent research also suggests that we already observe a declining efficiency of the sinks (Wang et al. 2020). Furthermore, even if such lowering occurs, it may not lead to a cessation of heating: because of the possible acceleration of

[1] https://www.esrl.noaa.gov/gmd/aggi/aggi.html

overheating once the 'global dimming effect' (from aerosols) is reduced (Xu, Ramanathan and Victor 2018); and because of vicious climate feedbacks that may already be underway (Lenton et al. 2019).

How much more overheat will result if CO_2 emissions alone stopped depends on both how rapidly the gas is removed from the atmosphere, and on the long-term climate response to the remaining CO_2 level. Model results (Matthews and Zickfeld 2012) indicate that in such a scenario, two-thirds of the human-caused excess CO_2 – i.e. above the pre-industrial level of 280 ppm – would still remain in the atmosphere after 190 years. For the case of stopping emissions in 2020 at a level of 415 ppm, this translates to more than 370 ppm by the year 2200. The earth during that time would continue to warm, but probably only by a few tenths of a degree. If all other greenhouse gas and aerosol emissions also stopped, the result might well be similar. However, the assumption that it *would* be excludes at least two further possibilities – possible stronger than expected carbon cycle feedback that we cannot reliably quantify, leading to higher than expected CO_2 levels (Lenton et al. 2019); and the possibility of a higher long-term sensitivity of the earth's temperature to CO_2 (Bjordal et al. 2020).

Because of the limitations of models, a more prudent approach is to derive climate sensitivity from past climates. Most commonly, this is based on the temperature and CO_2 changes during ice-age/warm-period fluctuations (Hansen et al. 2013). Results based on this approach generally support the model results (Sherwood et al. 2020). The problem, however, is that the earth is already in a different state from any time during those glacial cycles. Climate sensitivity could be higher in a warmer state due to positive climate system feedbacks, or tipping mechanisms, not yet quantified, which is the basis of the deeply alarming 'Hothouse Earth' hypothesis (Steffen et al. 2018). Support for this hypothesis comes from estimates for the Pliocene warm period, when CO_2 was between 365 and 415 ppm and temperatures about 3°C warmer than during the pre-industrial era (Pagani et al. 2010; Sherwood et al. 2020). According to those data – from the last time earth was in a similar climate state to now – an immediate stop of CO_2 emissions would still lead to substantial warming after today: about another 1°C for the higher end of the CO_2 estimate for the Pliocene, and more than 2°C at the lower end.[2]

The mechanisms that may have led to such a high climate sensitivity are unknown, but there is some evidence that Arctic sea-ice feedback could have contributed. It is possible that even if we stopped emitting CO_2 now, we could still experience an ice-free Arctic in the near future that could lock in significant warming for decades to come because of additional energy absorbed by the ice-free ocean in the long Arctic summer days. In the latest round of climate model simulations, those models that correctly simulate past sea-ice loss tend to have a higher climate sensitivity than usually assumed. Remarkably, even models driven by an extremely low-emissions scenario, approaching a stop-now scenario, still show an ice-free Arctic before 2050 (SIMIP Community 2020). The principal mechanism here is that even at declining CO_2 concentrations, excess heat stored in the oceans will only decline very slowly (Solomon et al. 2010).

It is important to stress that the scenario just discussed is largely speculative and only serves to illustrate how far we have already proceeded on a route to irreversibly altering our planet's climate state. Computer simulations of possible future climate states using certain scenarios of greenhouse gas emissions can be used to gain a general impression of how this trend might continue – as there is still no evidence of a lowered CO_2 level due to climate policy (Knorr 2019; Le Quéré et al. 2020).

A high-profile publication by a group of US scientists (Burke et al. 2018) confirms that we are indeed in the process of driving our climate system well into uncharted territory. Different to the approach followed by the IPCC (Hoegh-Guldberg et al. 2018), the group did not try to assess the impacts of projected changes directly by assessing impacts of past changes or using computer models. Instead, they compared expected climate warming patterns derived from model simulations with *what we know* from the

---

[2] The above 370 ppm CO_2 level would translate to about 3°C overall heating if we assume Pliocene CO_2 to be close to the lower estimate, 365 ppm, or 2°C further heating as we have already reached 1°C. At the high end of the estimate, 415 ppm, we assume that 415 – 280 =135 ppm excess CO_2 would lead to 3°C warming, but 370 – 280 = 90 ppm excess CO_2 to 90/135*3 = 2°C total, or 1°C additional warming.

geological past. They concluded that, at even 'moderate' degrees of warming, the climate in large parts of the planet will not resemble anything seen anywhere on earth since at least the onset of agricultural civilization. Instead, the combination of extreme heat and humidity due to be encountered in large parts of the world will have their closest analogue in deep time. In the case of a rapid and unprecedented decarbonization of the world economy, climate is expected to eventually stabilize at a state most closely resembling the already-discussed Mid-Pliocene warm period, some 3–5 million years ago. In a much more likely higher-emissions scenario, however, large parts of the earth will revert to a climate state last seen 'just' – in geological terms – after the demise of the dinosaurs: the early Eocene, some 50 million years ago.

This scary scenario is not all, because it only considers the start and end point of warming, but not the path on which we get there. If, within a few generations, we turn back the earth's geological CO_2 levels by tens of millions of years, then the *rapidity* of this change must surely have an impact on the way climate heating will play out. Unfortunately, this rate exceeds anything we know of from the deep geological past (Zeebe, Ridgwell and Zachos 2016), and therefore we cannot know in what ways dangerous anthropogenic climate change will occur in the coming decades. Which in itself is worrying (Read and O'Riordan 2017a). What is known, however, is that the large swings in temperature between ice ages and warm periods, bringing about temperature changes of up to 6°C peak to peak (Hansen et al. 2013), did not happen gradually – as the climate model runs underlying the above study suggest – but in bursts and bouts (Masson-Delmotte et al. 2005). Those climate oscillations were approximately as rapid as the warming we are seeing today and were created by various climate feedbacks, or tipping points. Then, about 10,000 years ago, a much more stable climate established itself. Some scholars argue that before this point, agriculture was impossible due to rapid climate fluctuations, but afterwards more or less unavoidable (Fagan 2004; Staubwasser and Weiss 2006).

In a recent commentary, prominent scientists have warned that tipping points and feedbacks similar to those that made the climate hostile to agriculture may have already been set in motion by the rapid increase in CO_2 levels (Lenton et al. 2019). During times of change, rapid collapse rather than gradual change is quite common for both ecosystems (Cooper, Willcock and Dearing 2020; Williams and Lenton 2010) and societies (Fagan 2008; Lee 2009). This suggests a triple threat to human civilization: agriculture has never existed in a strongly fluctuating climate; it also has never existed in climate states resembling distant geological warm period; and complex systems, such as human societies, can collapse even more rapidly than the ongoing speed of climate warming.

Recognizing the severity of the threat and following on from increasingly vocal and civilly disobedient climate protesters, several countries and countless organizations – from local councils to universities – have recently declared a state of climate emergency. Among those is the European Parliament, the first parliamentary representative of a major global emitter of greenhouse gases. Unfortunately, if this state of alertness exists, it has not been followed up by actions. Human emissions of CO_2, which had just started to pick up during the time of Arrhenius, continue to rise, apart from a decline due to the recent pandemic likely to be temporary (Le Quéré et al. 2020). Continuing investments in fossil fuel exploration and production (Tong et al. 2019) and continuing subsidies for fossil fuels make it unlikely that the situation will change any time soon (Farand 2018; ODI 2019; Trinomics 2018). Using past climate records and with some minimal use of climate models, it has been inferred that if we burn all fossil fuels, most of the earth will become uninhabitable for humans (Hansen et al. 2013). That's one reason for the name of the climate and ecological activism movement 'Extinction Rebellion'.

The remainder of this chapter will lay out the case that, when it comes to global heating, there is still no sign of any action that would resemble a true case of emergency. It will then be devoted to the question of why the gravity of the climate threat has largely been ignored or downplayed, even by many climate scientists themselves (Spratt and Dunlop 2018).

The root of denial may be found in the workings of climate science

The ownership of a story can best be judged by the prevailing news cycle. When it comes to global heating, there are three instances when the news machinery responds: publication of some groundbreaking scientific result, a climate policy decision or major climate policy meeting, or mass protests. Of the three groups that can trigger such news alerts – the scientists, the policy makers and the activists – only the first, at best, can generate news without the help of at least one of the others. Climate policy generally revolves around resolutions of the IPCC, a body of climate scientists (and politicians and civil servants). Climate protesters repeatedly cite scientific evidence to further their case. Therefore, rather than seeing climate heating as a symptom of industrial society and overconsumption, a framing many others could take part in, society typically views climate as an issue 'owned' by natural scientists.

The way in which the scientific community has approached the problem of global heating is therefore of primary importance for understanding the failure of climate policy to date. Physical scientists tend to see their role as to gain and ascertain new insights about the physical world we live in. Correspondingly, there are two principal ways for a scientist to rise in esteem: either being the first to make a significant discovery, or, something which can be much longer lasting, the first to propose a new theory that later withstands repeated attempts at proving it wrong.

Being disproven or having to retract a finding, on the other hand, is associated with a significant penalty in terms of loss of professional esteem. Consequently, scientists have been trained to be cautious before accepting new evidence or, even more so, new theories. This constitutes a certain type of 'precautionary principle': there is a certain fear of being seen to be exaggerating findings and promoting the possibility of less likely outcomes. 'False positives' are seen as worse than 'false negatives'. Unfortunately, this precautionary principle tends to point in the exact opposite direction from the needs of broader society: from, in other words, the Precautionary Principle proper (Read and O'Riordan 2017b). For, in 'post-normal' science, where the stakes for the broader society are high, 'false positives' are much less bad than 'false negatives'.[3] It is much worse for society if

---

[3] In normal science contexts, scientists tell the truth by being careful to avoid 'type 1' errors, 'false positives'. But in post-normal science, it is much more important to avoid 'type 2' errors, 'false negatives'. As we have explained, scientists find this

scientists fail to warn of an existential threat than if they end up sometimes having cried wolf.

When it comes to climate heating, the fear of being a scientist who goes well ahead of the pack has generally, and very unfortunately, proven stronger than the fear of catastrophic consequences of human-triggered climate change itself (Hansen 2007). How this mentality affects the way results are presented in major scientific assessments of societal threats is now well documented; it leads to a tendency to 'err on the side of least drama' (Brysse et al. 2013), i.e. to report only those threats where the scientist is fairly sure not to be refuted by his or her peers.

Ethical guidelines of certain professions, as for example emergency department physicians, can teach us what actions are required in a true emergency situation (Peacock 2018). The central piece of the applicable code of conduct is the application of the precautionary principle without delay, always with an eye on the worst-case outcome for the many, not just the few – for all those with a stake in the matter, not just those with a professional interest to defend. This type of precautionary principle works then, as we have said, in the exact opposite direction to the one followed by the scientific community; it demands being more tolerant, in particular where the stakes are high/ existential, to erring strongly on the side of 'maximum drama', rather than the opposite (Read and O'Riordan 2017a; Taleb et al. 2014).

Some processes that climate scientists study, such as the physics of atmospheric motion, of the earth's planetary energy balance or the chemistry of CO_2 dissolving in ocean water, are fundamentally understood, and we can safely assume that the same principles will apply in a warming/chaoticizing climate. But other processes, such as the melting and eventual collapse of ice sheets, or the reaction of crops and ecosystems to drought and warming and their possible collapse, are much less understood.

---

very uncomfortable. They are desperate to avoid being dubbed 'alarmists', while they are happy to allow that 'more research is needed'. This means that science is virtually always behind the curve – whereas in post-normal science we need to be always, precautionarily, ahead of the curve. Otherwise, we don't get to crush the curve, which is what we need to do: in regard to climate just as much as to epidemics.

There are often no analogues from the past, very limited experiments of necessarily small scale and computer models trained on severely limited data. It is thus a matter of precaution to rely mostly on theories and observations that are well established, that leave open the possibility of unforeseen developments where we know little, and that seek to implement 'no-regrets' policies of protection and precaution (and adaptation). The description of the current state of climate science given in the previous section therefore emphasizes the unknown character of even our immediate future and limits itself to what we know about past climate changes and a few findings that make use of climate model simulations in a limited way.

In order to tackle the problem of global heating, the United Nations instituted the IPCC and tasked it to provide regular comprehensive assessments of the state of climate science. The scientists writing those assessments are confronted with at least two big problems. First, that their normal model of conducting science contradicts the ethics of emergency situations; and second, that there are reasons to believe large parts of climate science necessarily remain speculative, for lack of known precedents or experimental techniques. Single plants or a small plot of land can be subject to artificially altered climates, but not entire societies or ecosystems.

But if predicting the impacts of a fundamentally novel climate state is impossible in principle, and given the stated reluctance of scientists to discuss findings that are highly uncertain, how could such reports even be attempted? And if global heating constitutes an emergency situation, how should the IPCC respond to it? Evidence suggests that that the IPCC in its assessments has on balance not tried to address those problems but has maintained a conservative attitude when dealing with less understood but plausible high-impact outcomes (Brysse et al. 2013). It may have split into three working groups, of which the first tackles the more tractable physical basis of climate change, but even here there are many processes we do not understand, such as the collapse of ice sheets that can lead to sea-level rise of several metres (Grégoire, Payne and Valdes 2012). In fact, the IPCC's reported range of 0.3–1.1 metres of sea-level rise by 2100 (IPCC 2019b) is much lower than the 2.4-metre rise that has been identified as the worst-case scenario (Bamber et al. 2019). All of the IPCC's scenarios of future man-made climate change tend to have one thing in common: the assumption that change happens smoothly and gradually, without any major disruptions. The possibility of such large-scale disruptions – such as ice-sheet collapse, dieback of the Amazon rainforest, or large-scale carbon release from permafrost – is acknowledged by the IPCC. But when the IPCC calculates a possible safe amount of CO_2 that could still be emitted, the possibility of such events actually happening is either not taken into account, relegated to footnotes, or labelled 'low confidence' in such a way as to make it seem as if those events need not be greatly worried about (Rogelj et al. 2018). But as we have stressed, and as those relatively few (but growing in number) climate scientists attest who speak out openly about the way their fears for the future exceed what they can conservatively prove, that is getting things the wrong way around. To be an effective early warning system, the IPCC or something like it would need to focus pretty strongly on making stark, and as rapidly as possible (rather than after years of slow deliberation), the risks inherent in allegedly low-probability but undoubtedly high-impact events or cascades.

Consider the IPCC report on climate change and land (IPCC 2019b). This assesses the question of how future climate change may impact yields. However, the studies rely on past observed changes or on models that are validated only by past change, and as such cannot take into account that the future climate in many crop-growing regions may be entirely novel, with combinations of extreme heat at high humidity not seen on earth for millions of years (Burke et al. 2018). There is also no assessment of what might happen if the climate becomes fundamentally unstable, as was the case before the adoption of agriculture. Instead, the assessment is limited to linking past climate warming to changes in crop yields, and the use of models to extrapolate those changes into the future. The possibility of major pest outbreaks of a scale not seen in the past, or large-scale drought hitting several major agricultural production regions at the same time (multi-breadbasket failure: Kornhuber et al. 2019), is not taken into account.

Such simple extrapolation of recent observations to make inferences about the future is also used in economic assessments. The extraordinary fact that the 2018 economics Nobel prize was given to William Nordhaus for his work with the DICE model (Nordhaus and Sztorc 2013) illustrates the scale of acceptance and dominance of this approach. Nordhaus's model includes a function that takes global mean-temperature change as input, and with it predicts the damage caused by climate change as a percentage of global gross domestic product (GDP). The data points used to motivate this damage function are derived either from observations of the GDP of different US states, or from quantification of damages of isolated effects, such as the building costs for dykes, or the costs of health care when there is an increase in the incidence of malaria (Tol 2009). If states with a hotter climate have a lower GDP, then the first method would infer that a warmer climate leads to 'damage' (Mendelsohn et al. 2000). As Richard Tol (Tol 2009) states, the authors of all included studies come from no more than three closely related groups of scholars and were published more than 20 years ago. The results of this and related analyses led William Nordhaus to conclude that 4°C warming is optimal for human welfare (Nordhaus 2018), and the IPCC to conclude that the impact of human-caused climate change will be small for most economic sectors (Arent et al. 2014).

It is important to recall that this exercise in 'foresight' is based on a number of unstated and unproven assumptions, including: first, that the welfare of a given place in today's interconnected world is independent of the climate of the rest of the world; second, that damages from climate change can be added up sector by sector, and that interconnectedness and its impact on vulnerability of the modern world can be ignored; third, that changes across time can be inferred from changes across space, for example, if the climate of Massachusetts changes to that of Florida, its GDP per capita would change accordingly; fourth, that it does not matter how quickly dangerous climate change occurs; and fifth, that there are no known thresholds or tipping points that could amplify the impact of climate change/chaos (Lenton et al. 2019). A recent analysis of this body of work also points out that large parts of the economy were excluded from the beginning as supposedly not dependent on climate, as well as other biases (Keene 2020).

A case for the virtue of scientific ignorance

How is it possible that a world of 4°C climate heating is judged to be uninhabitable or leading to societal collapse by some scientists (Steffen et al. 2018), but talked about in a professional matter-of-fact way by others, even seen as 'optimal' (Nordhaus 2018)? While the flaws and limitations of the economic approach are obvious, how can we understand the past reluctance of the IPCC to include worst-case scenarios and disruptive events or to accept the limits of its approach largely based on computer models?

Part of the answer may lie in the inherent tendency of professionals, such as climate scientists, to support the status quo (Schmidt 2000), something that clashes with the fact that averting a climate catastrophe requires society to change in radical ways, as advocated by some climate scientists (Rockström 2015). It is important to note that the change advocated is usually not radical enough to include a fundamental shift of the role of the scientists themselves. The possibility that climate science itself may have contributed to the current crisis, by overstating its knowledge and sketching out an often-theoretical road to solving the climate crisis, is seldom entertained. Evidence suggests, however, that climate policy makers and the IPCC have often co-created scenarios in which future, unproven technological solutions have provided justification for delaying action (McLaren and Markusson 2020).

It is obvious that climate scientists have done a generally pretty magnificent job in trying to detail the way the world has changed and is now under threat. It is obvious that some climate scientists have had to put up with appalling attacks from ignorant or well-funded citizens, media or 'think tanks' (*sic*). It is obvious that a limited but increasing number of climate scientists have become near-heroes for speaking out about the extreme gravity of the threat hanging over our planetary ecosystem. And yet . . . Could climate science, insofar as it has tended not to be properly precautionary, have even, on balance, *contributed* to a widespread denial of the severity of the threat from global overheating? It is an awkward but necessary question to ask. One experienced climatologist explains that one way 'we, as scientists, have contributed to the crisis concerns the excessive rationalization of a threat. In other words – we switch off common sense and produce scientific results borne of idealized models – be they mathematical or intellectual.' He continues:

> As citizens we all know the difference between a politician's words and deeds and we are all painfully aware of . . . a very real risk of a 4 or higher degree of warming. And yet, the IPCC's various assessment reports have repeatedly relied on highly idealized so-called integrated models that know and admit nothing of these things, and therefore [are] easily bent to produce results that fly in the face of common logic. (Knorr 2019)

Despite the existence of such criticism from within the climate science profession, at the time of writing it has proved to be largely unable to acknowledge the limits of its own approach to knowing about the climate crisis. It appears that the scientific community, while it continues to own the issue of global heating, does not own or abide by the fundamental importance of the precautionary principle for the functioning of human society. There is, however, a radically different approach that can be traced back almost two and half millennia to the ancient Greek philosopher Socrates, who taught the virtue of ignorance; of admitting what we don't know and don't understand. Collapse of complex systems such as human society is a chaotic process that we cannot fully understand, nor predict precisely through the scientific method. There are, to say the least, severe limits to what climate science can tell us about (say) the likelihood of 'populists' being elected who undermine climate sanity, or even about the likelihood of famines (which are going to be unprecedented in their nature, this century, as we move into the unknown – and which are always political events as well as 'natural' disasters).

Thus our emphasis above on the precautionary principle, properly understood, as decisive in cases of potential ruin. However, in scientific discourse, there is little room or incentive for admitting a significant level of ignorance. This may have contributed to a widespread and mistaken sense that the climate crisis is somehow under control. To emphasize probabilities rather than certainties from statistical calculations is not an effective way of accepting an inescapable ignorance. Rather, uncertainty within statistical methodology is widely translated into the message, whether by scientists or others, that an outcome is less than certain in the real world; and thus perhaps can be hedged or hoped against. Yet the important insight is that the method and language of science is unable to help us reach confident conclusions about highly complex systems (Servigne and Stevens 2020), and that this *underscores rather than undermines* the vital importance of taking rapid, profound, emergency action. Reaching and enacting conclusions is incredibly important on such matters, where the consequences are so immense; such conclusions should be reached on the basis of precaution, ethics and science, not 'outsourced' to science alone, which will be too slow, too conservative, too technocratic and too technocentric (Read 2020).

Two possible new approaches for survival and compassion

As our anxieties grow, it can be reassuring to work harder with the tools we have at our disposal. However, measuring ever more closely the nature of our predicament will deliver neither greater control nor safety. Rather, if the deeper assumptions and intentions underpinning those projects of measurement are not questioned, then they risk being the means for mass distraction. Therefore, we wonder if a new and happier approach to the climate crisis might emerge if one of the two following possibilities were to be attempted:

1) Society has been relying on scientists to blow the whistle on climate collapse. Mostly, scientists haven't yet done so (with honourable exceptions such as Hansen and Knorr). Scientists should admit that their approach, of trusting in the system, gradualism and reformism, and basically seeking to maintain the system (a system which enables them to be well paid, to feel important, to feel righteous, to *travel the world* giving warnings of how bad things are, while continuing to live well: Anderson 2018) has, on balance, badly failed. Now, scientists admitting this would have vertiginous consequences. The curtain would be pulled back, the veil removed, the pretence would be over. Many ordinary citizens would suddenly be scared. Might this have bad consequences?

Yes it might. But right now we are driving ourselves over a cliff. So it is time to take a few risks with communications (as we discuss further in the concluding chapter).

Imagine if more climate scientists stopped acting just as scientists, and started acting as citizens, as storytellers, as people. What would this look like? It might look like them breaking down with emotion on live TV. It might look like them doing civil disobedience en masse – and practising transformative or deep adaptation. It would look like them denouncing the absurdities not just of the Trumps but of the Nordhauses of this world – and of their own funders.[4]

Why hasn't this already happened at scale? No doubt there are many reasons, including some good ones; but we think the widespread mostly unspoken perception is that private feelings of terror are not supposed to enter professional conduct or judgement. We believe that that is a convention *outside of science itself*; and we are describing what it has led to.

We suspect that the desperate maintenance, to a large extent, of a veneer of normality as our civilization drives over a cliff edge indeed comes from despair – and from the desperate management of that despair. We suspect that the reason why professional facades are maintained through virtually all of this situation is not mainly because of a (highly and increasingly questionable) belief that that is the most pragmatically effective way to leverage change (through maintaining 'neutrality'), but mainly because such maintenance assists with *terror management*. A denial of death: in this case of the likely death of our civilization (which would of course almost certainly mean the death of many within it: Moses 2020; Read and Alexander 2019; and ch. 2 of this book).

---

[4] Reframed in terms of the agenda of Extinction Rebellion, what we are talking about in this chapter comes of course under the general heading of XR's first demand, 'Tell the truth'. We are saying: you aren't telling the truth unless you get serious about avoiding *type 2* errors. You aren't telling the truth unless you sketch scenarios, especially of/from fat-tails, to avoid at all costs. You aren't telling the truth, furthermore, if you undermine in the manner of your presentation the gravity of its content. If you describe a fat tail completely emotionlessly and with no suggestion that this impending scenario may require one to do something other than just keep turning up to work, then you aren't telling the truth.

The point can be made in terms of the concept of *incongruence*. It's incongruent to calmly announce potential apocalypse and then go back to work. It undermines the seriousness of the announcement. It's incongruent to speak of some horrendous eco-catastrophe and not get emotional – or political. It is incumbent upon scientists to seek to stop being incongruent.

2) Failing (1), another potential avenue to explore would be if climate scientists were to step back from their assumed role as the chief guardians of the climate debate. This would allow scholars, activists and policy makers to widen the view (as we hope is occurring in this very book) from the restrictions of a mechanistic scientific paradigm in which what counts are only quantifications suitable for the inclusion into mathematical models. Then people might give more attention to the known scientific fact that changes in complex systems often come about in an abrupt and unpredictable fashion (Servigne and Stevens 2020). Perhaps the climate agenda could better include other approaches and world views, in particular indigenous knowledge, as practised by the Intergovernmental Platform on Biodiversity and Ecosystem Services (Díaz et al. 2015). This would allow us to start learning from past breakdown and catastrophe, to thus better prepare for the inevitable disruptions ahead, and to start thinking about how to avoid the worst-case scenarios. Most importantly, we would stop underestimating the risks by overestimating the primacy of one means of knowing, and finally come to accept how precarious most human, animal and plant life has become on this planet.

In that epochal context, one might argue that it isn't good enough any more to restrict to a particular nexus of scientists and (especially) economists the ability to decide the kind of questions that issue from the climate-industrial complex. The talent pool should be considerably enlarged. It should include a *range* of philosophers, experts in precaution, ethicists. It should include systems thinkers and social scientists. It should go further still: it should include writers of imaginative fiction concerning the future. Further still: it should certainly, as we noted above, include indigenous people who have access to wisdom self-evidently little present in our civilization. Furthest of all: it should not be restricted to adults. Nordhaus, Stern, Mendessohn and Tol should for example consult with representatives of the young generation still at school about which future discount rate to use in their economic modelling. And not just that: the younger generation, who are not old enough to vote yet (which should be reconsidered) but aren't too young to die in climate disasters, should be given a role in *deciding* questions such as this.

There is no solid case, we are saying, given the failure around which this chapter revolves, for the climate debate to be taking place within nearly as restricted a group as it has been. Citizens' assemblies which include the young and the indigenous, the colonized and the marginalized, and which are empowered to make *decisions* about mitigation, adaptation, habitat-preservation, ecocide, discount rates and suchlike, are therefore one attractive way of reorienting the entire terrain.

Best of all, of course, would be to have a synthesis of both (1) *and* (2): climate scientists telling the truth, in the souped-up manner we outline above, *and* accepting the need to step aside somewhat to provide more space that the rest of us can rush into. We are encouraged, therefore, that many climatologists joined hundreds of other scholars in signing an international scholars' warning on collapse risk.

Box 1.1 The international scholars warning on collapse risk

As scientists and scholars from around the world, we call on policy-makers to engage with the risk of disruption and even of collapse of societies. After five years failing to reduce emissions in line with the Paris climate accord, we must now face the consequences. While bold and fair efforts to cut emissions and naturally draw down carbon are essential, researchers in many areas consider societal collapse a credible scenario this century. Different views exist on the location, extent, timing, permanence and cause of disruptions, but the way modern societies exploit people and nature is a common concern. Only if policy makers begin to discuss this threat of societal collapse might we begin to reduce its likelihood, speed, severity, harm to the most vulnerable – and to nature.

Some armed services already see collapse as an important scenario. Surveys show many people now anticipate societal collapse.

Sadly, that is the experience of many communities in the global South. However, it is not well reported in the media and mostly absent from civil society and politics. People who care about environmental and humanitarian issues should not be discouraged from discussing the risks of societal disruption or collapse. Ill-informed speculations about impacts on mental health and motivation will not support serious discussion. That risks betraying thousands of activists whose anticipation of collapse is part of their motivation to push for change on climate, ecology and social justice.

Some of us believe that a transition to a new society may be possible. That will involve bold action to reduce damage to the climate, nature and society, including preparations for disruptions to everyday life. We are united in regarding efforts to suppress discussion of collapse as hindering the possibility of that transition. We have experienced how emotionally challenging it is to recognize the damage being done, along with the growing threat to our own way of life. We also know the great sense of fellowship that can arise. It is time to have these difficult conversations so we can reduce our complicity in the harm and make the best of a turbulent future.

Signed by over 450 scientists and scholars from 30 countries, by the end of 2020, including more than 60 climatologists. Full letter and signatory list is at www.scholarswarning.net

Wider public awareness that climate scientists have been complicit with or victims of a system that has got the better of them *would* indeed produce some vertigo. But that truly does create a space. For *citizens*, suddenly realizing that they can't rely on scientists and the system to save them. Climate scientists confessing their great sorrow at the situation of the world and of their children, confessing their regret at having stayed inside the system for so long, expressing their actual emotions, confessing their impotence – would create a vertiginous void into which many citizens could and would step. *Stepping into their power.* Realizing that no one is riding to the rescue, and so instead *realizing* their agency. The game-changing narrative shift we are envisaging could unleash a scale of radical citizen activism so far only dreamed of. Extinction Rebellion has found thousands of people willing to be arrested for the cause of averting eco-driven civilizational collapse and mass extinction. Imagine hundreds of thousands, or even a million, or even more, ready to act in that way, if scientists come clean that only something like that is actually going to change the status quo in any serious way, and that science and policy-wonkery is not. And imagine how much more serious the new movements demanding and enacting adaptation would be if they were fuelled by a far more widespread realization that it's not five to midnight, but five *past* midnight. Academia as we have known it is fine for facilitating gradual change. But when you are faced with an *emergency*, with built-in time lags, then normal science is no longer appropriate. And that demands a new courage, in words and actions.

Many will quail at this call for courage – and disguise their quailing with literate scepticism (or name calling). One thing they will say is: 'But if we do as you say, and discard our "neutrality", then the Fox Newses of this world will come for us even worse than they already do.' True. But, we would say to scientists, they already come for you pretty badly as it is. They act as if you are systematically biased even when you are bending over backwards – much *too far* – not to be. It won't actually get much worse if you are simply truthful and congruent. But you will then also have a superpower, the superpower discovered by Greta Thunberg and XR in the public sphere: the superpower of authentic presence. Of what happens if you let your voice crack as you think of your nephews and nieces or of your beloved wilderness or whatever it is, when they ask you what is going to happen in the world . . .

We have been somewhat critical in this chapter of science as is. But we want to stress that, as we signalled above by speaking of scientists as *victims* of the situation, there is no desire whatsoever on our part to castigate individuals. In the spirit of XR, and in the spirit of deep adaptation, we come more from a place of love (another word which is very hard to mention without being warned that one is making a potentially career-destroying move . . . and this too is something that is wrong with science as it is). We should and do seek to not blame. Not shame. Rather, let's imagine a kind of truth and reconciliation process for the systemic failure which has resulted in generations now of climate science doing very little to bend the emissions curve, let alone crush it.

Given the grave human-induced precarity now of complex civilization and possibly of complex life on earth, the project of deep adaptation seems wonderfully and sadly timely. For the implication of what we have ventured to say in this chapter, with the sometimes quiet and sometimes public help of some still rather renegade climate scientists, is that the prospects for this society preventing itself from collapse are rather less rosy than virtually everyone still assumes. For there's a hegemonic story about how academic research and policy relevance is supposed to work: that climate scientists slowly establish the facts, and policy makers then act on them. The story *isn't true*. It isn't *working*. And: we're out of time.

There's an alternative possible story, or stories, that we've been sketching in the latter portion of this chapter. If such a new approach were embraced, then we would have a *chance*, at least of avoiding the direst impacts that otherwise we may be heading toward, such as Hothouse Earth. Whether scientist or citizen, we hope you will have the courage and goodwill to at least consider a new story.

References

Anderson, K. (2018) 'World's Richest Must Radically Change Lifestyles to Prevent Global Catastrophe'. *Democracy Now*. Available at: https://www.democracynow.org/2018/12/11/scientist_kevin_anderson_worlds_biggest_emitters

Arent, D. J., Tol, R. S. J., Faust, E., et al. (2014) 'Key Economic Sectors and Services', in C. B. Field, V. R. Barros, D. J. Dokken et al. (eds), *Climate Change 2014: Impacts, Adaptation, and Vulnerability. Part A: Global and Sectoral Aspects. Contribution of Working Group II to the Fifth Assessment Report of the Intergovernmental Panel on Climate Change*. Cambridge: Cambridge University Press.

Arrhenius, S. (2009 [1896]) 'On the Influence of Carbonic Acid in the Air upon the Temperature of the Ground'. *Philosophical Magazine* 5:41(251): 273–6. Available at: www.rsc.org/images/Arrhenius1896_tcm18-173546.pdf

Bamber, J. L., Oppenheimer, M., Kopp, R. E., Aspinall, W. P. and Cooke, R. M. (2019) 'Ice Sheet Contributions to Future Sea-Level Rise from Structured Expert Judgment'. *Proceedings of the National Academy of Sciences* 116: 11195–200.

Barbuzano, J. (2019) 'The Little Ice Age Wasn't Global, but Current Climate Change Is'. *EOS* 100. Available at: doi.org/10.1029/2019 EO129331

Betts, R., Jones, C., Jin, Y., et al. (2020) 'Analysis: What Impact Will the Coronavirus Pandemic Have on Atmospheric CO_2?'.

Carbon Brief. Available at: https://www.carbonbrief.org/analysis-wh
at-impact-will-the-coronavirus-pandemic-have-on-atmospheric-co2

Bjordal, J. Storelvmo, T., Alterskjaer, K. and Carlsen, T. (2020) 'Equilibrium Climate Sensitivity above 5°C Plausible Due to State-Dependent Cloud Feedback'. *Nature Geoscience*. 13: 718–21.

Brysse, K., Oreskes, N., O'Reilly, J. and Oppenheimer, M. (2013) 'Climate Change Prediction: Erring on the Side of Least Drama?'. *Global Environmental Change* 23: 327–37.

Burke, K. D., Williams, J. W., Chandler, M. A., et al. (2018) 'Pliocene and Eocene Provide Best Analogs for Near-Future Climates'. *Proc. Nat. Acad. Sci.* 115: 13288–93.

Cooper, G. S., Willcock, S. and Dearing, J. A. (2020) 'Regime Shifts Occur Disproportionately Faster in Larger Ecosystems'. *Nature Communications* 11: 1–10.

Díaz, S., Demissew, S., Carabias, J., et al. (2015) 'The IPBES Conceptual Framework – Connecting Nature and People'. *Current Opinion in Environmental Sustainability* 14: 1–16.

Fagan, B. (2004) *The Long Summer: How Climate Changed Civilization*. New York: Basic Books.

Fagan, B. (2008) *The Great Warming: Climate Change and the Rise and Fall of Civilizations*. New York: Bloomsbury Press.

Farand, C. (2018) 'G7 Fossil Fuel Subsidies Worth $100bn a Year to Industry, Study Finds'. *Climate Home News*. Available at: www.climate changenews.com/2018/06/04/uk-taxpayer-support-fossil-fuel-industry -exposed-ahead-g7

Global Carbon Project (2020) 'Carbon Budget 2020: Carbon Budget and Trends 2020'. Available at: www.globalcarbonproject.org/ carbonbudget

Grantham, H. S., Duncan, A., Evans, T. D., et al. (2020). 'Anthropogenic Modification of Forests Means Only 40% of Remaining Forests Have High Ecosystem Integrity'. *Nature Communications* 11: 5978. Available at: doi.org/10.1038/s41467-020-19493-3

Grégoire, L. J., Payne, A. J. and Valdes, P. J. (2012) 'Deglacial Rapid Sea Level Rises Caused by Ice-sheet Saddle Collapses'. *Nature* 487: 219–22.

Guardian (2020) 'A Warning on Climate and the Risk of Societal Collapse'. Available at: https://www.theguardian.com/enviro nment/2020/dec/06/a-warning-on-climate-and-the-risk-of-societal-co llapse

Hansen, J. E. (2007) 'Scientific Reticence and Sea Level Rise'. *Environmental Research Letters* 2, 024002. Available at: iopscience.iop. org/article/10.1088/1748-9326/2/2/024002

Hansen, J., Sato, M., Russell, G. and Kharecha, P. (2013) 'Climate

Sensitivity, Sea Level and Atmospheric Carbon Dioxide'. *Philosophical Transactions of the Royal Society A* 371(2001): 1–31.

Hoegh-Guldberg, O., Jacob, D., Taylor, M., et al. (2018) 'Impacts of 1.5°C Global Warming on Natural and Human Systems', in V. Masson-Delmotte, P. Zhai, H.-O. Pörtner, et al. (eds), *Global Warming of 1.5°C. An IPCC Special Report on the Impacts of Global Warming of 1.5°C above Pre-industrial Levels and Related Global Greenhouse Gas Emission Pathways, in the Context of Strengthening the Global Response to the Threat of Climate Change, Sustainable Development, and Efforts to Eradicate Poverty.* Cambridge: Cambridge University Press.

Huntingford, C., Williamson, M. and Nijsse, F. (2020) 'CMIP6 climate models imply high committed warming'. *Climatic Change* 162: 1515–1520. Available at: https://link.springer.com/article/10.1007/s10584-020-02849-5

IPCC (International Panel on Climate Change) (2019a) 'Summary for Policymakers', in H.-O. Pörtner, D. C. Roberts, V. Masson-Delmotte, et al. (eds), *IPCC Special Report on the Ocean and Cryosphere in a Changing Climate.* Cambridge: Cambridge University Press.

IPCC (International Panel on Climate Change) (2019b) *Climate Change and Land: An IPCC Special Report on Climate Change, Desertification, Land Degradation, Sustainable Land Management, Food Security, and Greenhouse Gas Fluxes in Terrestrial Ecosystems*, ed. P. R. Shukla, J. Skea, E. Calvo Buendia, et al. Cambridge: Cambridge University Press.

Keene, S. (2020) 'The Appallingly Bad Neoclassical Economics of Climate Change'. *Globalizations*. Available at: https://www.tandfonline.com/doi/full/10.1080/14747731.2020.1807856

Knorr, W. (2019) 'Climate Scientist: Our Profession is Letting Down Humanity – We Must Change the Way We Approach the Climate Crisis'. *The Conversation*. Available at: https://theconversation.com/climate-scientist-our-profession-is-letting-down-humanity-we-must-change-the-way-we-approach-the-climate-crisis-122479

Kornhuber, K., Coumou, D., Vogel, E., et al. (2019) 'Amplified Rossby Waves Enhance Risk of Concurrent Heatwaves in Major Breadbasket Regions'. *Nature Climate Change* 10: 48–53.

Lee, R. J. (2009) *Climate Change and Armed Conflict: Hot and Cold Wars.* London: Routledge.

Lenton, T. M., Rockström, J., Gaffney, O., et al. (2019) 'Climate Tipping Points – Too Risky to Bet Against'. *Nature* 575: 592–5.

Le Quéré, C., Jackson, R. B., Jones, M. W., et al. (2020) 'Temporary Reduction in Daily Global CO_2 Emissions during the COVID-19 Forced Confinement'. *Nature Climate Change* 10: 647–53.

Lunt, D. J., Foster, G. L., Haywood, A. M. and Stone, E. J. (2008)

'Late Pliocene Greenland Glaciation Controlled by a Decline in Atmospheric CO_2 Levels'. *Nature*. 454: 1102–5.

Marcott, S. A., Shakun, J. D., Clark, P. U. and Mix, A. C. (2013) 'A Reconstruction of Regional and Global Temperature for the Past 11,300 Years'. *Science* 339: 1198–1201.

Masson-Delmotte, V., Landais, A., Combourieu-Nebout, N., et al. (2005) 'Rapid Climate Variability during Warm and Cold Periods in Polar Regions and Europe'. *Comptes Rendus Geoscience* 337: 935–46.

Masson-Delmotte, V., Stenni, B., Pol, K., et al. (2010) 'EPICA Dome C Record of Glacial and Interglacial Intensities'. *Quaternary Science Reviews* 29(1–2): 113–28.

Matthews, H. D. and Zickfeld, K. (2012) 'Climate Response to Zeroed Emissions of Greenhouse Gases and Aerosols'. *Nature Climate Change* 2: 338–41.

McLaren, D. and Markusson, N. (2020) 'The Co-evolution of Technological Promises, Modelling, Policies and Climate Change Targets'. *Nature Climate Change* 20: 392–7.

Mendelsohn, R., Morrison, W., Schlesinger, M. E. and Andronova, N. G. (2000) 'Country-Specific Market Impacts of Climate Change'. *Climatic Change* 45: 553–69.

Moses, A. (2020) 'Collapse of Civilisation is the Most Likely Outcome: Top Climate Scientists'. Voice of Action. Available at: https://voiceofaction.org/collapse-of-civilisation-is-the-most-likely-outcome-top-climate-scientists/

Myhre, G., Shindell, D., Bréon, F.-M., et al. (2013) 'Anthropogenic and Natural Radiative Forcing', in T. F. Stocker, D. Qin, G.-K. Plattner, et al. (eds), *Climate Change 2013: The Physical Science Basis: Contribution of Working Group I to the Fifth Assessment Report of the Intergovernmental Panel on Climate Change*. Cambridge and New York: Cambridge University Press.

Neukom, R., Steiger, N., Gómez-Navarro, J. J., Wang, J. and Werner, J. P. (2019) 'No Evidence for Globally Coherent Warm and Cold Periods over the Preindustrial Common Era'. *Nature* 571: 550–4.

NOAA (National Oceanic and Atmospheric Administration) (2020a) *Global Temperature Time Series*. Available at: https://www.ncdc.noaa.gov/cag/global/time-series/globe/land_ocean/ann/2/1880-2020

NOAA (National Oceanic and Atmospheric Administration) (2020b) 'Global Atmospheric CO_2'. Available at: https://www.esrl.noaa.gov/gmd/ccgg/trends/global.html

Nordhaus, W. (2018) *Nobel Prize Lecture* Slide 6, Stockholm. Available at: https://www.nobelprize.org/prizes/economic-sciences/2018/nordhaus/lecture/

Nordhaus, W. and Sztorc, P. (2013) *DICE 2013R: Introduction and*

User's Manual, 2nd edn. Yale University. Available at: http://www.econ.yale.edu/~nordhaus/homepage/homepage/documents/DICE_Manual_100413r1.pdf

ODI (Overseas Development Institute) (2019) *Are the G7 on Track to Phase Out Fossil Fuel Subsidies by 2025?* Available at: https://www.odi.org/opinion/10482-are-g7-track-phase-out-fossil-fuel-subsidies-2025

Peacock, K. A. (2018) 'A Different Kind of Rigor: What Climate Scientists Can Learn from Emergency Room Doctors'. *Ethics, Policy & Environment* 21: 194–214.

Pagani, M., Liu, Z., LaRiviere, J. and Ravelo, A. C. (2010) 'High Earth-System Climate Sensitivity Determined from Pliocene Carbon Dioxide Concentrations'. *Nature Geoscience* 3: 27–30.

Pagani, M., Zachos, J. C., Freeman, K. H., Tipple, B. and Bohaty, S. (2005) 'Marked Decline in Atmospheric Carbon Dioxide Concentrations During the Paleogene'. *Science* 309: 600–3.

Read, R. (2020) 'Imagining the World after Covid-19'. *ABC Religion and Ethics*. Available at: https://www.abc.net.au/religion/rupert-read-imagining-a-world-after-coronavirus/12380676

Read, R. and Alexander, S. (2019) *This Civilization is Finished*. Melbourne: Simplicity Institute.

Read, R. and O'Riordan, T. (2017a) 'Understanding, Strengthening and Safeguarding the Precautionary Principle'. *APPG Limits to Growth*. Available at: http://limits2growth.org.uk/wp-content/uploads/2017/11/APPG-Briefing-Precautionary-Principle-online.pdf

Read, R. and O'Riordan, T. (2017b) 'The Precautionary Principle Under Fire'. *Environment* 59: 4–15.

Rockström, J. (2015) *Bounding the Planetary Future: Why We Need a Great Transition*. Great Transition Initiative. Available at: https://greattransition.org/publication/bounding-the-planetary-future-why-we-need-a-great-transition

Rogelj, J., Shindell, D., Jiang, K., et al. (2018) 'Mitigation Pathways Compatible with 1.5°C in the Context of Sustainable Development', in V. Masson-Delmotte, P. Zhai, H.-O. Pörtner, et al. (eds), *Global Warming of 1.5°C. An IPCC Special Report on the Impacts of Global Warming of 1.5°C above Pre-industrial levels and Related Global Greenhouse Gas Emission Pathways, in the context of Strengthening the Global Response to the Threat of Climate Change, Sustainable Development, and Efforts to Eradicate Poverty*. Cambridge: Cambridge University Press.

Schmidt, J. (2000) *Disciplined Minds: A Critical Look at Salaried Professionals and the Soul-Battering System that Shapes their Lives*. Oxford: Rowman & Littlefield.

Servigne, P and Stevens, R. (2020) *How Everything Can Collapse*. Cambridge: Polity Press.

Sherwood, S. et al. (2020) 'An Assessment of Earth's Climate Sensitivity Using Multiple Lines of Evidence'. *Reviews of Geophysics*. Available at: https://agupubs.onlinelibrary.wiley.com/doi/full/10.10 29/2019RG000678

SIMIP (Sea Ice Model Intercomparison Project) Community (2020) 'Arctic Sea Ice in CMIP6'. *Geophysical Research Letters* 47: e2019GL086749. Available at: doi.org/10.1029/2019GL086749

Slingo, J. (2017) 'The Evolution of Climate Science: A Personal View from Julia Slingo'. *World Meteorological Organization Bulletin* 66(1). Available at: https://public.wmo.int/en/resources/bulletin/ evolution-of-climate-science-personal-view-from-julia-slingo

Solomon, S., Daniel, J. S., Sanford, T. J., et al. (2010) 'Persistence of Climate Changes Due to a Range of Greenhouse Gases'. *Proceedings of the National Academy of Sciences* 107: 18354–9.

Spratt, D. and Dunlop, I. (2018) 'What Lies Beneath: The Understatement of Existential Climate Risk'. Breakthrough [National Centre for Climate Restoration]. Available at: https://www.break throughonline.org.au/whatliesbeneath

Staubwasser, M. and Weiss, H. (2006) 'Holocene Climate and Cultural Evolution in Late Prehistoric–Early Historic West Asia'. *Quaternary Research* 66: 372–87.

Steffen, W., Rockström, J., Richardson, K., et al. (2018) 'Trajectories of the Earth System in the Anthropocene'. *Proceedings of the National Academy of Science* 115: 8252–9.

Taleb, N., Read, R., Douady, R., Norman, J. and Bar-Yam, Y. (2014) 'The Precautionary Principle'. *Extreme Risk Initiative: NYU School of Engineering Working Paper Series*. Available at: https://arxiv.org/ abs/1410.5787

Tol, R. S. (2009) 'The Economic Effects of Climate Change'. *Journal of Economic Perspectives* 23: 29–51.

Tong, D., Zhang, Q., Zheng, Y., et al. (2019) 'Committed Emissions from Existing Energy Infrastructure Jeopardize 1.5°C Climate Target'. *Nature* 572: 373–7.

Trinomics (2018) *Study on Energy Prices, Costs and Subsidies and their Impact on Industry and Households, Final Report*. European Commission Directorate General for Energy. Available at: https://ec.europa.eu/ energy/sites/ener/files/documents/energy_prices_and_costs_-final_rep ort-v12.3.pdf

Wang, S. et al. (2020) 'Recent Global Decline of CO_2 Fertilization Effects on Vegetation Photosynthesis'. *Science* 370(6522): 1295–1300.

Williams, H. T. and Lenton, T. M. (2010) 'Evolutionary Regime Shifts in Simulated Ecosystems'. *Oikos* 119(12): 1887–99.

WMO (World Meteorological Organization) (2019) '2019 Concludes a Decade of Exceptional Global Heat and High-impact Weather'. Press release. Available at: https://public.wmo.int/en/media/press-release/2019-concludes-decade-of-exceptional-global-heat-and-high-impact-weather

Xu, Y., Ramanathan, V. and Victor, D. G. (2018) 'Global Warming Will Happen Faster Than We Think'. *Nature* 564: 30–2.

Zeebe, R. E., Ridgwell, A. and Zachos, J. C. (2016) 'Anthropogenic Carbon Release Rate Unprecedented During the Past 66 Million Years'. *Nature Geoscience* 9: 325–9.

2

Deep Adaptation:
A Map for Navigating Climate Tragedy

Jem Bendell

Preamble

This chapter presents the original deep adaptation paper, published on 27 July 2018, with revisions made on 27 July 2020. Although the paper went viral, with around a million downloads, I wrote it for people working in the corporate sustainability field and before I had knowledge of the wider fields of scholarship on societal collapse (see chapter 3). Therefore, despite my own wider interests, the paper did not address the many important issues of poverty, rights, humanitarian action, public policy, relocalization, monetary policy, anti-patriarchy and decolonization. However, it remains helpful for understanding the phenomenon of deep adaptation to consult this original text.

Introduction

Can professionals in sustainability management, policy and research – myself included – continue to work with the assumption or hope that we can slow down climate change or respond to it sufficiently to sustain our civilization? As disturbing information on climate change passed across my screen, this was the question I could no longer ignore, and therefore I decided to take a couple of months to analyse the latest climate science. As I began to conclude that we can no longer work with that assumption or hope, I asked a second question. Have professionals in the sustainability field discussed the possibility that it is too late to avert an environmental catastrophe and the implications for their work? A quick literature review revealed that my fellow professionals have not been publishing work that explores, or starts from, that perspective. That led to a third question, on why sustainability professionals are not exploring this fundamentally important issue to our whole field as well as to our personal lives. To explore that, I drew on psychological analyses, conversations with colleagues, reviews of debates amongst environmentalists in social media and self-reflection on my own reticence. Concluding that there is a need to promote discussion about the implications of a societal collapse triggered by an environmental catastrophe, I asked my fourth question on what are the ways that people are talking about collapse in social media. I identified a variety of conceptualizations and from that I asked myself what could provide a map for people to navigate this extremely difficult issue. For that, I drew on a range of reading and experiences over my 25 years in the sustainability field to outline an agenda for what I have termed 'deep adaptation' to climate change.

The result of these five questions is a chapter that does not contribute to one specific set of literature or practice in the broad field of sustainability management and policy. Rather, it questions the basis for all the work in this field. It does not seek to add to the existing research, policy and practice on climate adaptation, as I found that to be framed by the view that we can manage the impacts of a changing climate on our physical, economic, social, political and psychological situations. Instead, this chapter may contribute to future work on sustainable management and policy as much by subtraction as by addition. By that I mean the implication is for you to take time to step back, to consider 'what if' the analysis in these pages is true, to allow yourself to grieve and to overcome enough of the typical fears we all have, to find meaning in new ways of being and acting. That may be in the fields of academia or management – or could be in some other field that this realization leads you to.

First, I briefly explain the paucity of research in management studies that considers or starts from societal collapse due to environmental catastrophe, and I give acknowledgement to the existing work in this field that many readers may consider relevant. I am new to the topic of societal collapse and wish to define it as an uneven ending of our normal modes of sustenance, shelter, security, pleasure, identity and meaning. Second, I summarize what I consider to be the most important climate science of the last few years and how it is leading more people to conclude that we face disruptive changes in the near term. Third, I explain how that perspective is marginalized within the professional environmental sector – and so invite you to consider the value of leaving mainstream views behind. Fourth, I outline the ways that people in relevant social networks are framing our situation as one of facing collapse, catastrophe or extinction and how these views trigger different emotions and ideas. Fifth, I outline a deep adaptation agenda to help guide discussions on what we might do once we recognize climate change is an unfolding tragedy. Finally, I make some suggestions for how this agenda could influence our future research and teaching in the sustainability field.

As researchers and reflective practitioners, we have an opportunity and obligation to do not just what is expected by our employers and the norms of our profession but also to reflect on the relevance of our work within wider society. I am aware that some people consider statements from academics that we now face inevitable near-term societal collapse to be irresponsible, due to the potential impact that may have on the motivation or mental health of people reading such statements. My research and engagement in dialogue on this topic, some of which I will outline in this chapter, lead me to conclude the exact opposite. It is a responsible act to communicate this analysis now and invite people to support each other, myself included, in exploring the implications, including the psychological and spiritual implications.

Locating this study within academia

When discussing negative outlooks on climate change and its implications for human society, the response is often to seek insight through placing this information in context. That context is often assumed to be found in balancing it with other information. As the information on our climate predicament is so negative, the balance is often found in highlighting more positive information about progress on the sustainability agenda. This process of seeking to 'balance out' is a habit of the informed and reasoning mind. Yet that does not make it a logical means of deliberation if positive information being shared does not relate to the situation being described by the negative information. For instance, discussing progress in the health and safety policies of the White Star Line with the captain of the *Titanic* as it sank into the icy waters of the North Atlantic would not be a sensible use of time. Yet given that this balancing is often the way people respond to discussion of the scale and speed of our climate tragedy, let us first recognize the positive news from the broader sustainability agenda.

Certainly, there has been some progress on environmental issues in past decades, from reducing pollution, to habitat preservation, to waste management. Much valiant effort has been made to reduce carbon emissions over the last 20 years, one part of climate action officially termed 'mitigation' (Aaron-Morrison et al. 2017). There have been many steps forward on climate and carbon management – from awareness, to policies, to innovations (Flannery 2015). Larger and quicker steps must be taken. That is helped by the agreement reached in December 2015 at the COP21 intergovernmental climate summit and now that there is significant Chinese engagement on the issue. To support the maintenance and scaling of these efforts is essential. In addition, increasing action is occurring on adaptation to climate change, such as flood defences, planning laws and irrigation systems (Singh, Harmeling and Rai 2016). Whereas we can praise these efforts, their existence does not matter to an analysis of our overall predicament with climate change.

Rather than building from existing theories on sustainable business, this chapter is focusing on a phenomenon. That phenomenon is not climate change per se but the state of climate change in 2018, which I will argue from a secondary review of research now indicates near-term societal collapse. The gap in the literature that this chapter may begin to address is the lack of discussion within management studies and practice of the end of the idea that we can either solve or cope with climate change. In the *Sustainability Accounting Management and Policy Journal*

(SAMPJ), which this chapter was originally submitted to, there has been no discussion of this topic before, apart from my own co-authored paper (Bendell, Sutherland and Little 2017). Three papers mention climate adaptation in passing, with just one focusing on it by considering how to improve irrigated agriculture (de Sousa Fragoso and de Almeida Noéme 2018).[1]

Organization and Environment is a leading journal for discussion of the implications of climate for organizations and vice versa, where since the 1980s both philosophical and theoretical positions on environment have been discussed as well as organizational or management implications. However, the journal has not published any research papers exploring theories and implications of societal collapse due to environmental catastrophe.[2] Three articles mention climate adaptation. Two of those have adaptation as a context but explore other issues as their main focus, specifically social learning (Orsato, Ferraz de Campos and Barakat 2018) and network learning (Temby et al. 2016). Only one paper in that journal looks at climate adaptation as its main focus and the implications for organization. While a helpful summary of how difficult the implications are for management, the paper does not explore the implications of a widespread societal collapse (Clément and Rivera 2016).

Away from management studies, the field of climate adaptation is wide (Lesnikowski et al. 2015). To illustrate, a search on Google Scholar returns more than 40,000 hits for the term 'climate adaptation'. In answering the questions I set for myself in this chapter, I will not be reviewing that existing field and scholarship. One might ask 'Why not?' The answer is that the

[1] A full text search of the journal database shows that the following terms have never been included in articles in this journal: 'environmental collapse', 'economic collapse', 'social collapse', 'societal collapse', 'environmental catastrophe', 'human extinction'. 'Catastrophe' is mentioned in three papers, with two about Bangladesh factory fires and the other being Bendell, Sutherland and Little (2017).

[2] A full text search of the journal database shows that the terms 'environmental collapse', 'social collapse' and 'societal collapse' have occurred once, each in separate articles. 'Economic collapse' has been mentioned in three articles. 'Human extinction' is mentioned in two articles. 'Environmental catastrophe' is mentioned in twelve articles. A reading of these articles showed that they were not exploring collapse.

field of climate adaptation is oriented around ways to maintain our current societies as they face manageable climactic perturbations (ibid.). The concept of 'deep adaptation' resonates with that agenda where we accept that we will need to change, but breaks with it by taking as its starting point the inevitability of societal collapse (as I will explain below).

In addition, after the release of this chapter as a paper in 2018, I became aware of the fields of scholarship on catastrophic risks, existential risks and 'collapsology' (Servigne and Stevens 2020). I recommend readers explore the literature in those fields, as I am continuing to do. This chapter does not incorporate insights from those fields.

Our non-linear world

This chapter is not the venue for a detailed examination of all the latest climate science. However, I reviewed the scientific literature from the past few years and, where there was still large uncertainty, I then sought the latest data from research institutes. In this section, I summarize the findings to establish the premise that it is time we consider the implications of it being too late to avert a global environmental catastrophe in the lifetimes of people alive today.

The simple evidence of global ambient temperature rise is indisputable. Seventeen of the eighteen warmest years in the 136-year record up to 2018 have all occurred since 2001, and global temperatures have increased by 0.9°C since 1880 (NASA/GISS 2018). The most surprising warming is in the Arctic, where the 2016 land-surface temperature was 2.0°C above the 1981–2010 average, breaking the previous records of 2007, 2011, and 2015 by 0.8°C, representing a 3.5°C increase since the records began in 1900 (Aaron-Morrison et al. 2017).

These data are fairly easy to collate and not widely challenged, so swiftly find their way into academic publications. However, to obtain a sense of the implications of this warming on environment and society, one needs real-time data on the current situation and the trends that they may imply. Climate change and its associated impacts have, as we will see, been significant in the last few years. Therefore, to appreciate the situation we need to look directly to the research institutes, researchers and their websites for the most recent information. That means using, but not relying solely on, academic journal articles and the slowly produced reports of the Intergovernmental Panel on Climate Change (IPCC). This international institution has done useful work but has a track record of significantly underestimating the pace of change, which has been more accurately predicted over past decades by eminent climate scientists (Herrando-Pérez et al. 2019; Spratt and Dunlop 2018). Some researchers have concluded that climate change is happening and will happen much faster than the IPCC predicted (Xu et al. 2018). For instance, the IPCC previously assigned a probability of 17 per cent for crossing the 1.5°C global ambient warming mark by 2030, which underestimated a few key factors that 'bring forward the estimated date of 1.5°C of warming to around 2030, with the 2°C boundary reached by 2045' (Xu et al. 2018). The natural fluctuations in the Pacific 'raise[s] the odds of blasting through 1.5°C by 2025 to at least 10%', they wrote. A closer study of this 'interdecadal Pacific oscillation (IPO)' found that if it shifts to a positive warming phase, that 'would lead to a projected exceedance of the [1.5°C warming] target centered around 2026' (Henley and King 2017), which is statistical language for how it could be even sooner than that (but hopefully later).

Therefore, in this review, I will draw upon a range of sources outside of the IPCC, with a focus on data since 2014. That is because, unfortunately, data collected since then are often consistent with non-linear changes to our environment. Non-linear changes are of central importance to understanding climate change as they suggest both that impacts will be far more rapid and severe than predictions based on linear projections and that the changes no longer correlate with the rate of anthropogenic carbon emissions. While non-linear change does not necessarily mean exponential change, or that there might not be a curb or pause, in the natural world, changes like non-linear rises in sea level or non-linear changes in sea ice are the result of such massive processes with amplifying feedbacks, so it is reasonable to consider that such non-linear processes will be unstoppable. In other words, such changes would constitute both aspects and indicators of what is called 'runaway climate change'.

What do people mean by 'runaway' change? Scientists who study climate tipping points have found that 'we might already have crossed the threshold for a cascade of interrelated tipping points' (Lenton et al. 2019), which would begin taking the earth to a far hotter state. The researchers concluded that of the fifteen potential tipping points that they identified in 2008, seven now show signs of being active, meaning they may have already tipped into self-reinforcing and irreversible change – that is, along with two new ones they have added to their list (Lenton et al. 2019). With nine tipping points in total already active and interrelating, 'runaway' change is a reasonable term to use for that situation. New models are projecting that, on current emissions pathways, we are headed for more than 6°C of warming by the end of the century (Johnson 2019). Therefore, if people assess that we might be, probably are, or definitely are at the start of runaway climate change, these would be credible rather than extreme assessments.

The warming of the Arctic has reached wider public awareness as it has begun destabilizing winds in the higher atmosphere, specifically the jet stream and the northern polar vortex, leading to extreme movements of warmer air north into the Arctic and cold air to the south. At one point in early 2018, temperature recordings from the Arctic were 20°C above the average for that date (Watts 2018). The warming Arctic has led to dramatic loss in sea ice, the average September extent of which has been decreasing at a rate of 13.2% per decade since 1980, so that over two-thirds of the ice cover has gone (NSIDC/NASA 2018). These data are made more concerning by changes in sea-ice volume, which is an indicator of the resilience of the ice sheet to future warming and storms. It was at the lowest it has ever been in 2017, continuing a consistent downward trend (Kahn 2017).

Given a reduction in the reflection of the sun's rays from the surface of white ice, an ice-free Arctic is predicted to increase warming globally by a substantial degree. Writing in 2014, scientists calculated this change is already equivalent to 25% of the direct forcing of temperature increase from CO_2 during the past 30 years (Pistone, Eisenman and Ramanathan 2014). That means we could remove a quarter of the cumulative CO_2 emissions of the last three decades and it would already be outweighed by the loss of the reflective power of annual Arctic sea-ice cover. One of the most eminent climate scientists in the world, Peter Wadhams, believes an ice-free Arctic will occur for a summer in the next few years. Once that happens, the warming feedbacks make it near certain that, after some years, an entire year will be ice free in the Arctic, which he calculated will likely increase by 50% the warming caused by the CO_2 produced by human activity (Wadhams 2016).[3] Whereas some scientists assess warming implications to be lower than that (Hudson 2011), if correct, it would render the calculations of the IPCC redundant, along with the targets and proposals of the United Nations Framework Convention on Climate Change (UNFCCC). Between 2002 and 2016, Greenland shed approximately 280 gigatons of ice per year, and the island's lower-elevation and coastal areas experienced up to 13.1 ft (4 metres) of ice-mass loss (expressed in equivalent water height) over a 14-year period (NASA 2018). Along with other melting of land ice and the thermal expansion of water, this has contributed to a global mean sea-level rise of about 3.2 mm/year, representing a total increase of more than 80 mm since 1993 (JPL/PO.DAAC 2018). The IPCC has been found to have under-predicted sea-level rise as part of its general 'understatement of existential climate risk' (Spratt and Dunlop 2018). Recent data show that the upward trend is non-linear (Malmquist 2018). That means sea levels are rising due to non-linear increases in the melting of land-based ice.

The observed phenomena are both at the higher ranges and more extreme than what most climate models over the past decades were predicting for our current time. They are more extreme because the models did not predict the extent of the variability of weather, which is arising from phenomena such as the degree of changes to the jet streams (Kornhuber et al. 2019). The global average temperatures are at the higher edge of model predictions for the current time, especially if we consider the most recent years as indicating a new normal, rather than waiting for scientific convention to confirm decadal trends. 'The average temperature for the twelve months to June 2020 is close to 1.3°C above the level [of pre-industrial temperatures used by the IPCC] for its 1.5°C and 2°C degree thresholds' (Copernicus Programme 2020). These current measurements are consistent with non-linear changes in our environment that would then trigger uncontrollable impacts on human habitat and agriculture,

---

[3] This was corrected from 'double' in an earlier version.

with subsequent complex impacts on social, economic and political systems. I will return to the implications of these trends after listing some more of the impacts that are already being reported as occurring today.

Already we see impacts on storm, drought and flood frequency and strength due to a change in the balance of the thermal heat in the oceans and atmosphere, with the poles heating faster (Herring et al. 2018). In addition, the greater heat being trapped in the polar regions means the temperature gradient with the lower latitudes drops and therefore the jet streams weaken and become more wavy, thereby creating more blocks of high pressure that lead to extreme weather (Kornhuber et al. 2019). We are witnessing negative impacts on agriculture. Climate change has reduced growth in crop yields by 1–2 per cent per decade over the past century (Wiebe et al. 2015). The UN Food and Agriculture Organization (FAO) reports that weather abnormalities related to climate change are costing billions of dollars a year and growing exponentially. For now, the impact is calculated in money, but the nutritional implications are key (FAO 2018). We are also seeing impacts on marine ecosystems. About half of the world's coral reefs have died in the last 30 years as a result of a combination of factors, though higher water temperatures and acidification due to higher CO_2 concentrations in ocean water are key (Phys.org. 2018). In the ten years prior to 2016, the Atlantic Ocean soaked up 50 per cent more carbon dioxide than it did the previous decade, measurably speeding up the acidification of the ocean (Woosley, Millero and Wanninkhof 2016). This study is indicative of oceans worldwide, and the consequent acidification degrades the base of the marine food web, thereby reducing the ability of fish populations to reproduce themselves across the globe (Britten, Dowd and Worm 2015). Meanwhile, warming oceans are already reducing the population size of some fish species (Aaron-Morrison et al. 2017). Compounding these threats to human nutrition, in some regions we are witnessing an exponential rise in the spread of mosquito and tick-borne viruses as temperatures become more conducive to them (ECJCR 2018).

Looking ahead

Most of the impacts I just summarized are already upon us and, even without increasing their severity, they will nevertheless increase with respect to our ecosystems, soils, seas and our societies over time. It is difficult to predict future impacts. But it is more difficult not to predict them. The reported impacts today are at the very worst end of predictions being made in the early 1990s – back when I first studied climate change and model-based climate predictions as an undergraduate at Cambridge University. The models today suggest an increase in storm number and strength (Herring et al. 2018). They predict a decline of normal agriculture, including the compromising of mass production of grains in the northern hemisphere and intermittent disruption to rice production in the tropics. That includes predicted declines in the yields of rice, wheat and corn in China by 36.25%, 18.26% and 45.10%, respectively, by the end of this century (Zhang et al. 2016). Naresh Kumar et al. (2014) project a 6–23% and 15–25% reduction in the wheat yield in India during the 2050s and 2080s, respectively, under the mainstream projected climate change scenarios. The loss of coral and the acidification of the seas are predicted to reduce fishery productivity by more than half (Rogers et al. 2017). The rates of sea-level rise suggest they may soon become exponential (Malmquist 2018), which will pose significant problems for hundreds of millions of people living in coastal zones (Neumann et al. 2015). Environmental scientists are now describing our current era as the sixth mass extinction event in the history of planet Earth, with this one caused by us. About half of all plant and animal species in the world's most biodiverse places are at risk of extinction due to climate change (WWF 2018). The World Bank reported in 2018 that countries needed to prepare for more than 100 million internally displaced people due to the effects of climate change (Rigaud et al. 2018), in addition to millions of international refugees.

Despite you, me and most people we know in this field already hearing data on this global situation, it is useful to recap simply to invite a sober acceptance of our current predicament. It has led some commentators to describe our time as a new geological era shaped by humans – the Anthropocene (Hamilton et al. 2015).

It has led others to conclude that we should be exploring how to live in an unstable post-sustainability situation (Benson and Craig 2014; Foster 2015). This context is worth being reminded of, as it provides the basis upon which to assess the significance, or otherwise, of all the praiseworthy efforts that have been underway and reported in some detail here and in various journals over the past decade. I will now offer an attempt at a summary of that broader context insofar as it might frame our future work on sustainability.

The politically permissible scientific consensus is that we need to stay beneath 2°C warming of global ambient temperatures to avoid dangerous and uncontrollable levels of climate change, with impacts such as mass starvation, disease, flooding, storm destruction, forced migration and war. That figure was agreed by governments that were dealing with many domestic and international pressures from vested interests, particularly corporations. It is therefore not a figure that many scientists would advise, given that many ecosystems will be lost and many risks created if we approach 2°C global ambient warming (Wadhams 2018). The IPCC agreed in 2013 that if the world does not keep further anthropogenic emissions below a total of 800 billion tonnes of carbon, we are not likely to keep average temperatures below 2°C of global averaged warming. That left about 270 billion tonnes of carbon to burn (Pidcock 2013). Total global emissions remain at around 11 billion tonnes of carbon per year (which is 37 billion tonnes of CO_2). Those calculations appear worrying but give the impression we have at least a decade to change. It takes significant time to change economic systems, so if we are not already on the path to dramatic reductions, it is unlikely we will keep within the carbon limit. With an increase of carbon emissions of 2% in 2017, any decoupling of economic activity from emissions is not yet making a net dent in global emissions (Canadell et al. 2017). So we are not on the path to prevent going over 2°C warming through emissions reductions. In any case, the IPCC estimate of a carbon budget was controversial. One scientist has calculated that the IPCC had underestimated the amount of methane release, and therefore the carbon budget will be used up entirely by 2025 (Knorr 2019).

That situation is why some experts have argued for more work on removing carbon from the atmosphere with machines.

Unfortunately, the current technology needs to be scaled up by a factor of two million within two years, all powered by renewables, alongside massive emissions cuts, to reduce the amount of heating already locked into the system (Wadhams 2018). Biological approaches to carbon capture appear far more promising (Hawken and Wilkinson 2017). These include planting trees, restoring soils used in agriculture and growing seagrass and kelp, amongst other approaches. They also offer wider beneficial environmental and social side effects. Studies on seagrass (Greiner et al. 2013) and seaweed (Flannery 2015) indicate we could be taking millions of tons of carbon from the atmosphere immediately and continually if we had a massive effort to restore seagrass meadows and to farm seaweed. The net sequestration effect is still being assessed but in certain environments will be significant (Howard et al. 2017). Research into 'management-intensive rotational grazing' practices (MIRG), also known as holistic grazing, shows how a healthy grassland can store carbon. A 2014 study measured annual per hectare increases in soil carbon at 8 tons per year on farms converted to these practices (Machmuller et al. 2015). The world uses about 3.5 billion hectares of land for pasture and fodder crops. Using the 8-ton figure above, converting a tenth of that land to MIRG practices would sequester a quarter of present emissions. In addition, no-till methods of horticulture can sequester as much as 2 tons of carbon per hectare per year, so could also make significant contributions. It is clear, therefore, that our assessment of carbon budgets must focus as much on these agricultural systems as it does on emissions reductions.

Clearly, a massive campaign and policy agenda to transform agriculture and restore ecosystems globally is needed right now. It will be a huge undertaking, undoing 60 years of developments in world agriculture. In addition, it means the conservation of our existing wetlands and forests must suddenly become successful after decades of failure across lands outside of geographically limited nature reserves. Even if such will emerges immediately, the heating and instability already locked into the climate will cause damage to ecosystems, so it will be difficult for such approaches to curb the global atmospheric carbon level. The reality that we have progressed too far already to avert disruptions to ecosystems is highlighted by the finding that if CO_2 removal from the atmosphere could work at scale, it would not prevent massive damage to marine life, which is locked in for many years due to acidification from the dissolving of CO_2 in the oceans (Mathesius et al. 2015).

Despite the limitations of what humans can do to work with nature to encourage its carbon sequestration processes, the planet has been helping us out anyway. A global 'greening' of the planet has significantly slowed the rise of carbon dioxide in the atmosphere since the start of the century. Plants have been growing faster and larger due to higher CO_2 levels in the air and warming temperatures that reduce the CO_2 emitted by plants via respiration. The effects have led the proportion of annual carbon emissions remaining in the air to fall from about 50% to 40% in the last decade. However, this process only offers a limited effect, as the absolute level of CO_2 in the atmosphere is continuing to rise, breaking the milestone of 400 parts per million (ppm) in 2015. Given that changes in seasons, temperature extremes, flood and drought are beginning to negatively affect ecosystems, the risk exists that this global greening effect may be reduced in time (Keenan et al. 2016).

These potential reductions in atmospheric carbon from natural and assisted biological processes present a flickering ray of hope in our dark situation. However, the uncertainty about their impact needs to be contrasted with the uncertain yet significant impact of increasing methane release in the atmosphere. It is a gas that enables far more trapping of heat from the sun's rays than CO_2 but was significantly underestimated in most of the climate models since 2005 and ignored before then. Recent research is finding and predicting far higher levels of methane (Farquharson et al. 2019; Lamarche-Gagnon et al. 2019; Nisbet et al. 2019). The authors of the 2016 Global Methane Budget report found that in the early years of this century, concentrations of methane rose by only about 0.5 ppb each year, compared with 10 ppb in 2014 and 2015. Various sources were identified from fossil fuels to agriculture to melting permafrost (Saunois et al. 2016).

Given the contentiousness of this topic in the scientific community, it may even be contentious for me to say that there is no scientific consensus on the sources of current methane emissions or the potential risk and timing of significant methane releases from either surface or sub-sea permafrost. A recent attempt at consensus on methane risk from melting surface permafrost

concluded methane release would happen over centuries or millennia, not this decade (Schuur et al. 2015). Yet within three
years that consensus was broken by one of the most detailed
experiments which found that if the melting permafrost remains
waterlogged, which is likely, then it produces significant amounts
of methane within just a few years (Knoblauch et al. 2018). The
debate is now likely to be about whether other microorganisms
might thrive in that environment to eat up the methane – and
whether or not in time to reduce the climate impact.

The debate about methane release from clathrate forms, or
frozen methane hydrates, on the Arctic sea floor is even more
contentious. In 2010, a group of scientists published a study that
warned how the warming of the Arctic could lead to a speed and
scale of methane release that would be catastrophic to life on
earth through atmospheric heating of more than 5°C within just a
few years of such a release (Shakhova et al. 2010). The study triggered a fierce debate, much of which was ill considered, perhaps
understandable given the shocking implications of this information (Ahmed 2013). Since then, key questions at the heart of
this scientific debate (about what would amount to the probable
extinction of the human race) include the amount of time it will
take for ocean warming to destabilize hydrates on the sea floor,
and how much methane will be consumed by aerobic and anaero-
bic microbes before it reaches the surface and escapes into the
atmosphere. In a global review of this contentious topic, scientists concluded that there is not the evidence to predict a sudden
release of catastrophic levels of methane in the near term (Ruppel
and Kessler 2017). However, a key reason for their conclusion
was the lack of data showing actual increases in atmospheric
methane at the surface of the Arctic, which is partly the result of
a lack of sensors collecting such information. Most ground-level
methane measuring systems are on land. Could that be why the
unusual increases in atmospheric methane concentrations cannot
be fully explained by existing data sets from around the world
(Saunois et al. 2016)? The lack of easy-to-access and reputable
analysis of the potential implications of real-time atmospheric
measurements is bewildering to me.[4] However, there has been

---

[4] https://www.esrl.noaa.gov/gmd/ccgg/trends_ch4/

'very strong' growth in methane concentrations between 2014 and 2017 (Nisbet et al. 2019). A study in 2020 of methane release at the other pole, on the insufficient filtering effects of microbes, adds to concern that methane might be released in dangerous amounts from the sea bed (Thurber, Seabrook and Welsh 2020). These recent studies indicate to me that it would not be accurate to claim there is a consensus that it is highly unlikely we will see near-term massive release of methane from the Arctic Ocean. In 2017, scientists working on the Eastern Siberian sea shelf reported that the permafrost layer has thinned enough to risk destabilizing hydrates (Arctic News 2018). That report of sub-sea permafrost destabilization in the East Siberian Arctic sea shelf, the latest unprecedented temperatures in the Arctic and the recent data on non-linear rises in high-atmosphere methane levels combine to make it feel like we might be about to play Russian roulette with the entire human race, with two bullets already loaded. Nothing is certain. But it is sobering that humanity has arrived at a situation of our own making where we now debate the strength of analyses of our near-term extinction.

Apocalypse uncertain

The truly shocking information on the trends in climate change and their impacts on ecology and society are leading some to call for us to experiment with geoengineering the climate, from fertilizing the oceans so they consume more CO_2 through photosynthesis, to releasing chemicals in the upper atmosphere so the sun's rays are reflected. The unpredictability of geoengineering the climate through the latter method, in particular the dangers of disturbances to seasonal rains that billions of people rely on, makes it unlikely to be used (Keller, Feng and Oschlies 2014). The potential natural geoengineering from increased sulphur releases from volcanoes, due to isostatic rebound as weight on the earth's crust is redistributed, is not likely to make a significant contribution to earth temperatures for decades or even centuries.

It is a truism that we do not know what the future will be. But we can see trends. We do not know if the power of human ingenuity will help sufficiently to change the environmental trajectory we are on. Unfortunately, the recent years of innovation, investment and patenting indicate how human ingenuity has increasingly been channelled into consumerism and financial engineering. We might pray for time. But the evidence before us suggests that we are set for disruptive and probably uncontrollable levels of climate change, bringing starvation, destruction, migration, disease and war (Servigne and Stevens 2020).

It is difficult to assess how disruptive the impacts of climate change will be or where will be most affected, especially as economic and social systems will respond in complex ways. The evidence is mounting that the impacts will be catastrophic to our livelihoods and the societies that we live in. Our norms of behaviour, which we call our 'civilization', may also degrade. When I first wrote this chapter as a paper in early 2018, I did not know about the fields of scholarship that relate to catastrophic risks and what is now called 'collapsology' (Servigne and Stevens 2020). Those fields attempt to map how societies break down and how such collapses are likely to occur in future. I recommend exploring that literature, to look at how impacts on agriculture, international relations, social unease, crime, civil conflict, disease prevalence, financial stability and so on can cascade to create a breakdown of societies. In this chapter, I cannot prove the likelihood or certainty of societal collapse, and experts in the field of collapsology say that within such complex systems any attempt to prove within modalities of modern scholarship whether collapse will or will not happen would be futile. However, they also conclude that this does not mean that our limits in prediction within complex systems should restrict us from sense-making about our predicament.

When we contemplate this possibility of 'societal collapse', it can seem abstract. The previous paragraphs may seem, subconsciously at least, to be describing a situation to lament as we witness scenes on television or online. But when I say starvation, destruction, migration, disease and war, I mean in your own life. With the power down, soon you wouldn't have water coming out of your tap. You will depend on your neighbours for food and some warmth. You will become malnourished. You won't know whether to stay or go. You will fear being violently killed before starving to death.

These descriptions may seem overly dramatic. Some readers might consider them an unacademic form of writing, which would be an interesting comment on why we even write at all.

This is why the development of auto-ethnography within academia invites us to include in our academic prose some novel ways of communicating that might create emotional connection with the reader (Adams et al. 2015). I chose the words above as an attempt to cut through the sense that this topic is purely theoretical. As we are considering here a situation where the publishers of this book will no longer exist, the electricity to read its outputs won't exist and a profession to educate won't exist, I think it's time we break some of the conventions of this format.

However, some of us may take pride in upholding the norms of the current society, even amidst collapse. Even though some of us might believe in the importance of maintaining norms of behaviour as indicators of shared values, others will consider that the probability of collapse means that efforts to reform our current system are no longer the pragmatic choice. My conclusion to this situation has been that we need to expand our work on 'sustainability' to consider how communities, countries and humanity can adapt to the coming troubles. I have dubbed this the 'deep adaptation agenda' to contrast it with the limited scope of current climate adaptation activities. My experience is that a lot of people are resistant to the conclusions I have just shared. So before explaining the implications, let us consider some of the emotional and psychological responses to the information I have here summarized.

Systems of denial

It would not be unusual to feel a bit affronted, disturbed or saddened by the information and arguments I have just shared. In the past few years, many people have said to me that 'it can't be too late to stop climate change because, if it was, how would we find the energy to keep on striving for change?' With such views, a possible reality is denied because people want to continue their striving. What does that tell us? The 'striving' is based on a rationale of maintaining self-identities related to espoused values. It is understandable why that happens. If one has always thought of oneself as having self-worth through promoting the public good, then information that initially appears to take away that self-image is difficult to assimilate.

That process of strategic denial to maintain striving and identity is easily seen in online debates about the latest climate science. One particular case is illustrative. In 2017, the *New York Magazine* published an article that drew together the latest data and analysis of what the implications of rapid climatic warming would be for ecosystems and humanity. Unlike the many dry academic articles on these subjects, this popular article sought to describe these processes in visceral ways (Wallace-Wells 2017). The reaction of some environmentalists to this article did not focus on the accuracy of the descriptions or what might be done to reduce some of the worst effects that were identified in the article. Instead, they focused on whether such ideas should be communicated to the general public. Climate scientist Michael Mann warned against presenting 'the problem as unsolvable, and feed[ing] a sense of doom, inevitability and hopelessness' (in Becker 2017). Environmental journalist Alex Steffen (2017) tweeted that 'Dropping the dire truth . . . on unsupported readers does not produce action, but fear.' In a blog post, Daniel Aldana Cohen (2017), an assistant sociology professor working on climate politics, called the piece 'climate disaster porn'. Their reactions reflect what some people have said to me in professional environmental circles. The argument made is that to discuss the likelihood and nature of societal collapse due to climate change is irresponsible because it might trigger hopelessness amongst the general public. I always thought it odd to restrict our own exploration of reality and censor our own sense-making due to our ideas about how our conclusions might come across to others. Given that this attempt at censoring was so widely shared in the environmental field in 2017, it deserves some closer attention.

I see four particular insights about what is happening when people argue we should not communicate to the public the likelihood and nature of the catastrophe we face. First, it is not untypical for people to respond to data in terms of what perspectives we wish for ourselves and others to have, rather than what the data may suggest is happening. That reflects an approach to reality and society that may be tolerable in times of plenty but counterproductive when facing major risks. Second, bad news and extreme scenarios impact on human psychology. We sometimes overlook that the question of how they impact is a matter for informed discussion that can draw upon psychology and communications theories. Indeed, there are journals dedicated to environmental psychology. There is some evidence from social psychology to suggest that by focusing on impacts now, it makes climate change more proximate, which increases support for mitigation (McDonald, Chai and Newell 2015). That is not conclusive, and this field is one for further exploration. That serious scholars or activists would make a claim about impacts of communication without specific theory or evidence suggests that they are not actually motivated to know the effect on the public but are attracted to a certain argument that explains their view.

A third insight from the debates about whether to publish information on the probable collapse of our societies is that sometimes people can express a paternalistic relationship between themselves as environmental experts and other people whom they categorize as 'the public'. That is related to the non-populist antipolitics technocratic attitude that has pervaded contemporary environmentalism. It is a perspective that frames the challenges as one of encouraging people to try harder to be nicer and better rather than coming together in solidarity to either undermine or overthrow a system that demands we participate in environmental degradation.

A fourth insight is that 'hopelessness' and its related emotions of dismay and despair are understandably feared but wrongly assumed to be entirely negative and to be avoided whatever the situation. Alex Steffen warned that 'Despair is never helpful' (2017). However, the range of ancient wisdom traditions see a significant place for hopelessness and despair. Contemporary reflections on people's emotional and even spiritual growth as a result of their hopelessness and despair align with these ancient ideas. The loss of a capability, a loved one or a way of life, or the receipt of a terminal diagnosis, have all been reported, or personally experienced, as a trigger for a new way of perceiving self and world, with hopelessness and despair being a necessary step in the process (Matousek 2008). In such contexts 'hope' is not a good thing to maintain, as it depends on what one is hoping for. When the debate raged about the value of the *New York Magazine* article, some commentators picked up on this theme. 'In abandoning hope that one way of life will continue, we open up a space for alternative hopes,' wrote Tommy Lynch (2017).

This question of valid and useful hope is something that we must explore much further. Leadership theorist Jonathan Gosling has raised the question of whether we, in modern industrial consumer societies, need a more 'radical hope' in the context of climate change and a growing sense of 'things falling apart' (Gosling 2016). He invites us to explore what we could learn from other cultures that have faced catastrophe. Examining the way Native American Indians coped with being moved onto reservations, Lear (2008) looked at what he calls the 'blind spot' of any culture: the inability to conceive of its own destruction and possible extinction. He explored the role of forms of hope that involved neither denial nor blind optimism. 'What makes this hope radical is that it is directed toward a future goodness that transcends the current ability to understand what it is' (ibid.). He explains how some of the Native American chiefs had a form of 'imaginative excellence' by trying to imagine what ethical values would be needed in their new lifestyle on the reservation. He suggests that besides the standard alternatives of freedom or death (in service of one's culture) there is another way, less grand yet demanding just as much courage: the way of 'creative adaptation'. This form of creatively constructed hope may be relevant to our western civilization as we confront disruptive climate change (Gosling and Case 2013). It should be obvious to the reader that indigenous peoples today should be supported to fight such oppression and so not be forced to discover 'radical hope' in the same way. Quite the contrary, the coming collapse of industrial consumer societies means they can and must be both supported and learned about by people in modern urban cultures (Whyte, Talley and Gibson 2019).

Such deliberations are few and far between in either the fields of environmental studies or management studies. It is to help break this semi-censorship of our own community of inquiry on sustainability that motivated me to write this paper. Some scholarship has looked at the process of denial more closely. Drawing on sociologist Stanley Cohen, Foster (2015) identifies two subtle forms of denial – interpretative and implicative. If we accept certain facts but interpret them in a way that makes them 'safer' to our personal psychology, it is a form of 'interpretative denial'. If we recognize the troubling implications of these facts but respond by busying ourselves on activities that do not arise from a full assessment of the situation, then that is 'implicative denial'. Foster argues that implicative denial is rife within the environmental movement; from dipping into a local Transition Towns initiative to signing online petitions or renouncing flying, there are endless ways for people to be 'doing something' without seriously confronting the reality of climate change.

There are three main factors that could be encouraging professional environmentalists in their denial that our societies will collapse in the near term. The first is the way the natural scientific community operates. Eminent climate scientist James Hansen has always been ahead of the conservative consensus in his analyses and predictions. Using the case study of sea-level rise, he threw light on processes that lead to 'scientific reticence' to conclude and communicate scenarios that would be disturbing to employers, funders, governments and the public (Hansen 2007). A more detailed study of this process across issues and institutions found that climate-change scientists routinely underestimate impacts 'by erring on the side of least drama' (Brysse et al. 2013). Combined with the norms of scientific analysis and reporting to be cautious and avoid bombast, and the time it takes to fund, research, produce and publish peer-reviewed scientific studies, this means that the information available to environmental professionals about the state of the climate is not as frightening as it could be. In this chapter, I have had to mix information from peer-reviewed articles with recent data from individual scientists and their research institutions to provide the evidence which suggests we are now in a non-linear situation of climatic changes and effects.

A second set of factors influencing denial may be personal. George Marshall summarized the insights from psychology on climate denial, including the interpretive and implicative denial of those who are aware but have not prioritized it. In particular, we are social beings and our assessment of what to do about information is influenced by our culture. Therefore, people often avoid voicing certain thoughts when they go against the social norm around them and/or their social identity. Especially in situations of shared powerlessness, it can be perceived as safer to hide one's views and do nothing if it goes against the status quo. Marshall also explains how our typical fear of death means that we do not give our full attention to information that reminds us of that. According to anthropologist Ernest Becker (1973),

'A fear of death lies at the centre of all human belief.' Marshall explains: 'The denial of death is a "vital lie" that leads us to invest our efforts into our cultures and social groups to obtain a sense of permanence and survival beyond our death. Thus, [Becker] argued, when we receive reminders of our death – what he calls death salience – we respond by defending those values and cultures.' This view was recently expounded as part of the 'terror management theory' proposed by Jeff Greenberg, Sheldon Solomon and Tom Pyszczynski (2015). Although Marshall does not consider it directly, these processes would apply more so to 'collapse denial' than to climate denial, as the death involves not only oneself but all of what one could contribute to.

These personal processes are likely made worse for sustainability experts than the general public, given the typical allegiance of professionals to incumbent social structures. Research has revealed that people who have a higher level of formal education are more supportive of the existing social and economic systems that those that have less education (Schmidt 2000). The argument is that people who have invested time and money in progressing to a higher status within existing social structures are more naturally inclined to imagine reform of those systems than their upending. This situation is accentuated if we assume our livelihood, identity and self-worth are dependent on the perspective that progress on sustainability is possible and that we are part of that progressive process.

The third factor influencing denial is institutional. I have worked for more than 20 years within or with organizations working on the sustainability agenda, in non-profit, private and governmental sectors. In none of these sectors is there an obvious institutional self-interest in articulating the probability or inevitability of societal collapse. Not to members of your charity, not to consumers of your product, not to voters for your party. There are a few niche companies that benefit from a collapse discourse, leading some people to seek to prepare by buying their products. This field may expand in future, at various scales of preparedness, which I return to below. But the internal culture of environmental groups remains strongly in favour of appearing effective, even when decades of investment and campaigning have not produced a net positive outcome on climate, ecosystems or many specific species.

Let us look at the largest environmental charity, the World Wide Fund for Nature (WWF), as an example of this process of organizational drivers of implicative denial. I worked for them when we were striving towards all UK wood product imports being from sustainable forests by 1995. Then it became 'well-managed' forests by 2000. Then targets were quietly forgotten while the potensiphonic language[5] of solving deforestation through innovative partnerships remained. If the employees of the world's leading environmental groups were on performance-related pay, they would probably owe their members and donors money by now. The fact that some readers may find such a comment to be rude and unhelpful highlights how our interests in civility, praise and belonging within a professional community can censor those of us who seek to communicate uncomfortable truths in memorable ways (like that journalist in *New York Magazine*).

These personal and institutional factors mean that environmental professionals may be some of the slowest to process the implications of the latest climate information. In 2017, a survey of more than 8,000 people across eight different countries – Australia, Brazil, China, Germany, India, South Africa, the United Kingdom and the United States – asked respondents to gauge their perceived level of security as compared to two years before in regards to global risks. A total of 61% said they felt more insecure, while only 18% said they felt more secure. On climate change, 48% of respondents strongly agreed that it is a global catastrophic risk, with an additional 36% of people tending to agree with that. Only 14% of respondents disagreed to some degree with the idea that climate change presented a catastrophic risk (Hill 2017). This perspective on climate may help explain other survey data that suggest remarkable changes in how people view technology, progress, their society and the future prospects for their children. A 2017 global survey found that only 13% of the public think the world is getting better, which is a major change from ten years earlier (Ipsos MORI 2017). In the United States, polls indicate that belief in technology as a good force has been fading (Asay 2013). This information may reflect a wider

---

[5] Language that emphasizes power and supremacy.

questioning of the idea that progress is always good and possible. Such a shift in perspective is indicated by opinion polls showing that far fewer people today than in the last decade believe their children will have a better future than themselves (Stokes 2017). Another indicator of whether people believe in their future is if they believe in the basis of their society. Studies have consistently found that more people are losing faith in electoral democracy and in the economic system (Bendell and Lopatin 2016). The questioning of mainstream life and of progress is also reflected in the shift away from secular-rational values to traditional values that has been occurring worldwide since 2010 (World Values Survey 2016). How do children feel about their futures? I have not found a large or longitudinal study on children's views of the future, but one journalist who asked children from 6 to 12 years old to paint what they expect the world in 50 years to be like generated mostly apocalyptic images (Banos Ruiz 2017). This evidence suggests that the idea we 'experts' need to be careful about what to tell 'them', the 'unsupported public', may be a narcissistic delusion in need of immediate remedy.

Emotional difficulties with realizing the tragedy that is coming, and that is in many ways upon us already, are understandable. Yet these difficulties need to be overcome so we can explore what the implications may be for our work, lives and communities.

Framing after denial

As a sense of calamity grows within the environmental movement, some argue against a focus on 'carbon reductionism' for how it may limit our appreciation of why we face this tragedy and what to do about it (Eisenstein 2018). I agree that climate change is not just a pollution problem but an indicator of how our human psyche and culture became divorced from our natural habitat. However, that does not mean we should deprioritize the climate situation for a broader environmental agenda.

If we allow ourselves to accept that a climate-induced form of economic and societal collapse is now likely, then we can begin to explore the nature and likelihood of that collapse. That is when we discover a range of different views. Some frame the future as involving a collapse of this economic and social system, which does not necessarily mean a complete collapse of law, order, identity and values. Some regard that kind of collapse as offering a potential upside in bringing humanity to a post-consumerist way of life that would be more conscious of relationships between people and nature (Eisenstein 2013). Some even argue that this reconnection with nature will generate hitherto unimaginable solutions to our predicament. Sometimes that view comes with a belief in the power of spiritual practices to influence the material world according to human intent. The perspective that natural or spiritual reconnection might save us from catastrophe is, however, a psychological response one could analyse as a form of denial.

Some analysts emphasize the unpredictable and catastrophic nature of this collapse, so that it will not be possible to plan a way to transition at either collective or small-scale levels to a new way of life that we might imagine as tolerable, let alone beautiful. Those people who consider that we face 'near-term human extinction' can draw on the findings of geologists that the last mass extinction of life on earth, where 95% of species disappeared, was due to methane-induced rapid warming of the atmosphere (Brand et al. 2016; Lee 2014). Although a far distance from *inevitable* human extinction, two reputable climate scientists have calculated that the human race now has a 1 in 20 chance of going extinct this century (Xu and Ramanathan 2017).

With each of these framings – collapse, catastrophe, extinction – people describe different degrees of certainty. Different people speak of a scenario being possible, probable or inevitable. In my conversations with both professionals in sustainability or climate, and others not directly involved, I have found that people choose a scenario and a probability depending not on what the data and its analysis might suggest, but what they are choosing to live with as a story about this topic. This parallels findings in psychology that none of us are purely logic machines but merge information into stories about how things relate and why (Marshall 2014). None of us are immune to that process. Currently, I have chosen to interpret the information as indicating inevitable collapse, probable catastrophe and possible extinction. I do not prove in this chapter that societal collapse is inevitable, as that would require more discussion of complex social, economic, political and cultural processes, but it is my personal conclusion from an overview of those factors which I have not yet published (and which seems reasonable to share with the reader given the seriousness of the matter).

There is a growing community of people who conclude we face inevitable human extinction and treat that view as a prerequisite for meaningful discussions about the implications for our lives right now. For instance, there are thousands of people on Facebook groups who believe human extinction is near. In such groups, I have witnessed how people who doubt extinction is either inevitable or coming soon are disparaged by some participants for being weak and deluded. This could reflect how some of us may find it easier to believe in a certain than an uncertain story, especially when the uncertain future would be so different to today that it is difficult to comprehend. Reflection on the end of times, or eschatology, is a major dimension of the human experience, and the total sense of loss of everything one could ever contribute to is an extremely powerful experience for many people. How they emerge from that experience depends on many factors, with loving kindness, creativity, transcendence, anger, depression, nihilism and apathy all being potential responses. Given the potential spiritual experience triggered by sensing the imminent extinction of the human race, we can appreciate why a belief in the inevitability of extinction could be a basis for some people to come together.

In my work with mature students, I have found that inviting them to consider collapse as inevitable, catastrophe as probable and extinction as possible has not led to apathy or depression. Instead, in a supportive environment, where we have enjoyed community with each other, celebrating ancestors and enjoying nature before then looking at this information and possible framings for it, something positive happens. I have witnessed a shedding of concern for conforming to the status quo, and a new creativity about what to focus on going forward. Despite that, a certain discombobulation occurs and remains over time as one tries to find a way forward in a society where such perspectives are uncommon. Continued sharing about the implications as we transition our work and lives is valuable.

One further factor in the framing of our situation concerns timing. This also concerns geography. Where and when will the collapse or catastrophe begin? When will it affect my livelihood and society? Has it already begun? Although it is difficult to forecast and impossible to predict with certainty, that does not mean we should not try. The current data on temperature rise at the poles and impacts on weather patterns around the world suggest we are already in the midst of dramatic changes that will impact massively and negatively on agriculture within the next 20 years. Impacts have already begun. That sense of near-term disruption to our ability to feed ourselves and our families, and the implications for crime and conflict, adds another level to the discombobulation I mentioned. Should you drop everything now and move somewhere more suitable for self-sufficiency? Should you be spending time reading the rest of this chapter? Should I even finish writing it? Some of the people who believe that we face inevitable extinction believe that no one will read this chapter because we will see a collapse of civilization in the next twelve months when the harvests fail across the northern hemisphere. They see societal collapse leading to immediate meltdowns of nuclear power stations and thus human extinction being a near-term phenomenon, certainly not more than five years from now. The clarity and drama of their message is why 'inevitable near-term human extinction' (INTHE) has become a widely used phrase online for discussions about climate collapse.

Although I do not currently agree with them, writing about that perspective makes me sad. Even four years after I first let myself consider near-term extinction properly, not as something to dismiss, it still makes my jaw drop, eyes moisten and air escape my lungs. I have seen how the idea of INTHE can lead me to focus on truth, love and joy in the now, which is wonderful, but how it can also make me lose interest in planning for the future. And yet I always come around to the same conclusion – we do not know. Ignoring the future because it is unlikely to matter might backfire. 'Running for the hills' – to create our own eco-community – might backfire. But we definitely know that continuing to work in the ways we have done until now is not just backfiring – it is holding the gun to our own heads. With this in mind, we can choose to explore how to evolve what we do, without any simple answers. In my post-denial state, shared by increasing numbers of my students and colleagues, I realized that we would benefit from conceptual maps for how to address these questions. I therefore set about synthesizing the main things people talked about doing differently in light of a view of inevitable collapse and probable catastrophe. That is what I offer now as the 'deep adaptation agenda'.

The deep adaptation agenda

For many years, discussions and initiatives on adaptation to climate change were seen by environmental activists and policy makers as unhelpful to the necessary focus on carbon emissions reductions. That view finally changed in 2010 when the IPCC gave more attention to how societies and economies could be helped to adapt to climate change, and the United Nations Global Adaptation Network was founded to promote knowledge sharing and collaboration. Five years later, the Paris Accord between member states produced a 'global goal on adaptation' (GGA) with the aim of 'enhancing adaptive capacity, strengthening resilience and reducing vulnerability to climate change, with a view to contributing to sustainable development and ensuring an adequate adaptation response in the context of the global temperature goal' (cited in Singh, Harmeling and Rai 2016). Countries committed to develop national adaptation plans (NAPs) and to report on their creation to the UN.

Since then the funding being made available to climate adaptation has grown, with all the international development institutions active on adaptation finance. In 2018, the International Fund for Agricultural Development (IFAD), African Development Bank (AfDB), Asian Development Bank (ADB), Global Facility for Disaster Reduction and Recovery (GFDRR) and the World Bank each agreed major financing for governments to increase the resilience of their communities. Some of their projects include the Green Climate Fund, which was created to provide lower-income countries with assistance. Typical projects include improving the ability of small-scale farmers to cope with weather variability through the introduction of irrigation and the ability of urban planners to respond to rising sea levels and extreme rainfall events through re-engineering drainage systems (Climate Action Programme 2018). These initiatives are falling short of the commitments made by governments over the past eight years, and so more is being done to promote private bonds to finance adaptation (Bernhardt 2018) as well as stimulate private philan-thropy on this agenda (Williams 2018).

These efforts are paralleled by an increased range of activities under the umbrella of 'disaster risk reduction' which has its own international agency – the United Nations Office for Disaster Risk Reduction (UNDRR). The aim of its work is to reduce the damage caused by natural hazards, like earthquakes, floods, droughts and cyclones, through reducing sensitivity to these hazards as well as increasing the capacity to respond when dis-asters hit. That focus means significant engagement with urban planners and local governments. In the business sector, this dis-aster risk-reduction agenda meets the private sector through the well-established fields of risk management and business continu-ity management. Companies ask themselves what the points of failure might be in their value chains and seek to reduce those vulnerabilities or the significance of something failing.

Given the climate science we discussed earlier, some people may think this action is too little too late. Yet, if such action reduces some harm temporarily, that will help people just like you and me, and therefore such action should not be disregarded. Nevertheless, we can look more critically at how people and organizations are framing the situation and the limitations that such a framing may impose. The initiatives are typically described as promoting 'resilience' rather than sustainability. Some definitions of resilience within the environmental sector are sur-prisingly upbeat. For instance, the Stockholm Resilience Centre (2015) explains that 'resilience is the capacity of a system, be it an individual, a forest, a city or an economy, to deal with change and continue to develop. It is about how humans and nature can use shocks and disturbances like a financial crisis or climate change to spur renewal and innovative thinking.' In offering that definition, they are drawing on concepts in biology, where ecosystems are observed to overcome disturbances and increase their complexity (Brand and Jax 2007).

Two issues require attention at this point. First, the upbeat allegiance to 'development' and 'progress' in certain discourses about resilience may not be helpful as we enter a period when material 'progress' may not be possible and so aiming for it might become counterproductive. Second, apart from some limited soft skills development, the initiatives under the resilience banner are nearly all focused on physical adaptation to climate change, rather than considering a wider perspective on psychological resilience. In psychology, 'resilience is the process of adapting well in the face of adversity, trauma, tragedy, threats or significant sources of stress – such as family and relationship problems, serious health problems or workplace and financial stressors. It means "bouncing back" from difficult experiences' (American Psychology Association 2018). How a person 'bounces back' after difficulties or loss may be through a creative reinterpretation of identity and priorities. The concept of resilience in psychology does not, therefore, assume that people return to how they were before. Given the climate reality we now face, this less progressivist framing of resilience is more useful for a deeper adaptation agenda.

In pursuit of a conceptual map of 'deep adaptation', we can conceive of resilience of human societies as the capacity to adapt to changing circumstances so as to survive with valued norms and behaviours. Given that some analysts are concluding that a societal collapse is now likely, inevitable or already occurring, the question becomes: What are the valued norms and behaviours that human societies will wish to maintain as they seek to survive? That highlights how deep adaptation will involve more than 'resilience'. It brings us to a second area of this agenda, which I have named 'relinquishment'. It involves people and communities letting go of certain assets, behaviours and beliefs where retaining them could make matters worse. Examples include withdrawing from coastlines, shutting down vulnerable industrial facilities, or giving up expectations for certain types of consumption. The third area can be called 'restoration'. It involves people and communities rediscovering attitudes and approaches to life and organization that our hydrocarbon-fuelled civilization eroded. Examples include re-wilding landscapes so they provide more ecological benefits and require less management, changing diets back to match the seasons, rediscovering non-electronically powered forms of play, and increased community-level productivity and support. A fourth area for deep adaptation is what could be termed 'reconciliation', in recognition of how we do not know whether our efforts will make a difference, while we also know that our situations will become more stressful and disruptive ahead of the ultimate destination for us all. How we reconcile with each other and with the predicament we must now live with will be key to how we avoid creating more harm by acting from suppressed panic (Bendell 2019).

It is not my intention in this chapter to map out more specific implications of a deep adaptation agenda. Indeed, it is impossible to do so, and to attempt it would assume we are in a situation for calculated attempts at management, when what we face is a complex predicament beyond our control. Rather, I hope the deep adaptation agenda of resilience, relinquishment and restoration can be a useful framework for community dialogue in the face of climate change. Resilience asks us 'How do we keep what we really want to keep?' Relinquishment asks us 'What do we need to let go of in order to not make matters worse?' Restoration asks us 'What can we bring back to help us with the coming difficulties and tragedies?' Reconciliation asks 'With what and with whom can we make peace as we face our shared mortality?' In 2017, part of this deep adaptation agenda was used to frame a festival of alternatives organized by Peterborough Environment City Trust. It included a whole day devoted to exploring what relinquishment could involve. As such, it allowed more open conversation and imagination than a narrower focus on resilience. Further events are planned across the United Kingdom. Whether it will be useful framing for a broader-level policy agenda is yet to be seen.

How does this 'deep adaptation agenda' relate to the broad conceptual framework of sustainable development? It is an explicitly post-sustainability framing, and part of the restoration approach to engaging with social and environmental dilemmas, as I outlined elsewhere (Bendell, Sutherland and Little 2017).

Research futures in the face of climate tragedy

I was only partly joking earlier when I questioned why I was even writing this chapter. If all the data and analysis turn out to be misleading, and this society continues nicely for the coming decades, then this chapter will not have helped my career. If the predicted collapse comes within the next decade, then I won't have a career. It is the perfect lose–lose. I mention this to highlight how it will not be easy to identify ways forward as academic researchers and educators in the field of organizational sustainability. For the academics reading this chapter, most of you will have increasing teaching loads in areas where you are expected to cover certain content. I know you may have little time and space for reinventing your expertise and focus. Those of you who have a mandate to research might discover that the deep adaptation agenda is not an easy topic for finding research partners and funders. This restrictive situation was not always the reality faced by academics. It is the result of changes in higher education that are one expression of an ideology that has made the human race so poor at addressing a threat to its well-being and even existence. It is an ideology that many of us have been complicit in promoting if we have been working in business schools. It is important to recognize that complicity before considering how to evolve our research in the face of the climate tragedy (Bendell 2020).

The West's response to environmental issues has been restricted by the dominance of neoliberal economics since the 1970s. That led to hyper-individualist, market fundamentalist, incremental and atomistic approaches. By hyper-individualist, I mean a focus on individual action as consumers, switching light bulbs or buying sustainable furniture, rather than promoting political action as engaged citizens. By market fundamentalist, I mean a focus on market mechanisms like the complex, costly and largely useless carbon cap and trade systems, rather than exploring what more government intervention could achieve. By incremental, I mean a focus on celebrating small steps forward such as a company publishing a sustainability report, rather than strategies designed for a speed and scale of change suggested by the science. By atomistic, I mean a focus on seeing climate action as a separate issue from the governance of markets, finance and banking, rather than exploring what kind of economic system could permit or enable sustainability (Bendell 2020).

This ideology has now influenced the workloads and priorities of academics in most universities, which restricts how we can respond to the climate tragedy. In my own case, I took an unpaid sabbatical, and writing this chapter is one of the outcomes of that decision. We no longer have time for the career games of aiming to publish in top-ranked journals to impress our line managers or to improve our CVs if we enter the job market. Nor do we have a need for the narrow specialisms that are required to publish in such journals. So, yes, I am suggesting that in order to let oneself evolve in response to the climate tragedy one may have to quit a job – and even a career. However, if one is prepared to do that, then one can engage with an employer and professional community from a new place of confidence.

If staying in academia, I recommend you begin to ask some questions of all that you research and teach. When reading others' research, I recommend asking: 'How might these findings inform efforts for a more massive and urgent pursuit of resilience, relinquishment and restoration in the face of social collapse?' You may find that most of what you read offers little on that question and, therefore, you no longer wish to engage with it. On one's own research, I recommend asking: 'If I didn't believe in incremental incorporation of climate concerns into current organizations and systems, what might I want to know more about?' In answering that question, I recommend talking to non-specialists as much as people in your own field so that you are able to talk more freely and consider all options.

In my own work, I stopped researching corporate sustainability. I learned about leadership and communications and began to research, teach and advise on these matters in the political arena. I began to work on systems to enable relocalization of economies and support for community development, particularly those systems using local currencies. I sought to share that knowledge more widely and therefore launched a free online course (The Money and Society Mass Open Online Course). I began to spend more time reading and talking about the climate tragedy and what I might do, or stop doing, with that in mind. This rethinking and repositioning is ongoing, but I can no longer work on subjects that do not have some relevance to deep adaptation. Looking ahead, I see the need and opportunity for more work at multiple levels. People will need more support to access information and networks on how to attempt a shift in their livelihoods and lifestyles. Existing approaches to living off-grid in intentional communities are useful to learn from, but this agenda needs to go further in asking questions such as how small-scale production of drugs like aspirin is possible. Free online and in-person courses as well as support networks on self-sufficiency need to be scaled. Local governments will need similar support on how to develop the capabilities today that will help their local communities to collaborate, not fracture, during a collapse. For instance, they will need to roll out systems for productive cooperation between neighbours, such as product and service exchange platforms enabled by locally issued currency. At the international level, there is the need to work on how to responsibly address the wider fallout from collapsing societies (Harrington 2016). The aspects will be many but will obviously include the challenges of refugee support and the securing of dangerous industrial and nuclear sites at the moment of a societal collapse.

Other intellectual disciplines and traditions may be of interest going forward. Human extinction and the topic of eschatology, or the end of the world, is something that has been discussed in various academic disciplines, as you might expect. In theology, it has been widely discussed, while it also appears in literary theory as an interesting element to creative writing, and in psychology during the 1980s as a phenomenon related to the threat of nuclear war. The field of psychology seems to be particularly relevant going forward.

Whatever we choose to work on in future will not be a simple calculation. It will be shaped by the emotional or psychological implications of this new awareness of a societal collapse being likely in our own lifetimes. I have explored some of these emotional issues and how they have been affecting my work choices in a reflective essay on the spiritual implications of climate despair (Bendell 2018). I recommend giving yourself time for such reflection and evolution, rather than rushing in to a new agenda of research or teaching. If you are a student, then I recommend sending your lecturers this chapter and inviting a class discussion about these ideas. It is likely that those who are not embedded within the existing system will be the ones more able to lead this agenda.

I think it may be our vanity as academics to think that anyone but academics and students read academic papers. Therefore, I have chosen to leave my recommendations for managers, policy makers and lay persons for another outlet (see www.jembendell.com for my writings on various aspects of the deep adaptation agenda and community, including topics of campaign strategy, social justice, relocalization, decolonization, financial reform, psychology and spirituality).

Conclusions

Since records began in 1850, seventeen of the eighteen hottest years have occurred, all since 2000. Important steps on climate mitigation and adaptation have been taken over the past decade. However, these steps could now be regarded as equivalent to walking up a landslide. If the landslide had not already begun, then quicker and bigger steps would get us to the top of where we want to be. Sadly, the latest climate data, emissions data and data on the spread of carbon-intensive lifestyles show that the landslide has already begun. As the point of no return can't be fully known until after the event, ambitious work on reducing carbon emissions and extracting more from the air (naturally and synthetically) is more critical than ever. That must involve a new front of action on methane.

Disruptive impacts from climate change are now inevitable. Geoengineering is likely to be ineffective or counterproductive. Therefore, the mainstream climate policy community now recognizes the need to work much more on adaptation to the effects of climate change. That must now rapidly permeate the broader field of people engaged in sustainable development as practitioners, researchers and educators. In assessing how our approaches could evolve, we need to appreciate what kind of adaptation is possible. Recent research suggests that human societies will experience disruptions to their basic functioning within fewer than ten years due to climate stress. Such disruptions include increased levels of malnutrition, starvation, disease, civil conflict and war – and will not spare affluent nations. This situation makes redundant the reformist approach to sustainable development and related fields of corporate sustainability that has underpinned the approach of many professionals (Bendell, Sutherland and Little 2017). Instead, a new approach which explores how to reduce harm and not make matters worse is important to develop. In support of that challenging, and ultimately personal, process, understanding a deep adaptation agenda may be useful.

References

Aaron-Morrison, A. et al. (2017) State of the Climate in 2016. *Bulletin of the American Meteorological Society* 98(8): Si-S280.

Adams, T. et al. (2015) *Autoethnography.* New York, NY: Oxford University Press.

Ahmed, N. (2013) 'Seven Facts You Need to Know about the Arctic Methane Timebomb'. *Guardian.* Available at: https://www.theguardi an.com/environment/earth-insight/2013/aug/05/7-facts-need-to-know -arctic-methane-time-bomb

American Psychology Association (2018). *The Road to Resilience.* Available at: www.apa.org/helpcenter/road-resilience.aspx

Arctic News (2018) 'Warning Signs'. Available at: https://arctic-news. blogspot.co.id/2018/03/warning-signs.html

Asay, M. (2013) *Americans Losing Faith in Technology, but Can't Break the Addiction.* Readwrite.com. Available at: https://readwrite. com/2013/09/12/americans-losing-faith-in-technology-but-cant-brea k-the-addiction/

Banos Ruiz, I. (2017) 'This Apocalyptic Is How Kids are Imagining Our Climate Future'. DW.com. Available at: www.dw.com/en/this-apoca lyptic-is-how-kids-are-imagining-our-climate-future/a-40847610

Becker, E. (1973) *The Denial of Death.* New York: Simon & Schuster.

Becker, R. (2017) *Why Scare Tactics Won't Stop Climate Change: Doomsday Scenarios Don't Inspire Action.* The Verge. Available at: https://www. theverge.com/2017/7/11/15954106/doomsday-climate-science-apocal ypse-new-york-magazine-response

Bendell, J. (2018) 'After Climate Despair – One Tale of What Can Emerge'. Jembendell.com. Available at: https://jembendell.wordpress. com/2018/01/14/after-climate-despair-one-tale-of-what-can-emerge/

Bendell, J. (2019) 'Hope and Vision in the Face of Collapse: The 4th R of Deep Adaptation'. Jembendell.com. Available at: https://jembendell. com/2019/01/09/hope-and-vision-in-the-face-of-collapse-the-4th-r-of -deep-adaptation/

Bendell, J. (2020) 'The Collapse of Ideology and the End of Escape'. Jembendell.com. Available at: https://jembendell.com/2020/06/28/ the-collapse-of-ideology-and-the-end-of-escape/

Bendell, J. and Lopatin, M. (2016) 'Democracy Demands a Richer Britain'. *Huffington Post.* Available at: http://www.huffingtonpost. co.uk/jem-bendell/democracy-demands-a-riche_b_13348586.html

Bendell, J., Sutherland, N. and Little, R. (2017) 'Beyond Unsustainable Leadership: Critical Social Theory for Sustainable Leadership'. *Sustainability Accounting, Management and Policy Journal* 8(4): 418–44. Available at: https://doi.org/10.1108/SAMPJ-08-2016-0048

Benson, M. and Craig, R. (2014) 'The End of Sustainability'. *Society and Natural Resources* 27: 777–82.

Bernhardt, A. (2018) 'Bonds: How to Finance Climate Adaptation'. Brinknews.com. Available at: http://www.brinknews.com/bonds-how-to-finance-climate-adaptation/

Brand, F. S. and Jax, K. (2007) 'Focusing the Meaning(s) of Resilience: Resilience as a Descriptive Concept and a Boundary Object'. *Ecology and Society* 12(1): 23. Available at: http://www.ecologyandsociety.org/vol12/iss1/art23/

Brand, U., Blarney, N., Garbelli, C., et al. (2016) 'Methane Hydrate: Killer Cause of Earth's Greatest Mass Extinction'. *Palaeoworld* 25(4): 496–507.

Britten, G. L., Dowd, M. and Worm, B. (2015) Changing Recruitment Capacity in Global Fish Stocks. *Proceedings of the National Academy of Sciences*. Published ahead of print, 14 December. Available at: www.pnas.org/content/early/2015/12/09/1504709112

Brysse, K., Reskes, N., O'Reilly, J. and Oppenheimer, M. (2013) 'Climate Change Prediction: Erring on the Side of Least Drama?' *Global Environmental Change* 23(1): 327–37. Available at: https://www.sciencedirect.com/science/article/pii/S0959378012001215

Canadell, P., Le Quéré, C., Peters, G., et al. (2017) 'Global Carbon Budget 2017'. Globalcarbonproject.org. Available at: http://www.globalcarbonproject.org/carbonbudget/index.htm

Clément, V. and Rivera, J. (2016) 'From Adaptation to Transformation: An Extended Research Agenda for Organizational Resilience to Adversity in the Natural Environment'. *Organisation and Environment* 30(4): 346–65.

Climate Action Programme (2018) '$1 Billion of New Funding Announced for Climate Adaptation Projects'. Climateactionprogramme.org. Available at: http://www.climateactionprogramme.org/news/1-billion-of-new-funding-announced-for-climate-adaptation-projects

Cohen, D. A. (2017) 'The Power and Peril of "Climate Disaster Porn"'. New Republic. Available at: https://newrepublic.com/article/143788/power-peril-climate-disaster-porn

Copernicus Programme (2020) 'Surface Air Temperature for June 2020'. Available at: https://climate.copernicus.eu/surface-air-temperature-june-2020

de Sousa Fragoso, R. M. and de Almeida Noéme, C. J. (2018) 'Economic Effects of Climate Change on the Mediterranean's Irrigated Agriculture'. *Sustainability Accounting, Management and Policy Journal* 9(2): 118–38.

ECJCR (European Commission Joint Research Centre) (2018) 'Climate Change Promotes the Spread of Mosquito and

Tick-borne Viruses'. ScienceDaily. Available at: www.sciencedaily.
com/releases/2018/03/180316111311.htm

Eisenstein, C. (2013) *The More Beautiful World Our Hearts Know Is
Possible*. Berkeley, CA: North Atlantic Books.

Eisenstein, C. (2018) *Climate – A New Story*. Berkeley, CA: North
Atlantic Books.

FAO (Food and Agriculture Organization) (2018) 'Disasters Causing
Billions in Agricultural Losses, with Drought Leading the Way'. Press
release, 15 March.

Farquharson, L. M., Romanovsky, V. E., Cable, W. L., et al. (2019)
'Climate Change Drives Widespread and Rapid Thermokarst
Development in Very Cold Permafrost in the Canadian High Arctic'.
Geophysical Research Letters 46(12): 6681–9. Available at: https://doi.
org/10.1029/2019GL082187

Flannery, T. (2015) *Atmosphere of Hope: Searching for Solutions to the
Climate Crisis*. New York: Atlantic Monthly Press.

Foster, J. (2015) *After Sustainability*. Abingdon: Earthscan/Routledge.

Gosling, J. (2016) 'Will We Know What Counts as Good Leadership
if "Things Fall Apart?" Questions Prompted by Chinua Achebe's
Novel'. *Leadership* 13(1): 35–47.

Gosling, J. and Case, P. (2013) 'Social Dreaming and Ecocentric Ethics:
Sources of Non-Rational Insight in the Face of Climate Change
Catastrophe'. *Organization* 20(5): 705–21.

Greenberg, J., Solomon, S. and Pyszczynski, T. (2015) *The Worm at the
Core: On the Role of Death in Life*. New York: Random House.

Greiner, J. T., McGlathery, K. J., Gunnell, J. and McKee, B. A. (2013)
'Seagrass Restoration Enhances "Blue Carbon" Sequestration in
Coastal Waters'. *PLoS ONE* 8(8). Available at: http://journals.plos.
org/plosone/article?id=10.1371/journal.pone.0072469

Hamilton, C. et al. (eds) (2015) *The Anthropocene and the Global
Environmental Crisis*. Abingdon: Routledge.

Hansen, J. E. (2007) 'Scientific Reticence and Sea Level Rise'.
Environmental Research Letters 2(2). Available at: http://iopscience.iop.
org/article/10.1088/1748-9326/2/2/024002

Harrington, C. (2016) 'The Ends of the World: International Relations
and the Anthropocene'. *Millennium: Journal of International Studies*
44(3): 478–98.

Hawken, P. and Wilkinson, K. (2017) *Drawdown*. London: Penguin Books.

Henley, B. J. and King, A. D. (2017) *Geophysical Research Letters* 44(9):
4256–62. Available at: https://agupubs.onlinelibrary.wiley.com/doi/
full/10.1002/2017GL073480

Herrando-Pérez, S., Bradshaw, C. J. A., Lewandowsky, S. and
Vieites, D. R. (2019) 'Statistical Language Backs Conservatism in

Climate-Change Assessments'. *BioScience* 69(3): 209. Available at: https://www.sciencedaily.com/releases/2019/03/190320102010.htm

Herring, S. C., Christidis, N., Hoell, A., et al. (2018) 'Explaining Extreme Events of 2016 from a Climate Perspective'. *Special Supplement to the Bulletin of the American Meteorological Society*, 99(1): S1–S157.

Hill, J. S. (2017) 'Global Attitudes to Climate Change Risks Show Increasing Concern'. Cleantechnica. Available at: https://cleantech nica.com/2017/05/29/global-attitudes-climate-change-risks-show-inc reasing-concern

Howard, J. L. et al. (2017) 'CO_2 Released by Carbonate Sediment Production in Some Coastal Areas May Offset the Benefits of Seagrass "Blue Carbon" Storage'. *Limnology and Oceanography* 63(1): 160–72.

Hudson, S. R. (2011) 'Estimating the Global Radiative Impact of the Sea Ice–Albedo Feedback in the Arctic'. *Journal of Geophysics Research* 116(D16).

Ipsos MORI (2017) 'Only 13% of the Public Think the World is Getting Better (Belgians Most Gloomy = "Must be the Booze" Says @benatipsosmori)'. #ipsosmorilive. Twitter, 7 December. Available at: https://twitter.com/IpsosMORI/status/938492368659116033

Johnson, J. (2019) '"Terrifying" New Climate Models Warn of 6–7°C of Warming by 2100 If Emissions Not Slashed'. Common Dreams. Available at: https://www.commondreams.org/news/2019/09/17/ter rifying-new-climate-models-warn-6-7degc-warming-2100-if-emissions -not-slashed

JPL/PO.DAAC (2018) 'Key Indicators: Global Mean Sea Level'. NASA. gov. Available at: https://sealevel.nasa.gov/understanding-sea-level/ key-indicators/global-mean-sea-level

Kahn, B. (2017) 'The Arctic has Been Crazy Warm All Year. This Is What It Means for Sea Ice'. Climate Central. Available at: www.climatecentral.org/news/arctic-crazy-warm-sea-ice-21599

Keenan, T. F., Prentice, I. C., Canadell, J. G., et al. (2016) 'Recent Pause in the Growth Rate of Atmospheric CO_2 due to Enhanced Terrestrial Carbon Uptake'. *Nature Communications* 7. Available at: https://www. nature.com/articles/ncomms13428

Keller, D. P., Feng, E. Y. and Oschlies, A. (2014) 'Potential Climate Engineering Effectiveness and Side Effects during a High Carbon Dioxide-Emission Scenario'. *Nature Communications* 5. Available at: https://www.nature.com/articles/ncomms4304

Knoblauch, C., Beer, C., Liebner, S., et al. (2018) 'Methane Production as Key to the Greenhouse Gas Budget of Thawing Permafrost'. *Nature Climate Change* 8: 309–12. Available at: http://www.nature. com/articles/s41558-018-0095-z

Knorr, W. (2019) 'Climate Scientists Should Admit Failure and Move

On'. IFLAS, University of Cumbria. Available at: http://iflas.blogspot. com/2019/09/climate-scientists-should-admit-failure.html

Kornhuber, K., Coumou, D., Vogel, E., et al. (2019) 'Amplified Rossby Waves Enhance Risk of Concurrent Heatwaves in Major Breadbasket Regions'. *Nature Climate Change* 10: 48–53. Available at: https://www. nature.com/articles/s41558-019-0637-z

Lamarche-Gagnon, G. et al. (2019) 'Greenland Melt Drives Continuous Export of Methane from the Ice-Sheet Bed'. *Nature*: 73–7. Available at: https://www.nature.com/articles/s41586-018-0800-0

Lear, J. (2008) *Radical Hope: Ethics in the Face of Cultural Devastation.* Boston, MA: Harvard University Press.

Lee, H. (2014) 'Alarming New Study Makes Today's Climate Change More Comparable to Earth's Worst Mass Extinction'. *Skeptical Science.* Available at: https://skepticalscience.com/Lee-commentary-on-Burgess-et-al-PNAS-Permian-Dating.html

Lenton, T. M. et al. (2019) 'Climate Tipping Points – Too Risky to Bet Against: The Growing Threat of Abrupt and Irreversible Climate Changes Must Compel Political and Economic Action on Emissions'. *Nature* 595: 592–95. Available at: https://www.nature.com/articles/ d41586-019-03595-0

Nisbet, E. G. et al. (2019) 'Very Strong Atmospheric Methane Growth in the Four Years 2014–2017: Implications for the Paris Agreement'. *Global Biogeochemical Cycles* 3(33): 318–42. Available at: https://doi. org/10.1029/2018GB006009

Lynch, T. (2017) 'Why Hope Is Dangerous When It Comes to Climate Change: Global Warming Discussions Need Apocalyptic Thinking'. Slate. Available at: www.slate.com/Arcticles/technology/ future_tense/2017/07/why_climate_change_discussions_need_apocaly ptic_thinking.html

Lesnikowski, A. C., Ford, J. D., Berrang-Ford, L., et al. (2015) 'How Are We Adapting to Climate Change? A Global Assessment'. *Mitigation and Adaptation Strategies for Global Change* 20(2): 277–93.

Machmuller, M. B., Kramer, M. G., Cyle, T. K., et al. (2015) 'Emerging Land Use Practices Rapidly Increase Soil Organic Matter'. *Nature Communications* 6. Available at: https://www.nature.com/articles/nco mms7995

Malmquist, D. (2018) 'Researchers Issue First-Annual Sea-Level Report Cards'. Phys.org. Available at: https://m.phys.org/news/2018-03-is sue-first-annual-sea-level-cards.html

Marshall, G. (2014) *Don't Even Think About It: Why Our Brains Are Wired to Ignore Climate Change.* New York: Bloomsbury.

Mathesius, S., Hofmann, M., Caldeira, K. and Schellnhuber, H. J. (2015) 'Long-Term Response of Oceans to CO_2 Removal from the

Atmosphere'. *Nature Climate Change* 5: 1107–13. Available at: www.nature.com/articles/nclimate2729

Matousek, M. (2008) *When You Are Falling, Dive: Lessons in the Art of Living*. New York: Bloomsbury.

McDonald, R. I., Chai, H. Y. and Newell, B. R. (2015) 'Personal Experience and the "Psychological Distance" of Climate Change: An Integrative Review'. *Journal of Environmental Psychology* 44: 109–18.

Kumar, N. et al. (2014) 'Vulnerability of Wheat Production to Climate Change in India'. *Climate Research* 59(3): 173–87.

NASA (2018) *Greenland Ice Loss 2002–2016*. NASA.gov. Available at: https://grace.jpl.nasa.gov/resources/30

NASA/GISS (2018) 'Vital Signs: Global Temperature'. NASA.gov. Available at: https://climate.nasa.gov/vital-signs/global-temperature

Neumann, B., Vafeidis, A. T., Zimmermann, J. and Nicholls, R. J. (2015) 'Future Coastal Population Growth and Exposure to Sea-Level Rise and Coastal Flooding – A Global Assessment'. *PLoS One* 10(3). Available at: https://doi.org/10.1371/journal.pone.0118571

NSIDC/NASA (2018) 'Vital Signs: Arctic Sea Ice'. NASA.gov. Available at: https://climate.nasa.gov/vital-signs/arctic-sea-ice

Orsato, R. J., Ferraz de Campos, J. G. and Barakat, S. R. (2018) 'Social Learning for Anticipatory Adaptation to Climate Change: Evidence from a Community of Practice'. *Organisation and Environment* 32(4): 416–40.

Phys.org. (2018) 'The Sorry State of Earth's Species, in Numbers'. Available at: https://phys.org/news/2018-03-state-earth-species.html

Pidcock, R. (2013) 'Carbon Briefing: Making Sense of the IPCC's New Carbon Budget'. Carbonbrief.org. Available at: https://www.carbonbrief.org/carbon-briefing-making-sense-of-the-ipccs-new-carbon-budget

Pistone, K., Eisenman, I. and Ramanathan, V. (2014) 'Observational Determination of Albedo Decrease Caused by Vanishing Arctic Sea Ice'. *Proceedings of the National Academy of Sciences of the United States of America* 111: 3322–6.

Rigaud, K. K., de Sherbinin, A., Jones, B., et al. (2018) 'Groundswell: Preparing for Internal Climate Migration'. World Bank. Available at: https://openknowledge.worldbank.org/handle/10986/29461

Rogers, A. et al. (2017) 'Fisheries Productivity under Progressive Coral Reef Degradation'. *Journal of Applied Ecology* 55(3): 1041–9. Available at: https://doi.org/10.1111/1365-2664.13051

Ruppel, C. D. and Kessler, J. D. (2017) 'The Interaction of Climate Change and Methane Hydrates'. *Review of Geophysics* 55(1): 126–68. Available at: https://agupubs.onlinelibrary.wiley.com/doi/full/10.1002/2016RG000534

Saunois, M. et al. (2016) 'The Global Methane Budget 2000–2012'. *Earth System Scientific Data* 8(2): 697–751. Available at: www.earth-syst-sci-data.net/8/697/2016/

Schmidt, J. (2000) *Disciplined Minds – A Critical Look at Salaried Professionals and the Soul-Battering System that Shapes Their Lives.* Lanham, MD: Rowman & Littlefield.

Schuur, E. A. G. et al. (2015) 'Expert Assessment of Vulnerability of Permafrost Carbon to Climate Change'. *Climatic Change* 119(2): 359–74.

Servigne, P. and Stevens, R. (2020) *How Everything Can Collapse.* Cambridge: Polity Press.

Shakhova, N. et al. (2010) 'Extensive Methane Venting to the Atmosphere from Sediments of the East Siberian Arctic Shelf'. *Science, New Series* 327(5970): 1246–50.

Singh, H., Harmeling, S. and Rai, S. C. (2016) *Global Goal on Adaptation: From Concept to Practice.* A report written on behalf of CARE International, ActionAid and WWF. Available at: http://careclimatechange.org/wp-content/uploads/2016/11/Global-Goal-on-Adaptation-From-Concept-to-Practice-v2-DesktopPrint-NoCrops.pdf

Spratt, D. and Dunlop, I. (2018) 'What Lies Beneath: The Understatement of Existential Climate Risk'. National Centre for Climate Restoration. Available at: https://www.breakthroughonline.org.au

Steffen, A. (2017) 'My Reservations, in a Nutshell: Despair is Never Helpful, and This Is Essentially One Long Council of Despair'. Twitter. 10 July. Available at: https://twitter.com/AlexSteffen/status/884262230279176193

Stockholm Resilience Centre (2015) 'What is Resilience?' Available at: www.stockholmresilience.org/research/research-news/2015-02-19-what-is-resilience.html

Stokes, B. (2017) 'Global Publics More Upbeat about the Economy, but Many are Pessimistic about Children's Future'. Pew Global. Available at: www.pewglobal.org/2017/06/05/global-publics-more-upbeat-about-the-economy/

Temby, O., Sandall, J., Cooksey, R. and Hickey, G. M. (2016) 'Examining the Role of Trust and Informal Communication on Mutual Learning in Government: The Case of Climate Change Policy in New York'. *Organization & Environment* 30(1): 71–97.

Thurber, A. R., Seabrook, S. and Welsh, R. M. (2020) 'Riddles in the Cold: Antarctic Endemism and Microbial Succession Impact Methane Cycling in the Southern Ocean'. *Proceedings of the Royal Society B* 287(1931). Available at: https://doi.org/10.1098/rspb.2020.1134

Wadhams, P. (2016) *A Farewell to Ice*. Oxford: Oxford University Press.

Wadhams, P. (2018) 'Saving the World with Carbon Dioxide Removal'. *Washington Post*. Available at: https://www.washington post.com/news/theworldpost/wp/2018/01/08/carbon-emissions/?utm _term=.308256f2236c

Wallace-Wells, D. (2017) 'The Uninhabitable Earth: Famine, Economic Collapse, a Sun that Cooks Us: What Climate Change Could Wreak – Sooner than You Think'. *New York Magazine*. Available at: http:// nymag.com/daily/intelligencer/2017/07/climate-change-earth-too-hot -for-humans.html

Watts, J. (2018) 'Arctic Warming: Scientists Alarmed by "Crazy" Temperature Rises'. *Guardian*. Available at: https://www.thguardian. com/environment/2018/feb/27/arctic-warming-scientists-alarmed-by-crazy-temperature-rises

Whyte, K. P., Talley, J. and Gibson, J. (2019) 'Indigenous Mobility Traditions, Colonialism and the Anthropocene'. *Mobilities* 14(3): 319–35.

Wiebe, K. et al. (2015) Climate Change Impacts on Agriculture in 2050 under a Range of Plausible Socioeconomic and Emissions Scenarios'. *Environmental Research Letters* 10(8). Available at: https://iopscience. iop.org/article/10.1088/1748-9326/10/8/085010

Williams, T. (2018) 'Adapt or Die: How Climate Funders Are Falling Short on a Key Challenge'. Insidephilanthropy.com. Available at: https://www.insidephilanthropy.com/home/2018/2/15/climate-adapta tion-field-faces-large-gap-in-action-and-funding

Woosley, R. J., Millero, F. J. and Wanninkhof, R. (2016) 'Rapid Anthropogenic Changes in CO_2 and pH in the Atlantic Ocean: 2003– 2014'. *Global Biogeochemical Studies* 30(1): 70–90. Available at: https:// agupubs.onlinelibrary.wiley.com/doi/abs/10.1002/2015GB005248

World Values Survey (2016) 'Findings and Insights'. Available at: http:// www.worldvaluessurvey.org/WVSContents.jsp

WWF (World Wide Fund for Nature) (2018) 'Half of Plant and Animal Species at Risk from Climate Change in World's Most Important Natural Places'. Available at: http://wwf.panda.org/wwf_ news/?324471/Half-of-plant-and-animal-species-at-risk-from-climate -change-in-worlds-most-important-natural-places

Xu, Y. and Ramanathan, V. (2017) 'Well Below 2°C: Mitigation Strategies for Avoiding Dangerous to Catastrophic Climate Changes'. *Proceedings of the National Academy of Sciences* 114(39): 10315–23. Available at: https://www.pnas.org/content/114/39/10315

Xu, Y., Ramanathan, V. and Victor, D. G. (2018) 'Global Warming Will Happen Faster Than We Think'. *Nature* 564: 30–2. Available at: https://www.nature.com/articles/d41586-018-07586-5

Zhang, P. et al. (2016) 'Economic Impacts of Climate Change on Agriculture: The Importance of Additional Climatic Variables Other than Temperature and Precipitation'. *Journal of Environmental Economics and Management* 83: 8–31.

3

Reasons for Anticipating Societal Collapse

*Pablo Servigne, Raphaël Stevens, Gauthier Chapelle
and Daniel Rodary*

Introduction

Since the original deep adaptation paper 'went viral' in 2018, not only has the field of people anticipating collapse grown, but also has the number of people who criticize that perspective for not having a sound basis in science (Nicholas, Hall and Schmidt 2020). Typically, the criticisms focus on climate science, rather than the broader range of scholarship on the pressures on societies and how they could collapse as a result. As such, they privilege the voices of a narrow range of natural scientists and ignore a wide range of social science. The aim of this chapter is to provide further background on the possibility of societal collapse due in part to the direct and indirect influence of rapid climate change. This chapter draws upon a book (Servigne and Stevens 2015) which reviewed dozens of peer-reviewed publications and institutional reports on global catastrophic risks.

In the book we asked: What are the catastrophic risks? Can we predict their occurrence? What tools and methods are used? How did past societies face them? Are they inevitable? Near term? Should we plan and prepare? Many disciplines had touched these questions through thousands of scholarly papers and, whereas many books had already been published, none had a transdisciplinary approach. This is why we coined a neologism, *collapsology*,[1] in order to invite scholars, academic or independent experts, and the public alike, to join together and engage in a meaningful conversation on these urgent and vital questions. They are so vital they must be studied as seriously as possible and we should prepare for every eventuality. Indeed, climate change that is too abrupt, a mass extinction of species, a collapse of biodiversity, a multiple breadbasket failure, a major pandemic, an artificial intelligence or geoengineering scheme that has gone out of control, a nuclear winter, a major disruption of fossil fuel supply, amongst other scenarios, are not risks that we can manage with our conventional risk management tools and methods (Wagner and Weitzman 2015). They are part of a special risk class – the 'Global Catastrophic Risks' – defined as those that could kill at least 10 per cent of the global population (Bostrom and Cirkovic 2011; Ord 2020). This is a field of scholarship and research that has been ignored by some critics of the deep adaptation agenda, framework and community.

What we highlighted in our multiple and academically supported reviews is that these aspects of collapse could happen in our lifetime, for the *present generation*. In that sense, our findings aligned with the deep adaptation analysis that invited people to understand that those alive today in all parts of the world are becoming vulnerable to climate disruption. Our aim has been to inform as many people as possible of what scientists and institutions are saying about these little-considered hazardous scenarios so that society can organize itself politically to mitigate these existential risks.

Some commentators have called us 'alarmists' or 'doomers'. Perhaps the best form of response is a metaphor about how it is normal to prepare for the worst in order to reduce the hazard. When your insurer or the fire department tells you that there is a possibility that your home could go up in smoke and kill your family, you do not silence them by calling them alarmists. You take this risk seriously, take out insurance, check appliances and furnishings, assess cladding and escape routes, advise or train

---

[1] A neologism we proposed to refer to the field of research in the scientific community that studies Global Catastrophic Risks (GCRs), the category of risks that could lead to the collapse of industrial civilization and cause mass deaths and disasters on a global scale.

colleagues, and install smoke detectors and extinguishers. Perhaps you notice and discuss your concerns. You try to make sure a fire never happens, and you adapt to this possibility in a concrete way.

In our view, the key to understanding the subject lies in the subtlety of the notion of uncertainty and the paradoxes it generates in the current situation. We are obviously in a period of radical uncertainty, and as we have shown in our book (and as many other authors did: Oreskes 2015), science will never have absolute certainty about the future. By using the status of science to criticize anyone talking about the possibility of societal collapse, some scientists have been promoting falsehoods. It is impossible to prove scientifically that collapse will not happen. The debate on the possibility of collapse will never be settled. Since this is an existential risk, we cannot afford to experience it in practice as the usual scientific approach would require. Making society collapse in order to know for sure if and how it can collapse is obviously not possible or desirable. This view resonates with the concept of the precautionary principle in science as applied to public policy. As Rupert Read, co-editor of this book, explains, 'collapse would probably be so dreadful that not preparing for it to make it less so is now gross irresponsibility' (Read 2020; Read and Alexander 2019).

With this perspective in mind, there are two problematic narratives coming from some scientists: the first is to engage in endless scientific discussion before preparing for such an eventuality; the second is to take this scientific uncertainty as an excuse for not acting, or to simply ignore the question. As Professors Rupert Read and Jem Bendell note in chapter 1, it is illogical that many climate scientists assume that the burden of proof in relation to anticipated collapse is with those who warn and ask us to prepare, rather than with those who do not want to discuss the matter.

So how might we respond to the growing evidence that our societies may collapse in our lifetimes? Your house fire isn't certain, but it's because you take it seriously (it *certainly* can happen) that you act accordingly. And, if you act, it is then more likely not to happen. In other words, you had better take it for granted to have any chance of avoiding it or, at worst, of mitigating it if it occurs, for instance, by reducing the casualties. This is the paradox that the philosopher Jean-Pierre Dupuy called 'enlightened catastrophism', and it is this philosophical pirouette that causes so much misunderstanding. If the norms of science mean that something can only be concluded as likely (and therefore still fundamentally uncertain), this should not translate into the general public awareness as a reason to hesitate. Unfortunately, this is where scientific modes of analysis and communication do not translate well into the public sphere. For non-scientists, many people hear expressions of uncertainty as meaning something that it is not necessary to engage with. With the emergence of the deep adaptation concept, we witnessed the power of a scholar expressing the view that an outcome appears unavoidable, despite not being able to prove a prediction about the future as completely certain within the normal mode of scientific analysis.

But wait. Which collapse? Here is another source of confusion. On the one hand, societies (as shown in the past: e.g. Diamond 2005; Middleton 2017; Tainter 1988; Turchin 2018; Yoffee and Cowgill 1991) and industrial civilization (as projected by numerous models: e.g. Brandt and Merico 2013; Brown, Seo and Rounsevell 2019; Capellán-Pérez et al. 2015; Meadows et al. 1972; Motesharrei, Rivas and Kalnay 2014; Yu et al. 2016) can collapse. On the other hand, the biosphere could also switch irreversibly towards an unliveable state for many populations and species, including our own (Barnosky et al. 2012; Lenton et al. 2019; Steffen et al. 2018; Xu et al. 2020). But these two dynamics are asymmetrically linked: if we choose to 'save' the industrial civilization by pursuing growth of consumption of materials and energy (Garrett 2014, 2015), the earth systems will even faster encounter a possible tipping threshold, which in turn could end life as we know it. If, on the contrary, we choose to preserve the biosphere, it means that we must stop the race of our civilization within a few months, which would amount to an intentional social and economic collapse.[2] Imagine: that would mean extending (and even strengthening) for 10 years the strongest economic

---

[2] Indeed, following the recommendations of the IPCC on the necessary mitigation efforts would in a way amount to bringing about the end of thermo-industrial civilization. With such a forced decrease, the world's economies would not survive in their current structure. The necessary reduction in emissions is −7.6% per year for 10 years to maintain a 66% probability of remaining below 1.5°C (−2.7% per year for 10 years to maintain a 66% probability of remaining below 2°C) (United Nations Environment Programme 2019).

effect of the Covid-19 lockdown.[3] Whatever happens, if one is paying proper attention, it has become difficult to imagine a future for our civilization.

In 2015, the rational and scientific approach of 'collapsology' was considered plausible but pessimistic by the political landscape and most of the media in France (Gadeau 2019). Nevertheless, the general public and some people in every institution (administrations, unions, corporations, the army and so on) were really open and ready to discuss the matter. We saw a growing number of people reaching the conclusion that trying to solve our problems with more economic growth would speed up our demise, yet stopping economic growth could also speed up our demise. In other words, we face a predicament.

Five years later, not only has collapsology entered the French dictionaries and provoked a significant transformation of the French social and political landscape (for instance, the prime minister and other ministers repeatedly mentioned collapse in public speeches: Laurent 2018), but the scientific findings about catastrophic shifts and risks are unfortunately even more robust. The idea that societies around the world could collapse in the coming years is now widespread. In February 2020, an opinion poll on 'collapsology' conducted by the Institut français d'opinion publique (IFOP) on 5,000 persons in France, the United States, the United Kingdom, Italy and Germany found that 56% of British people and 65% of French think that western civilization as we know it will soon collapse (23% of British people expect it within 20 years, and 9% before 2030) (Cassely and Fourquet 2020)[4].

Hints of the end of *this* world are appearing everywhere, in recent scientists' warnings (Cardoso et al. 2020; Cavicchioli et al. 2019; Heleno, Ripple and Traveset 2020; Jenny et al. 2020; Ripple et al. 2017, 2019; Wiedmann et al. 2020), in independent scholars (Ahmed 2017; Alexander 2019; Korowicz and

---

[3] The Covid-19 effect offers valid comparisons: 'The impact on 2020 annual emissions depends on the duration of the confinement, with a low estimate of −4% (−2 to −7%) if pre-pandemic conditions return by mid-June, and a high estimate of −7% (−3 to −13%) if some restrictions remain worldwide until the end of 2020' (Le Quéré et al. 2020). The World Bank estimates the 2020 recession at 5.2% due to the pandemic (7% for advanced economies), and indicates that it is unparalleled since 1945, and often even 1870 (World Bank 2020).

[4] For a press dispatch in English, see https://bit.ly/2XKNWaU

Calantzopoulos 2018) and reporters' writings (Franzen 2019; Haque 2020; Wallace-Wells 2017), in the speeches of activist Greta Thunberg and Antonio Guterres (2018), the Secretary General of the United Nations, in World Bank and army reports (Brockmann et al. 2010; Burger 2012; Femia and Werrell 2020), in Davos conversations (Granados Franco et al. 2020), and in ongoing media commentaries on the fires in Australia, Brazil and Siberia, as well as in relation to the Covid-19 pandemic.

A growing number of scientists now consider that the most likely outcome of climate change, if the atmospheric greenhouse gas concentrations keep growing from human activities as they always have, is a global societal collapse (Future Earth 2020a, 2020b). This awful possibility doesn't even take into account the other global systemic risks, their tipping points and their nexus. Hundreds of scientists and experts agree that global systemic risks, among which are climate change, biodiversity, resource depletion, financial crisis and societal breakdown, need to be taken seriously (Future Earth 2020b). It is a nascent field of scholarship and neither peculiar nor unscientific (Ahmed 2019; Bardi, Falsini and Perissi 2019; Barnosky, Ehrlich and Hadly 2016; Cumming and Peterson 2017; Rees 2013; Shackelford et al. 2020).

Recently, the Doomsday Clock, which symbolizes the imminence of a planetary cataclysm, was brought forward to midnight minus 100 seconds.[5] As Will Steffen, a leading professor of climate science and co-author of major studies on tipping points and earth system trajectories, concludes, 'collapse is the most likely outcome of the present trajectory of the current system' (Moses 2020).

What do we do with this?

It is high time to fully acknowledge the existence and the nature of these risks and act as if it was the most likely future. From

---

[5] The Doomsday Clock was created during the Cold War and is maintained by the editors of the Bulletin of the Atomic Scientists at the University of Chicago. Since 23 January 2020, the clock has been displaying midnight minus 100 seconds (11:58:20 pm), the first time since 1953, due to the inability of world leaders to deal with the imminent threats of nuclear war and climate change and the proliferation of 'fake news' as a weapon to destabilize democracies.

that starting point, two questions become important to clarify: (1) how do we live with recurrent bad news of these mega threats? And (2) how do we organize in order to respond to catastrophic risks and events?

The first question emerges because almost everybody finds themselves running on a perpetual treadmill of emotions, including anger, fear, sadness, grief and guilt. Yet, for Will Steffen, 'the science of global warming has failed spectacularly to emotionally connect with much of society, particularly those in the most powerful positions – rendering policymakers ineffective despite repeated warnings' (Jones and Steffen 2019).

Our recent book *Another End of the World is Possible* (Servigne, Stevens and Chapelle 2018) tries to answer this first question with psychological, emotional, metaphysical and spiritual answers. It is about our relationship to the world, about interdependencies between humans as well between humans and non-humans, about meaning, narratives, grief, rituals, and so on. There is wisdom that can and must emerge from this predicament.

One important controversy deals with whether bad news necessarily leads to inaction or whether fear does always paralyze. Many critics of collapsology and now deep adaptation often assume that negative effect, without using scholarly insight in support of their assumptions. On the contrary, we argue that fear, despair or rage are (and always will be) part of the process of action. We have to get through, together.

Many studies show that so-called 'positive' emotions (such as hope, joy, compassion and so on) promote well-being, fulfilment, taking action, developing networks and skills and relating to others and to nature (Salama and Aboukoura 2018). They are undoubtedly indispensable for the rough weather to come. On the other hand, unpleasant emotions are the logical and healthy responses of a human being who is witnessing the destruction of what he or she cares about. They also help us to stay alert and seek out information (Yang and Kahlor 2013) (a fundamental step before setting out on a journey), to refine our perception of risks (Leiserowitz 2006; Smith and Leiserowitz 2014) and to turn indifference into urgency (Thomas, McGarty and Mavor 2009).

In a comprehensive meta-analysis of fear, a team of researchers led by the psychologist Melanie Tannenbaum concluded that '(a) fear appeals are effective at positively influencing attitude, intentions, and behaviours, (b) there are very few circumstances under which they are not effective, and (c) there are no identified circumstances under which they backfire and lead to undesirable outcomes' (Tannenbaum et al. 2015). For more than 40 years, the work of Joanna Macy, environmental activist and eco-psychologist, and contributor to this book, has been to show that no longer hiding the facts, no longer holding back in the expression of our truths, and sharing within a benevolent collective all that we feel, provokes a revival of energy and a kind of release of enthusiasm leading to joy and action. This is something we have experienced ourselves, which helped us to deal with the constant flux of 'bad news' and connect to another kind of hope. Emotions are not enemies; denial is. Moreover, as Joanna Macy and Chris Johnstone say, hope does not come from good news or from hiding emotions but from community and action (Bendell 2019; Macy and Johnstone 2012).

Last year in France, a psychologist and a professor of economy created 'the Observatory of Collapse Experiences' (OBVECO[6]). They conduct surveys, questionnaires and lexical analysis, concluding that contrary to popular belief, the anguish of finitude is a driving force for action. 'Far from making them pessimistic and passive, after a vacuum caused by the anguish of finitude, the collapsological narrative has made [people] optimistic and active, because through their concrete and organized action they show that it is possible to envisage a life after the collapse rather than an apocalypse where only death would be at the rendezvous' (Sutter and Steffan 2020).

These findings are in agreement with research by Jem Bendell and Dorian Cave on the perceptions of participants in the Deep Adaptation Forum which found that, as a result of their involvement, far more people feel less apathetic and less isolated than the reverse (Bendell and Cave 2020). Many describe taking leadership to help their communities become more resilient to future disruption. Two recent studies on collapse-centred communities in France (Bidet 2019) and the United Kingdom (Barker 2019) concluded that the cliché 'people do not react well when hearing bad news' should not be taken for granted anymore, although the

[6] https://obveco.com

science on this subject is certainly not settled, and further studies are needed. How we might organize to better respond to catastrophic risks and cascading events is essential to explore. To help people engage with that matter creatively, the deep adaptation movement began in 2018 by proposing that we explore the 4Rs of resilience, relinquishment, restoration and reconciliation. People involved in such conversations and initiatives have been holding space for discussions infused with attention to anti-patriarchy, social justice, decolonization and inequality. Debates around collapse issues should not be western-centred as they concern all living communities (and species) on earth. Indigenous communities have been experiencing collapses for centuries, and modern middle classes can learn from them (see chapter 6). In the same way, collapse narratives must not become the only vision of our future. We need a diversity of points of view, and even dissensus.

As noted by the editors in the concluding chapter of this book, the political question is the great work of the months and years to come. The task ahead is devising policies of resilience to cope with the unpredictable roller coasters of the Anthropocene, managing great 'collapses' and imagining what could come 'after'.

We know that some people continue to look for some technofix solutions while some billionaires pursue a form of space escapism (Yu 2017). Others are building closed communities (Hogg 2015). But for most people, who wish to care for the commons and each other, it is time for both collapse mitigation and adaptation policies, even if the window of opportunity of the first is rapidly shrinking.[7] We have simultaneously to slow down the predicament and to prepare for the consequences *that are already here.*

Deep adaptation is very close to the analyses and postures that we have been developing in parallel since 2015: synthesizing scientific information on major risks and on the possibilities of collapse, taking these risks seriously (considering that it is *certain*

---

[7] Mitigation efforts show this to be really hard to achieve in a short time frame as we must face a series of wicked problems such as rebound effects, seemingly unfeasible decoupling and socio-technological, cognitive and psychological lock-ins (Biewendt, Blaschke and Böhnert 2020; Gifford 2011; Parrique et al. 2019; Unruh and Carrillo-Hermosilla 2006; Vadén et al. 2020).

is part of it), taking care of emotional, psychological and spiritual aspects, and organizing ourselves to develop resources and policy ideas.

When the deep adaptation paper (chapter 2) came out in 2018 and went viral, we were pleased to see the levels of enthusiasm in the public. Quietly and without promotion, the deep adaptation movement managed, in a very short time, to talk about the scientific, emotional and spiritual issues, as well as possible political proposals, with a measured and subtle attitude and while touching the themes of injustice, colonialism, patriarchy, and so on. This rapidity has been a strength (for the English-speaking movement), but it also proves to be a weakness in terms of the issues at stake and the amount of information to be processed. The need is therefore to help the movement mature and evolve so that it reaches even more people. In contributing to this book, we hope to be bringing more people together for meaningful dialogue and initiative to reduce harm in the face of societal collapse.

References

Ahmed, N. M. (2017) *Failing States, Collapsing Systems: BioPhysical Triggers of Political Violence*. Cham: Springer International Publishing.
Ahmed, N. (2019) *The Collapse of Civilization May Have Already Begun*. Vice. Available at: https://bit.ly/2BmI3s6
Alexander, S. (2019) *The Rebellion Hypothesis: Crisis, Inaction, and the Question of Civil Disobedience*. Melbourne: Simplicity Institute. Available at: https://bit.ly/2CNjcyC
Bardi, U., Falsini, S. and Perissi, I. (2019) 'Toward a General Theory of Societal Collapse: A Biophysical Examination of Tainter's Model of the Diminishing Returns of Complexity'. *BioPhysical Economics and Resource Quality* 4(1). Available at: 10.1007/s41247-018-0049-0
Barker, K. (2019) 'How to Survive the End of the Future: Preppers, Pathology and the Everyday Crisis of Insecurity'. *Transactions of the Institute of British Geographers* 45(2). Available at: 10.1111/tran.12362
Barnosky, A. D. et al. (2012) 'Approaching a State Shift in Earth's Biosphere'. *Nature* 486(7401). Available at: 10.1038/nature11018
Barnosky, A. D., Ehrlich, P. R. and Hadly, E. A. (2016) 'Avoiding Collapse: Grand Challenges for Science and Society to Solve by 2050'. *Elementa: Science of the Anthropocene* 4(1). Available at: 10.12952/journal.elementa.000094

Bendell, J. (2019) *Hope in a Time of Climate Chaos: Keynote Speech at the UK Council of Psychotherapy*. Available at: https://bit.ly/30GH5jh

Bendell, J. and Cave, D. (2020) *Does Anticipating Societal Collapse Motivate Pro-Social Behaviours?* University of Cumbria: Initiative for Leadership and Sustainability. Available at: https://bit.ly/3jyJEMY

Bidet, A. (2019) 'Faut-il "avertir de la fin des temps pour exiger la fin des touillettes"'? *Multitudes* 76(3): 134–41. Available at: 10.3917/mult.076.0134

Biewendt, M., Blaschke, F. and Böhnert, A. (2020) 'The Rebound Effect – A Systematic Review of the Current State of Affairs'. *European Journal of Economics and Business Studies* 6(1). Available at: 10.26417/ejes.v6i1.p106-120

Bostrom, N. and Cirkovic, M. M. (2011) *Global Catastrophic Risks*. Oxford: Oxford University Press.

Brandt, G. and Merico, A. (2013) 'Tipping Points and User-Resource System Collapse in a Simple Model of Evolutionary Dynamics'. *Ecological Complexity* 13. Available at: 10.1016/j.ecocom.2012.12.003

Brockmann, K. et al. (2010) *Peak Oil: Sicherheitspolitische Implikationen knapper Ressourcen*. [pdf] Berlin: Planungsamt der Bundeswehr. Available at: https://bit.ly/30Se2JF

Brown, C., Seo, B. and Rounsevell, M. (2019) 'Societal Breakdown as an Emergent Property of Large-Scale Behavioural Models of Land Use Change'. *Earth System Dynamics* 10(4). Available at: 10.5194/esd-10-809-2019

Burger, A. (2012) *Turn Down the Heat: Why a 4°C Warmer World Must Be Avoided*. Washington, DC: World Bank. Available at: https://openknowledge.worldbank.org/handle/10986/11860

Capellán-Pérez, I. et al. (2015) 'More Growth? An Unfeasible Option to Overcome Critical Energy Constraints and Climate Change'. *Sustainability Science* 10(3). Available at: 10.1007/s11625-015-0299-3

Cardoso, P. et al. (2020) 'Scientists' Warning to Humanity on Insect Extinctions'. *Biological Conservation* 242. Available at: 10.1016/j.biocon.2020.108426

Cassely, J.-L. and Fourquet, J. (2020) *La France : Patrie de la collapsologie ?* Fondation Jean-Jaurès. Available at: https://bit.ly/37jzvOv

Cavicchioli, R. et al. (2019) 'Scientists' Warning to Humanity: Microorganisms and Climate Change'. *Nature Reviews Microbiology* 17: 569–86. Available at: 10.1038/s41579-019-0222-5

Cumming, G. S. and Peterson, G. D. (2017) 'Unifying Research on Social-Ecological Resilience and Collapse'. *Trends in Ecology & Evolution* 32(9). Available at: 10.1016/j.tree.2017.06.014

Diamond, J. (2005) *Collapse: How Societies Choose to Fail or Succeed*. London: Penguin.

Femia, F. and Werrell, C. E. (2020) *A Security Threat Assessment of Global Climate Change: How Likely Warming Scenarios Indicate a Catastrophic Security Future*. Washington, DC: National Security, Military and Intelligence Panel on Climate Change. The Center for Climate & Security. Available at: https://climateandsecurity. org/a-security-threat-assessment-of-global-climate-change/

Franzen, J. (2019) 'What if We Stopped Pretending the Climate Apocalypse Can Be Stopped?' *The New Yorker*. Available at: https:// bit.ly/3jxqKGa

Future Earth (2020a) *Our Future on Earth*. Available at: https://bit. ly/30npSg6

Future Earth (2020b) *Risks Perceptions Report 2020*. Available at: https:// futureearth.org/wp-content/uploads/2020/02/RPR_2020_Report.pdf

Gadeau, O. (2019) 'Brève chronologie de la médiatisation de la collapso-logie en France (2015–2019)'. *Multitudes* 76(3). Available at: 10.3917/ mult.076.0121

Garrett, T. J. (2014) 'Long-Run Evolution of the Global Economy: 1. Physical Basis'. *Earth's Future* 2(3). Available at: 10.1002/2013 EF000171

Garrett, T. J. (2015) 'Long-Run Evolution of the Global Economy: 2: Hindcasts of Innovation and Growth'. *Earth System Dynamics* 6(2). Available at: 10.5194/esd-6-673-2015

Gifford, R. (2011) 'The Dragons of Inaction: Psychological Barriers that Limit Climate Change Mitigation and Adaptation'. *American Psychologist* 66(4). Available at: 10.1037/a0023566

Granados Franco, E. et al. (2020) *The Global Risks Report 2020*, 15th edn. WEF. Available at: https://www.weforum.org/reports/ the-global-risks-report-2020

Gutteres, A. (2018) 'Secretary-General's Remarks on Climate Change [as Delivered]'. United Nations Secretary-General. Available at: https://bit.ly/2X0xv9I

Haque, U. (2020) 'The Age of Collapse'. Eudaimonia&Co. Available at: https://bit.ly/3fUsvL7

Heleno, R. H., Ripple, W. J. and Traveset, A. (2020) 'Scientists' Warning on Endangered Food Webs'. *Web Ecology* 20(1). Available at: 10.5194/we-20-1-2020

Hogg, A. (2015) 'As Inequality Soars, the Nervous Super Rich Are Already Planning Their Escapes'. *Guardian*. Available at: https://bit. ly/3huip4m

Jenny, J.-P. et al. (2020) 'Scientists' Warning to Humanity: Rapid Degradation of the World's Large Lakes'. *Journal of Great Lakes Research* 46(4): 686–702. Available at: 10.1016/j.jglr.2020.05.006

Jones, A. and Steffen, W. (2019) 'Our Climate is like Reckless Banking before the Crash – It's Time to Talk about Near-Term Collapse'. The Conversation. Available at: https://bit.ly/32MVlJP

Korowicz, D. and Calantzopoulos, M. (2018) 'Beyond Resilience: Global Systemic Risk, Systemic Failure, & Societal Responsiveness'. [pdf] White Paper, Geneva Global Initiative. Available at: https://t.co/F6AmRrY5FN

Laurent, A. (2018) 'Quand Edouard Philippe et Nicolas Hulot papotent théorie de l'effondrement'. Usbek & Rica. Available at: https://bit.ly/32QejiA

Leiserowitz, A. (2006) 'Climate Change Risk Perception and Policy Preferences: The Role of Affect, Imagery, and Values'. *Climatic Change* 77(1). Available at: 10.1007/s10584-006-9059-9

Lenton, T. M. et al. (2019) 'Climate Tipping Points – Too Risky to Bet Against'. *Nature* 575(7784). Available at: 10.1038/d41586-019-03595-0

Le Quéré, C. et al. (2020) 'Temporary Reduction in Daily Global CO$_2$ Emissions during the COVID-19 Forced Confinement'. *Nature Climate Change* 10(7). Available at: 10.1038/s41558-020-0797-x

Macy, J. and Johnstone, C. (2012) 'Active Hope: How to Face the Mess We're in Without Going Crazy'. New World Library. Available at: https://www.activehope.info/

Meadows, D. H. et al. (1972) 'The Limits to Growth'. New York: Universe Books. Available at: https://clubofrome.org/publication/the-limits-to-growth/

Middleton, G. D. (2017) *Understanding Collapse: Ancient History and Modern Myths*. Cambridge: Cambridge University Press.

Moses, A. (2020) 'Collapse of Civilisation is the Most Likely Outcome': Top Climate Scientists. Voice of Action. Available at: https://voiceofaction.org/collapse-of-civilisation-is-the-most-likely-outcome-top-climate-scientists/

Motesharrei, S., Rivas, J. and Kalnay, E. (2014) 'Human and Nature Dynamics (HANDY): Modeling Inequality and Use of Resources in the Collapse or Sustainability of Societies'. *Ecological Economics* 101: 90–102. Available at: 10.1016/j.ecolecon.2014.02.014

Nicholas, T., Hall, G. and Schmidt, C. (2020) 'The Faulty Science, Doomism, and Flawed Conclusions of Deep Adaptation'. Open Democracy. Available at: https://www.opendemocracy.net/en/oureconomy/faulty-science-doomism-and-flawed-conclusions-deep-adaptation/

Ord, T. (2020) *The Precipice: Existential Risk and the Future of Humanity*. New York: Hachette Books.

Oreskes, N. (2015) 'The Fact of Uncertainty, the Uncertainty of Facts and the Cultural Resonance of Doubt'. *Philosophical Transactions of the Royal Society A: Mathematical, Physical and Engineering Sciences* 373(2055). Available at: 10.1098/rsta.2014.0455

Parrique, T. et al. (2019) 'Decoupling Debunked – Evidence and Arguments against Green Growth as a Sole Strategy for Sustainability'. European Environmental Bureau. Available at: https://eeb.org/library/decoupling-debunked/

Read, R. (2020) 'It's a matter of the #precautionaryprinciple. Collapse will/would probably be so dreadful that not preparing for it to make it less so is now gross irresponsibility. This is why, despite our important differences, I work alongside Jem as a colleague'. 19 July. Available at: https://twitter.com/GreenRupertRead/status/1284790888955367426

Read, R. and Alexander, S. (2019) *This Civilisation is Finished: Conversations on the End of Empire – and What Lies Beyond*. Melbourne: Simplicity Institute.

Rees, M. (2013) 'Denial of Catastrophic Risks'. *Science* 339(6124). Available at: 10.1126/science.1236756

Ripple, W. J. et al. (2017) 'World Scientists' Warning to Humanity: A Second Notice'. *BioScience* 67(12): 1026–8. Available at: 10.1093/biosci/bix125

Ripple, W. J. et al. (2019) 'World Scientists' Warning of a Climate Emergency'. *BioScience*. 70(1): 8–12. Available at: 10.1093/biosci/biz088

Salama, S. and Aboukoura, K. (2018) 'Role of Emotions in Climate Change Communication', in W. Leal Filho, E. Manolas, A. Azul, et al. (eds), *Handbook of Climate Change Communication: Vol. 1*. Cham: Springer.

Servigne, P. and Stevens, R. (2015) *Comment tout peut s'effondrer. Petit manuel de collapsologie à l'usage des générations présentes*. Paris: Editions du Seuil. Available at: https://www.seuil.com/ouvrage/comment-tout-peut-s-effondrer-pablo-servigne/9782021223316

Servigne, P., Stevens, R. and Chapelle, G. (2018) *Une autre fin du monde est possible*. Paris: Seuil. Available at: https://bit.ly/2P3iC28

Shackelford, G. E. et al. (2020) 'Accumulating Evidence Using Crowdsourcing and Machine Learning: A Living Bibliography about Existential Risk and Global Catastrophic Risk'. *Futures* 116. Available at: 10.1016/j.futures.2019.102508

Smith, N. and Leiserowitz, A. (2014) 'The Role of Emotion in Global Warming Policy Support and Opposition'. *Risk Analysis* 34(5): 937–48.

Steffen, W. et al. (2018) 'Trajectories of the Earth System in the Anthropocene'. *Proceedings of the National Academy of Sciences* 115(33). Available at: 10.1073/pnas.1810141115

Sutter, P. and Steffan, L. (2020) 'Qui a peur de l'effondrement?' *Revue Project* 375(2): 34–7.

Tainter, J. (1988) *The Collapse of Complex Societies*. Cambridge: Cambridge University Press.

Tannenbaum, M. B. et al. (2015) 'Appealing to Fear: A Meta-Analysis of Fear Appeal Effectiveness and Theories'. *Psychological Bulletin* 141(6). Available at: 10.1037/a0039729

Thomas, E. F., McGarty, C. and Mavor, K. I. (2009) 'Transforming "Apathy into Movement": The Role of Prosocial Emotions in Motivating Action for Social Change'. *Personality and Social Psychology Review: An Official Journal of the Society for Personality and Social Psychology, Inc.* 13(4). Available at: 10.1177/1088868309343290

Turchin, P. (2018) *Historical Dynamics: Why States Rise and Fall.* Princeton, NJ and Woodstock: Princeton University Press.

United Nations Environment Programme (2019) *Emissions Gap Report 2019.* UNEP. Available at: https://bit.ly/3hxkrjR

Unruh, G. and Carrillo-Hermosilla, J. (2006) 'Globalizing Carbon Lock-in'. *Energy Policy* 34(10): 1185–97.

Vadén, T., Lähde, V., Majava, A., et al. (2020) 'Decoupling for Ecological Sustainability: A Categorisation and Review of Research Literature'. *Environment and Society* 112: 236–44.

Wagner, G. and Weitzman, M. (2015) *Climate Shock: The Economic Consequences of a Hotter Planet.* Princeton University Press: Princeton and Oxford.

Wallace-Wells, D. (2017) 'The Uninhabitable Earth'. *New York Magazine.* Available at: https://nym.ag/2X4Ajmh

Wiedmann, T. et al. (2020) 'Scientists' Warning on Affluence'. *Nature Communications* 11(1). Available at: 10.1038/s41467-020-16941-y

World Bank (2020) *Global Economic Prospects, June 2020.* Available at: https://bit.ly/2CZFdKh

Xu, C., Kohler, T., Lenton, T., et al. 'Future of the Human Climate Niche'. *Proceedings of the National Academy of Sciences* 117(21): 11350–5.

Yang, Z. J. and Kahlor, L. (2013) 'What, Me Worry? The Role of Affect in Information Seeking and Avoidance'. *Science Communication* 35(2). Available at: 10.1177/1075547012441873

Yoffee, N. and Cowgill, G. L. (1991) *The Collapse of Ancient States and Civilizations.* Chicago, IL: University of Arizona Press.

Yu, H. H. (2017) 'What Tech's Survivalist Billionaires Should Be Doing Instead'. IMD Business School. Available at: https://bit.ly/2CWToQj

Yu, Y. et al. (2016) 'System Crash as Dynamics of Complex Networks'. *Proceedings of the National Academy of Sciences* 113(42). Available at: 10.1073/pnas.1612094113

Part II

Shifts in Being

4

Climate Psychology and Its Relevance to Deep Adaptation

Adrian Tait

This chapter describes the psychological and cultural problems which climate psychology aims to address. It recounts the origins of the Climate Psychology Alliance (CPA) – a venture with imaginal, academic and therapeutic strands. Of central importance is the psychotherapeutic approach of 'deep listening', which can be applied equally to the hydra-like phenomenon of denial and the growing incidence of ecological or climate distress.

Underlying these three strands of practice is a major recognition and response challenge. What humankind is collectively doing to our planetary home is undeniable, but its significance is also unthinkable and unbearable. In the face of this, we are all liable to be caught up in and surrounded by denial in some form and to some degree.

The chapter points to some key links between climate psychology and the Deep Adaptation Forum. It celebrates these links as an example of the alliances which CPA has, since its inception in 2014, seen as essential to facing the emergency and to any effective response through mitigation or adaptation.

Why climate psychology?

Climate psychology came into being not so much because the climate and ecological emergency is the greatest challenge which humanity has ever faced but because its scale and nature make it uniquely difficult for us to find a proportionate response.

We do not lack information on the subject. As one of the characters in Rosemary Randall's novel *Transgression* remarked, 'All you need to know about climate change is that it's real, it's caused by us and it's very, very dangerous' (Randall 2020).

The obviousness and severity of the problem ought to be a compelling case for action. But the word 'case' threatens to take us down a blind alley because it leads so easily to the false assumption that we human beings are primarily motivated by the reasoning, analytical part of our brains.

CPA has two main objectives.[1] The first is to promote understanding of the irrational or uncaring element in our minds which combines with economic and cultural forces to block appropriate, timely and proportionate action in the face of climate disruption. The second objective is a more therapeutic one: to develop support systems for those who are committed to the exhausting, disturbing and painful task of sustained engagement.

Support is essential. Climate science backs up the evidence of our senses, but scientific *detachment* is definitely not what's needed in the journey of comprehension which climate psychology sees as necessary. If we have not been racked by grief over what is happening, then we are shutting its meaning out of our hearts and bodies. But if we remained immersed in grief alone, we would become part of the wreckage. The loss is continuous and mounting, which prevents us from moving on as in normal mourning. We need relief from the pain. At best and with luck, we return gratefully to the everyday delights of life that are still there, even in a Covid-afflicted world. Relief is necessary but is not emotionally very different from the defences of denial which cause a problem by shutting out reality. We are all on the spectrum; our place on it is determined by our willingness to ignore or forget external reality. Led by ex-CPA Chair Chris Robertson and drawing on a title of Donna Haraway's (Haraway 2016), attention has been focused on our capacity to *stay with the trouble*. But knowing that our ability to do this has limits can help us to find empathy, rather than pointing fingers of blame and adding

---

[1] Climate Psychology Alliance, https://www.climatepsychologyalliance.org/

to the divisiveness of the subject, which is not to say that anger at wilful ignorance and deliberate deceit (denialism) can or should be avoided.

The storms and firestorms of a destabilized climate are echoed by our own internal storms as the earth is tipped by our collective actions out of the stability of the Holocene era into the Anthropocene, in which humankind has become an earth system in its own right. This scenario is explored in depth by Clive Hamilton (Hamilton 2017).

We are liable to feel not just grief and anger, but guilt and fear, perhaps depression too. Lurking in the shadows there might be a touch of excitement, feelings of vengeance, even a death wish.

All of this emotion gets bundled up in the unsatisfactory terms 'eco-anxiety' and 'climate anxiety'. In an as yet unpublished paper, CPA member Breda Kingston has written an incisive critique of these labels. But we do need concise terms, so long as we remember that they are signifiers of a range of disruptive feeling states. Climate distress or eco-distress probably work better as container words for the range of feelings involved. Rosemary Randall has recently, as part of a series of short videos on engagement with climate change, also advocated the term 'distress', explaining and elaborating her view and suggesting ways of making the feelings more tolerable.[2]

Shiva – seeing what we need to see from inside a sick culture

We could benefit from a philosophical or imaginative tool to better comprehend humankind's grossly disordered interaction with the more-than-human world. The economics of plunder and incursion has fed a set of myths and assumptions – for instance, the notion that it is fine to externalize costs and to dump them into the global commons. These myths and assumptions are denial systemically enshrined; they blind us to the situation or encourage us to accept it as inevitable. The trick is to understand the fallibility of those myths, then to make choices based on that

[2] Ro Randall on climate distress: https://www.climatepsychologyalliance.org/explorations/blogs/477-coping-with-the-climate-crisis

understanding. We need, for instance, to face the terrible fact that the creative and inventive powers of the human mind, which have contributed so much and so diversely to culture, are in current danger of being overshadowed by the channelling of energy into a drive for acquisition, domination and consumption.

Climate psychology is necessarily an imaginal venture as well as a rational one. The Hindu deity Shiva, the creator and destroyer of worlds, may help us in that direction. The point behind this invocation is that, thanks largely to the power we have acquired through fossil fuels and technology, we have assumed a god-like status, a sense of omnipotence. But it is a classic case of hubris and nemesis because we have been revelling in our superhuman power with little concern for the consequences. Now, when we cannot help but know about these consequences, most of us turn away from them. The destruction in the shadow of our inventiveness and ingenuity is starting to envelop us and is demolishing the beautiful, complex web of life on earth.

We are in theory capable of stepping back from our technological hubris. 'Stepping back' is not a rejection of technology but more like a revisiting of what E. F. Schumacher called 'appropriate technology' (Schumacher 1973). However pervasive the trance exerted by consumer culture and the post-Schumacher digitalization of everything, it is clear from other cultures that we are capable of realizing a different identity as co-creators with wider Nature in its extraordinary capacity for regeneration (see chapter 12). But proactive economic and cultural change, though it could lessen damage, is neither certain nor a guarantee that societal collapse can be avoided.

Climate psychology can be construed as embodying a painful, ambitious and unpredictable engagement with Shiva. We are witnesses to the destruction and threat all around us. Drawing on psychotherapy, we can seek to offer 'holding' of the grief, anger, guilt and fear which are afflicting so many of us as we open our eyes and minds – not just to the consequences of our collective behaviour but also to the stupefaction which has enabled it. What often makes the task more bearable is the empowerment and uplift which comes from creative action such as regenerative work on the land or observing animals in the wild. The more-than-human world is usually to hand and brings priceless gifts.

Finally, and perhaps uniquely, climate psychology seeks to

map the interface of destruction and creation. Here we encounter an existential paradox. The grim forensic journey of witnessing the arrogant rampage of our species reveals what Paul Hoggett, borrowing from W. B. Yeats's 'The Second Coming', refers to as the 'rough beast' lurking in our culture,[3] what Sally Weintrobe calls 'the culture of uncare'.[4] We have to know, to understand and own our own capacity for uncaring in order to find a path to reducing harm during societal breakdown and possible regeneration. Otherwise, such creative impulses will be subject to the fatal flaws of naivety and idealism – a version of what psychoanalysts call dissociation or Jungians might classify as a refusal to face the shadow side of our nature. We are at a point of maximum peril and need to be training our eyes in the shadows even as we search longingly for the light. Ultimately, Shiva is a signpost to the duality of our nature.

Formation

The climate psychology field began to form in the United Kingdom around 2009. Several people were doing innovative work, but there was not yet much of a 'body' to offer connection, stimulus, support and coherence. There was a shared sense amongst a number of psychotherapists and academics in the United Kingdom and elsewhere that the moment for this had come. The group which gathered around this idea gave birth in 2012–13 to CPA.

An axiom of depth psychology is that the human mind is a site of contradictions and conflicts, of creativity and destructiveness. We take as a given that understanding beliefs and behaviour means recognizing the existence of unconscious processes (things that cannot easily be thought about) and the crucial role of meaning, emotion and identity in human experience. This does not

---

[3] Paul Hoggett, 'Slouching Towards the Anthropocene', Ecology, Psychoanalysis and Global Warming – Present and Future Traumas at the Tavistock Clinic, London. 8–9 December 2018, https://www.climatepsychologyalliance.org/events/298-ecology-psychoanalysis-and-global-warming-present-and-future-traumas

[4] Uncare, https://www.climatepsychologyalliance.org/handbook/326-un-care

preclude respect for science, but very often what really counts cannot be counted and requires deep listening in order to be discerned. In his CPA podcast with Verity Sharp and Caroline Hickman, Paul Hoggett explains his view that the listening style of psychotherapy is at the heart of climate psychology.[5] It is also integral to research methods aimed at registering the complexity and subtlety of personal engagement with such a challenging subject. Climate psychologists therefore consider not only why people are not listening to the science but *how* people are listening when they do or, when they're not, *why* they're not.

Secondly, climate psychology draws on psycho-social studies, which brings in the cultural matrix in which we operate as individuals. This is something I will illustrate in a moment in the context of denial. Our third main wellspring is eco-psychology. This tradition recognizes the interconnection between the human psyche and all the other beings, systems and elements of planet Earth. Eco-psychology offers, amongst other things, an antidote to humanity's hubris. It gives us a perspective on symptoms and causes that is not anthropocentric, helping us to see that both global heating and humankind's assault on the natural world are symptomatic of our collective forgetfulness of unity with nature (something discussed further in chapters 5, 6, 7 and 8). What we forget is that the earth systems we are busy vandalizing not only have a magnificence far beyond our own but are our very life support system. There is a great philosophical and intellectual diversity of voices within CPA, but these three fields have been the main formative influences.

CPA's early years were largely devoted to establishing a network of interested people, a body of ideas and links with key groups like scientists, activists and policy makers. Since 2018, there has been a marked shift of energy into outreach work, partly triggered by our connection with the Deep Adaptation Forum and Extinction Rebellion (XR). Preparation for this outreach activity has included 'Through the Door'[6] – a series of workshops for therapists and counsellors who are interested in

[5] Deep listening, https://www.climatepsychologyalliance.org/podcasts/406-what-is-climate-psychology-a-way-of-listening
[6] Through the Door, https://www.climatepsychologyalliance.org/events/470-through-the-door-a-therapeutic-practice-for-the-commons-18th-july-2020

CLIMATE PSYCHOLOGY AND DEEP ADAPTATION   111

taking their skills out of the consulting room and engaging, in a range of settings, with people who are striving to come to terms with the emergency. 'Through the Door' is a careful, facilitated and flexible process. At its heart is the psychotherapeutic goal of finding ways to bear and think about things that feel unbearable. It is a step towards CPA's goal of helping to enable therapeutic work in societies that are increasingly troubled by climate and ecological disruption.

Other strands of CPA's outreach include talks to professional bodies, workshops and consultancy with environmental NGOs, climate cafes, engaging with media and also collaboration with schools and community associations. Conversation with children and young people continues to be a critically important feature of CPA's work; it is informed by the perception not only that the emergency has triggered a seismic change in inter-generational dynamics at a mass level, but that the mix of vulnerability and leadership coming from our children needs to be appreciated and met. Caroline Hickman's account of her research work with children opens a window here, as well as illustrating the relevance of 'deep listening' to research (Hickman 2019).

CPA's outreach work has included facing a child abuse narrative in the media – allegations that adults in the climate movement are spreading an exaggerated and alarmist picture of the threat and causing unnecessary trauma to our young. We might spot a cynical inversion of the truth here! But along with robustness in our perspective we have to be open to learning. Do we, for instance, have a contribution to make when the problem is children bringing home from school information and anxiety that their parents are ill equipped to handle? We need to be alert to the danger of systemic inter-generational disorder.[7]

The robustness we need means staying grounded in the knowledge that climate distress is, broadly speaking, not pathological nor something to be massaged away but a sane response to danger and harm on a global scale. Alongside this argument is the view within CPA that, whilst it is rational to be alarmed and ethically necessary to be sounding the alarm, dismissing the possibility of finding meaningful forms of action is unhelpful.

[7] I am grateful to my colleague Paul Zeal for raising this issue.

This very brief sketch of CPA's purpose, methodology and scope illustrates the values and understandings we have in common with deep adaptation. The word 'alliance' in our name is not just about the need for common cause amongst the different traditions of depth psychology. It is also about a far wider alliance in re-imagining a future where we face up to the consequences of irreversible harm, accept limitation and learn from past mistakes. For such a revolution in economic and political thinking and aspirations to have a chance of success, a wide-ranging alliance of people and movements is going to be essential. Gail Bradbrook, co-founder of XR, voiced this awareness in the BBC programme *The Big Questions* on 9 January 2020.[8] The Transition movement, in its original handbook (Hopkins 2008), said something very similar with reference to harnessing the genius of the community. Many strands of consultation and engagement are needed. Citizens' assemblies – one of XR's demands – are a promising step towards widening and informing the conversation, though they are no magic bullet when it comes to renunciation of consumer entitlement at a mass level.

Alliances are needed to find ways to address questions such as how do we go about visualizing the future which is approaching and to which we will have to adapt? Can that imaginative and proactive effort help us to collectively shape or mitigate what is coming? How do we deal with genuine uncertainties as to what it will mean to inhabit an earth with an inhospitable climate system and a devastated natural world (albeit with potential for partial recovery)? What adjustments to our lives are likely to be meaningful at this point? How do we support each other, both in our own internal journeys and in the face of avoidance or hostility from those to whom the prospect of reduced entitlement, let alone collapse, is unthinkable? What agency do we truly have in relation to those who govern us and those who influence them, covertly or overtly, against the common good? Given the many uncertainties about the earth and human scenarios that will evolve, what options are available to improve our resilience?

The answers to these questions are debatable and probably unknowable, but holding them in mind can help to inform our

---

[8] Gail Bradbrook, https://www.youtube.com/watch?v=B4Y-mRznK2w&feature=youtu.be

strivings and ease the anxiety which comes with so much uncertainty and upheaval. The fact that the future is uncertain, to a degree, challenges us imaginatively and emotionally. Eco-distress has in it a variable perception and reaction to the prospect of collapse – whether people view it as possible, probable, inevitable or already occurring. The feelings which people mention include anguish and conflict over bringing children into the world and persistent anxieties about collapse that are vying for position with a deep-seated need to believe that all will be well in the end. One challenge is staying with uncertainty and ambiguity. Psychotherapists working in this field must adjust to sharing the same predicament with their clients, while being able to handle (and not identify with) the position of the one who is supposed to know (Lacan 1981).

The devil has the best tunes

Language matters. 'Biodiversity loss' and 'destruction of Nature' refer to the same thing but have very different resonances. Scientific and academic texts are governed by the need for precision, by appeals to reason rather than emotion. But decades of increasingly accurate climate science have not been effective in communicating the risks of climate change to the general public. Public-facing commentary is now improving and promoters of climate awareness, led by Climate Outreach,[9] have turned away from rarefied scientific language to evolve more listener-friendly ways of communicating about the climate crisis.

A caveat is needed here. Climate psychology offers richly informed insights. But the ethos of alliance includes recognition that important knowledge comes from other quarters and intellectual cultures. Two linked examples are: firstly, the need for frequent repetition of messages. Anthony Leiserowitz stresses this, in the context of the US public not having, by 2015, grasped basic facts such as the very high consensus amongst scientists.[10] The second and connected point is that a huge part of the problem is the vastly well-funded and highly effective disinformation

[9] Climate Outreach, https://climateoutreach.org
[10] Leiserowitz interview, https://www.youtube.com/watch?v=398tGbFcqOs

campaign which has been operating for decades, since before James Hanson presented his testimony to Congress in 1988. This is particularly well documented in the book *Merchants of Doubt* (Oreskes and Conway 2011). I attempt to integrate these points below, under the headings 'Denialism' and 'A Nexus of Denial'. There may be a bias in the climate movement against recognizing the extent and power of climate disinformation and, if so, this is likely to involve a default assumption amongst those operating in good faith and concern for planet Earth. It can be hard to believe the depth of (short-term) self-interest, cynicism and perverse disregard for the public good being exhibited by the denial industry.

In the past, efforts at climate communication have often lost out to debunkers who, even when they were talking rubbish, intuitively understood that denial reassured and appealed to many at an emotional level, therefore carrying more persuasion than quiet, careful presentation of facts. But until recently climate communicators and activists must have sometimes had a sense that you can't win because efforts to simplify the message and raise the alarm have been met with accusations of hysteria, being prophets of doom, opponents of progress, and so on.

All that seems to have shifted under the cumulative effect of a number of factors. First, the analysis has changed, with the 2018 IPCC report (which was startling, despite the political censorship and conservatism caused by the cumbersome review process), commentaries from the likes of David Wallace-Wells and Jem Bendell (chapter 2) and the ratchetting up of David Attenborough's warnings. Second, there has been a further escalation in extreme events like Australia's and the western United States' most devastating ever fire seasons, the inundation in July 2020 of much of Bangladesh and record flooding in 2015–2016 in the United Kingdom. Third, there has been a new kind of mass activism by XR and the school strikers. This shift means that more people are likely to be experiencing eco-distress from the witnessing or anticipation of disruption, loss and devastation, which makes the development of climate psychology even more important.

Denial

Despite rising awareness of the climate predicament, many people still ignore it outright. Negation is the most basic form of denial, in which the individual says, 'It can't be true', 'I refuse to believe it' or 'This is nothing to do with me.' We're all familiar with spontaneous emotional reactions of this kind in response to shocking news. They're self-protective at an individual level even if, as in this context, their collective effect is lethal. Sections of the media weigh in with accusations of alarmism to support negation. Political leaders exploit people's susceptibility to false reassurance because the threatened shock to the system (individual and body politic) is radical, undermining as it does not just entitlement but self-belief and sense of security.

Given climate psychology's focus on questions of emotion, meaning and identity, the field of denial is a place where we have something unique to contribute. But a grasp of denial, though it improves our chances of counteracting it, by no means guarantees that. The communication challenges are formidable. The very term 'denial', whilst it may be entirely accurate, can inflame the antagonism, political polarization and culture war which has so contaminated the subject of climate change.

Understanding needs to come first, followed by questions of communication strategy. But the two tasks interconnect because a careful exploration of denial reveals the spectrum mentioned earlier, in which most if not all of us have self-protective manoeuvres to defend against the horrors of our collective destruction and self-induced threat. Self-awareness facilitates the calling out of crimes and gives us more chance of establishing common ground in everyday discourse with others who relate differently to the subject. This is one of the key points underlying the Carbon Conversations project.[11] Self-awareness also helps to diminish the fear of social rejection which feeds a socially constructed silence.

---

[11] Carbon Conversations, http://www.carbonconversations.co.uk/p/materials.html

Forms of denial

Deep listening is as relevant to understanding denial as it is to meeting climate distress. Everyone has their own set of defences and idiom of communication. But listening can be informed by background questions like 'What is actually being denied here?', 'What is the feeling tone, as distinct from the content?' and, perhaps most important of all, 'How is this communication making me feel and how am I going to handle that?' Much can be learnt from on-the-spot appraisal of this kind, but much is hidden (from self and others), which is where depth psychology can be helpful in revealing some of the hidden blocks to facing and negotiating reality.

One blocking factor is fear of dependence. We all come into the world utterly dependent on caregivers who are attuned to our needs and dedicated to meeting them. All being well, we progress to a maturity in which we can tolerate the fact of lifelong interdependence, with attendant responsibility and vulnerability. When this process fails, we erect mental defences against unpleasant experiences of *not* being in safe hands (Winnicott 1990). To feel secure, we draw on the material and virtual worlds to create illusions of invulnerability, the price being that this cuts us off from much sense of relatedness with all that 'not me' world out there. In psychoanalytic parlance, we have, with the encouragement of a psychologically savvy advertising industry, entered a state of narcissism and omnipotence.

Denial of dependence cuts both ways. The notion of the health of the world out there being dependent on how we behave is liable to be just as disturbing as feeling dependent on an environment which is indifferent to our needs.

Perhaps a certain amount of healthy narcissism is necessary for us to feel good about ourselves, but beyond a certain point it will make us resistant to the suggestion that we are part of an ecocidal and self-destructive system. Any suggestion that our sense of entitlement in the rich world results in the abuse of millions of less fortunate people and of our planetary home is abhorrent and can arouse resentful feelings in people, as noted by Bendell in chapter 5 and a collective of decolonial scholars in chapter 6. Put simply, we have too much to lose by going there, even if we have everything to lose by *not* going there – irony, paradox and tragedy rolled into one.

Denialism

This is a term referring to the cynical promotion of denial, based on ideology and/or commercial self-interest. Such acts are designed to sow doubt and confuse the public, to block or delay climate-informed policy making, using lobbying, bribes and other means to influence politicians. The most obvious and egregious example is the fossil fuel industry in the United States, which has a well-chronicled record of such behaviour (Oreskes and Conway 2012) even while the industry was climate-proofing its own operations. Denialism can morph into a kind of 'so what?' nihilism, evident in the political leadership of both Russia and America. In the United Kingdom, too, efforts to interpret the mixed messages of the Johnson government include the observation that denial is taking a new form. Direct challenges to climate science are being replaced by covert undermining of green policies and decarbonization measures, despite these being acknowledged as necessary.

Disavowal

Refocusing on the individual, for those who are not somehow insulated against actual news (as when relying for information primarily on a social media echo chamber), it has become increasingly difficult to deny climate chaos and ecological collapse or our own hand in them. Disavowal is a more subtle and resilient line of defence – a capacity to know and not know, to turn a blind eye, to acknowledge the truth whilst minimizing its personal significance and implications for how we lead our lives (Weintrobe 2013). This form of denial has been termed 'everyday denial'.[12]

---

[12] Ro Randall on disavowal: everyday denial, https://www.youtube.com/watch?v= xMH3SgO4rKY&feature=youtu.be

A nexus of denial

It should be clear from the above outline that these mechanisms of denial shade into and support each other. Between them, they provide a formidable set of defences for those who seek to block out reality or feel that they have too much to lose by taking the hard path of engagement. It is this conclusion which gives rise to the notion of a *nexus of denial*.

Australia provides a striking example. A lacklustre conservative political leadership nevertheless held onto power in the country's May 2019 general election. Despite widespread dissatisfaction with the government's record on many social and environmental issues, mega-donors and the Murdoch media helped the incumbents to spin the choice as one between economic stability and a reckless, idealistic gamble with the nation's security and well-being. Australia has been on the climate frontline for a long time, but a shoot-the-messenger strategy worked as part of a 'better the devil you know' argument. The Labour opposition lacked the courage or imagination to face up to the immensely powerful coal lobby with a persuasive or imaginative vision for the country.

What followed was the worst fire season in the country's history in terms of hectares burnt and animal deaths. The fires scorched the edges of Sydney and Canberra. The government, again ably supported by the media, diverted attention with stories about arson and counterproductive green policies. Its intransigence in the face of the climate narrative was voiced in February 2020 by the new resources minister calling for more coal, gas and uranium exports. The country's greenhouse gas emissions for a year doubled because of the fires – a classic feedback loop. There has been a subsequent defunding of renewables in favour of gas, against advice from practically every quarter apart from the Economic Recovery Commission, which is stacked with fossil fuel executives.

These observations were distilled from a series of conversations with colleagues in Australia. Man Booker prizewinning author Richard Flanagan, in a *New York Times* article titled 'How Does a Nation Adapt to its Own Murder?', makes similar points (Flanagan 2020).

The political tactics and media antics referred to can be successful because they seek to amplify and harness existing cultural norms, or what Chris Robertson has referred to as cultural complexes – drawing on the concepts of Singer and Kimbles (Singer and Kimbles 2004). My own interpretation of cultural complexes, in the context of climate psychology, is that they are akin to the myths which maintain a collective blindness about our disordered relation to our fellow humans and to the more-than-human world. (For a fuller exploration of the cultural role of myths, see Sally Gillespie's *Climate Crisis and Consciousness*.) Below are seven examples of cultural complex:

(i)   the assumption that value is determined by monetary wealth and the monetization of everything;

(ii)   the consumerist paradigm of well-being, in which desire for sex, status and fantasies of security are exploited. One example is the current boom in sport utility vehicle (SUV) sales, obliterating the emissions savings due to electrification of transport;

(iii)   the 'no such thing as society' trope which defines us as isolates rather than members of a collective. The myth is one of liberation and motivation, but its main effect is to dehumanize;

(iv)   the generalized belief that competition rather than cooperation is the natural condition for humanity and the main driver of progress. Competitive sport often (but not always) reinforces this;

(v)   the 'culture of uncare', as outlined by Sally Weintrobe;

(vi)   entitlement – the notion that we are not just special but at complete liberty to dominate, exploit and destroy. This myth has some religious underpinnings. It is also a close relative of colonialism. Entitlement includes expansion and incursion – a prime factor in zoonotic diseases like Covid-19 (Tait 2020);

(vii)   species autonomy – the delusion that, with our brilliance, ingenuity, technology and built environment, we have created the world, a bubble in which we're above wider nature, rather than being dependent on the natural world in myriad ways.

This brief analysis reveals a strong connection with the deep adaptation thesis because it offers some leverage to the idea of relinquishment. Climate and ecological degeneration is already causing massive suffering and loss (to ourselves and other species), but the critique of cultural complexes invites us to look at how we arrived at this situation, thereby enlarging our capacity for more ecologically informed choices. Coming from psychology, it is resonant with the critique from sociology, offered by Bendell as the 'ideology of e-s-c-a-p-e' in chapter 5.

The psychotherapy profession – another case study?

The fact that depth psychology and psychotherapy provide such rich material for climate psychology does not mean that psychotherapists have less difficulty than anyone else in adapting to how profoundly our world is changing. This has implications for practice in the face of eco-distress. There may be a specific problem in that people who are assiduously trained to challenge the individual's projection outwards of internal issues will struggle to accept as valid a person's distress at collective destruction of the more-than-human world.

Good psychotherapy always cross-references personal history, current life issues and the here-and-now field of the session (Malan 1995). But dismissal (by interpretation) of disturbance which is rooted in global concerns is not good psychotherapy.

Our professional bodies are lagging behind others in the health-care field. Judith Anderson and Tree Staunton – two CPA members – have long been lobbying the United Kingdom's main regulatory body to adopt a climate change and sustainability policy, and Tree has introduced new frameworks requiring trainings to include sustainability and environmental awareness in their curricula. The UK Council for Psychotherapy's 2019 conference 'Sleepwalking through the Anthropocene' raised important questions for the profession. But it is not enough.

Disturbing accounts of psychotherapists or their supervisors taking a formulaic, reductionist approach to eco-distress in the consulting room can be expected to dwindle. But the consulting room may not necessarily even be the best place for the expression and hearing of such feelings. CPA's 'Through the Door' initiative has already been mentioned. And as Steffi Bednarek, writing in the *British Gestalt Journal*, observes, 'a collective wound may require collective healing'. My own experience of group facilitating, working with CPA colleague Gisela Lockie, supports this view.

In her passionate and powerfully reasoned article, Bednarek employs a psycho-social perspective to good effect, for instance in describing a malignant normality and, like Hickman, in casting the symptoms of eco-distress as a sign of health. She calls urgently for creation of a space in which the state of the world can be allowed and facilitated as a subject, warning, 'If we wait until it's too late and keep colluding with business as usual, we may well have a mental health crisis at a global scale on our hands very soon, with both therapists and clients utterly unprepared to bear the consequences' (Bednarek 2019).

Psychotherapy is seldom if ever an easy task, but there are securities and empowerment for the practitioner in familiar concepts, setting, methods and technique. However sensitive the therapist may be to power imbalance in the consulting room, it is probably a difficult step to acknowledge a situation where we are all in the same boat. Therapists whose training and approach preclude 'me too' responses may find themselves struggling to meet eco-anxiety usefully.

I hope I have shown that the fields of learning and practice which constitute depth psychology can throw much light on why it is so hard for us to face and respond to the existential crisis that is now confronting human and other life on earth. What remains to be seen is whether, as a professional and clinical field, it can find the courage and imagination to play a full part in the cultural healing on which so much now depends.

References

Bednarek, S. (2019) '"This is an Emergency" – Proposals for a Collective Response to the Climate Crisis'. *British Gestalt Journal* 28(2). Available at: https://www.climatepsychologyalliance.org/explorations/papers/448-by-steffi-bednarek

Flanagan, R. (2020) 'How Does a Nation Adapt to its Own Murder?' *New York Times*. Available at: https://www.nytimes.com/2020/01/25/opinion/sunday/australia-fires-climate-change.html

Gillespie, S. (2020) *Climate Crisis and Consciousness – Re-imagining our World and Ourselves*. Oxford and New York: Routledge.

Hamilton, C. (2017) *Defiant Earth – The Fate of Humans in the Anthropocene*. Cambridge and Malden, MA: Polity.

Haraway, D. (2016) *Staying with the Trouble*. Durham, NC: Dukes University Press.

Hickman, C. (2019) 'Children and Climate Change', in Paul Hoggett (ed.), *Climate Psychology: On Indifference to Disaster*. Cham: Palgrave Macmillan.

Hopkins, R. (2008) *The Transition Handbook*. Totnes: Green Books.

Lacan, J. (1981) *The Seminar of Jacques Lacan, Book XI: The Four Fundamental Concepts of Psychoanalysis*. New York: Norton.

Malan, D. H. (1995) *Individual Psychology and the Science of Psychodynamics*, 2nd edn. London: Hodder Arnold.

Oreskes, N. and Conway, E. M. (2011) *Merchants of Doubt*. London: Bloomsbury.

Randall, R. (2020) *Transgression*. Amazon e-book. Available at: https://rorandall.org/2020/02/02/my-new-novel-is-out-now/

Schumacher, E. F. (1973) *Small is Beautiful: A Study of Economics as if Humans Mattered*. New York: Routledge.

Singer, T. and Kimbles, S. (eds) (2004) *The Cultural Complex: Contemporary Jungian Perspectives on Psyche and Society*. Hove and New York: Brunner-Routledge.

Tait, A. (2020) 'Covid-19 and the Climate and Ecological Emergency'. Climate Psychology Alliance. Available at: https://www.climatepsychologyalliance.org/explorations/blogs/453-covid-19-and-the-climate-and-ecological-emergency-cee

Weintrobe, S. (ed.) (2013) *Engaging with Climate Change*. London: Routledge.

Winnicott, D. W. (1990) *The Maturational Processes and the Facilitating Environment*. London: Karnac Books.

5

Deeper Implications of Societal Collapse: Co-liberation from the Ideology of E-s-c-a-p-e

Jem Bendell

That modern humans have been oppressing and destroying life on earth is indisputable (Ceballos, Ehrlich and Dirzo 2017). That more of us around the world are increasingly anxious and depressed is also a global fact (Menzies and Menzies 2019). These realities should be cause enough to invite our deep reflection on what it is about modern cultures that means we have been oppressing and destroying so much. Yet the ability of politicians, business people, scientists and others to have known about the damage and dangers yet either to have ignored them or persisted with failing efforts at change suggests something quite powerful has been captivating their minds. Some analysts may assess that the fault is with nationalism, consumerism, capitalism or neoliberalism and so forth. However, I share the view of many scholars and activists in feminist, decolonial, spiritual and eco-centric traditions that the cause of our predicament is found deeper within the culture created from and upon the human psyche (Servigne, Stevens and Chapelle 2020). That view does not mean that human nature should be regarded as essentially exploitative, but that our potential for 'good' and 'bad' behaviours is shaped by the culture we grow up and live within – and which we reproduce (or disengage) through every moment of our emotions and thoughts.

In this chapter, I will explain an ideology at the root of human-caused climate chaos and one systemic reason why it proliferated. I will suggest how we might live creatively and meaningfully by consciously freeing ourselves and each other from that ideology.

My hope is that if more of us become more aware of this 'omni-cidal' ideology and the mental habits that maintain it, we could help each other to avoid making matters worse as a tur-bulent future unfolds. I call this the ideology of e-s-c-a-p-e, which comprises our assumptions of, or beliefs in, the follow-ing: Entitlement, Surety (which is another word for certainty), Control, Autonomy, Progress, and Exceptionalism.

The 'ideology of e-s-c-a-p-e' is a summary of mental habits that arise from, and maintain, restrictions on our affinity with all life – human and beyond. The acronym e-s-c-a-p-e is inten-tional and convenient, as the mental habits arise from a desire to escape from unavoidable aspects of our reality – impermanence and death – as well as our aversion to those realities, which arise because we experience our existence as separate mortal entities (Jenkinson 2016). These mental habits of e-s-c-a-p-e give rise to attitudes like individualism, nationalism, fundamentalist religios-ity and selfish spiritualities, as well as systems like colonialism, capitalism and neoliberalism. They are also involved in processes of unconscious bias, helping to reproduce prejudices and oppres-sions of various kinds.

By distilling the ideology into six components, my aim is to offer a simple synthesis of insights from relevant sociology, psy-chology and philosophy. I attempt to combine and adapt ideas from many different schools of thought, such as feminist critical theory (Stanley and Wise 1993), critical social theory (Adorno and Horkheimer 1997), critical discourse theory (Fairclough 2014), existentialism (Bakewell 2016), decolonial studies (Andreotti 2014), Buddhism (Hagen 1998) and mysticism in both Christian and other traditions (Abhayananda 2002). I offer the concept of e-s-c-a-p-e as a complement to analysis of, and efforts in, anti-patriarchy, decolonization, anti-imperialism, co-liberation and radical postmodernism.

There are a growing number of academic texts on the philo-sophical implications of climate change (Budolfson, McPherson and Plunkett forthcoming). Unlike most of these academic texts, in this chapter I will not offer a discussion of what one philosophi-cal tradition or theory could imply for our predicament. That is because I am not interested in communicating to you what I know of a particular literature, and instead wish to offer a framework that can help you explore your own engagement with our predicament.

In this chapter, I do not give examples of people and organizations that are perpetuating the ideology of e-s-c-a-p-e. My reason for that is I do not want to suggest that this ideology is outside of us or that the fault is with 'others'. Instead, this ideology is within all of us, including myself, and is shaping how I approach my life even as I type these words. Therefore, in this chapter I will illustrate the elements of e-s-c-a-p-e ideology from my own life, in an auto-ethnographic approach (Hughes and Pennington 2017). Although my experience is that the ideas outlined in this chapter can only be understood well through facilitated experiences and dialogue, I hope reading about them will offer a useful means for your own sense-making.

Entitlement in E-s-c-a-p-e ideology

There is a widespread assumption that we are entitled not to feel emotional pain and suffering; that we are entitled to have our inner worlds heard and validated; that we are entitled to have more than our basic needs met. I certainly would like those things, but am I entitled to them? When so many people in the world are suffering? When injury, pain, loss and death are as much a part of life as their opposites? Why should I assume my needs, whether material or for self-expression, are always priorities? A sense of entitlement can enable people to express their views and needs to others and the world, which would be fine if it were not that this sense of entitlement is socially conditioned and is therefore more prevalent amongst the 'white', male and rich of our species. That means we hear so much more from such people. Like me. Yes, one reason I thought I could write this chapter and expect it to arrive in front of your face is because of the sense of entitlement produced in me by my culture. With that awareness, I wrote this chapter anyway, which is a paradox I will return to later.

People sometimes ask, 'But why is entitlement a problem?' First, because it is unevenly distributed according to social conditioning, which aligns with inequalities in society so is therefore a mechanism of the interpersonal reproduction of systems of inequality. For example, women do not just need to 'lean in'; we men need to lean the heck back. By reinforcing power differentials, the cultural contributions of the masculine, the rich, the 'white' and the confident define what is considered 'normal', and the current 'normal' is the most heinous destruction of life on earth. Oh, the paradox of continuing writing here! But I want to explain that there is a second issue, which means that the democratizing of entitlements is not the answer. The expectation that we should have positive emotional experiences and that our emotional difficulties will be resolved means that we can expect external support for our inner emotional worlds. It is wonderful when such support is available and when we are able to offer that to each other. However, the expectation, and sense that we are entitled to not feel bad, is problematic because it creates insatiable appetites for new experiences and the pursuit of manic distractions. There can be no achievement of lasting 'happiness' by pursuing it. The sense that we are entitled to happiness means we contribute to the destruction of the planet through constant consumption, and we instinctively feel that it is justified to push away information that we might feel bad about, such as information on our complicity in the oppression of others, the destruction of life on earth and the unlikeliness of avoiding societal collapse.

Noticing the problematic assumption and belief in entitlement does not mean we do not want to try to meet our own and others' needs. Instead, being aware of this ideological assumption means that we begin to question our own sense of entitlement; we can loosen our expectation that what we feel or think is a priority for others to know or address. Questioning entitlement does not go against the belief in human rights or in an openness in human relating but brings attention to uneven expectations of participation, audience and power. Although the sense of entitlement of people who are 'white', male and rich has been increasingly challenged since the 1960s, the assumption of entitlement per se is not, and it may mean people are not open to the painful situations that unfold as our societies are disrupted.

I learned about my own sense of entitlement to not feel pain about other people's experience of emotional pain when I attended a 'breathwork' session. It involves people lying down and hyperventilating to achieve an altered state of consciousness. That might sound odd but, for me, when well facilitated, it has helped me connect with loving consciousness and gain new insights. In previous sessions, I had often become distracted and somewhat annoyed when people lying in the room next to me would start wailing or screaming as they expressed emotional pain, sometimes within minutes of the start. A wise friend suggested I might be averse to my own emotional difficulty with other people's emotional pain. That came to mind in one breathwork session when two women started to cry very close to me. I noticed my annoyance and then invited a more loving response in me. I sat up and, cross-legged, silently witnessed their crying and pain. I accepted it was how they were feeling right now, for whatever reason, and without judgement I witnessed their emotion and began to cry with them.

Achieving more equanimity about the suffering in the world, and our own sense of vulnerability, would be so welcome, but are we entitled to prioritize that at this time? It is a difficult question. I believe it is important to seek equanimity for many reasons, but prioritizing it at a time of turmoil might in some cases be an entitled response to our predicament. One statement I particularly liked from Mohandas Gandhi was when he explained that while he knew he had a lot more inner work he could do on himself, he felt that his inner world was less important than the pressing matters of India's liberation and non-violence between its peoples (Gandhi 1993). He did not mean that spiritual inquiry and heart-opening practices were not important but, while such work is never complete, we live in this world and have other matters to attend to.

Surety in e-S-c-a-p-e ideology

I will use the word 'surety' to describe the threefold assumption that we can be certain of reality, that it is good to be certain, and that there is a universal standard through which we can all agree what reality is and how to know it. One way this assumption manifests is in relation to the idea of 'rationality', which posits that we can be certain of reality by using rational intellect and, secondly, that more use of rational intellect and the artefacts it creates, such as computer models, are always positive in the pursuit of knowledge. The third aspect of this is the idea that knowledge claims are better because they relate to an imagined notion of 'objectivity', which is universal by virtue of not being influenced by subjective bias. These are all myths, debunked by critics of logical positivism and scientific empiricism over many decades (Doucet and Mauthner 2006). At first, the new powers of institutions that promoted the rational scientific method were widely welcomed, as they provided opposition to religion and superstition. Today this approach persists in most cultures, which means people and organizations privilege measurement over depth of understanding. It persists because it is convenient for the power of some, particularly because it requires significant resources to produce the knowledge that will be considered valid in fields like medicine, economy, engineering, planning and suchlike (Atkinson 2002).

However, on one matter, rationality and religion are not so dissimilar because institutionalized religion typically involves its own repressive 'surety'. It suggests we can, with human concept and language, make concrete the nature of reality that is universal and transcendent. Any invitation to adhere to simple stories of reality, whether with a religious, nationalist or political flavour, is an invitation away from staying fully present to experiences, complexity, ambiguity and unknowability. With spirituality, sadly, religions can F the ineffable.

This unhelpful focus on certainty underlies debates about human nature, which some people assume are involved whether one anticipates societal collapse or not. Some religions and political philosophies claim that we are inherently bad and need to be protected or saved from that, while other religions and philosophies suggest that we are essentially good and need to remove barriers to that. All of these approaches assume that there is one kind of human nature, that it can be known and that it can be objectively and usefully described as good or bad. These assumptions arise from a desire to map complexity and define reality in one way in order to control and belong. Instead, one could consider that there is no human nature, while all of nature and its possibilities reside within each human. Such a view may seem obvious when observing a world of good and bad behaviours and the billions of views on what is good and bad.

The cross-cutting theme for all of the many 'delusions of surety' is that they arise from an attachment to stable forms and an aversion to fluidity. A key part of the ideology of surety is that we assume that because a word describes a concept which describes a reality, that the word is somehow 'true' about a reality, rather than being a contingent, fallible and provisional tool for helping us communicate about things whose real nature we don't fully comprehend through language. The formulas of science and creeds of religion are all too easily used as escapes from the ambiguity of our infinitely complex existence that is only revealed to us through our limited senses, limited capabilities of cognition and limited modes of conceptualization and communication with language (Rorty 1989).

This desire for surety has led humanity to fixate on our stories of reality and add new information into those stories, rather than staying curious about realities. It has encouraged us to look for sensory information that affirms our stories of reality and ignore sensory information that does not affirm those stories (Lakoff 2002). Because of that, we can pay more attention to our stories of good and bad than what might be happening around us and how we might be feeling if we did not let those stories shape or deny those feelings. In the realm of rational thinking, we see this emphasis on surety manifest in a focus on what can be considered credible knowledge claims according to established norms, above attentiveness to what might be happening in the world. Chapter 1 describes this process amongst climatologists. Perhaps it is best highlighted by how climate scientists who popularized the 'hockey stick' curve of exponential carbon emissions years ago appear not to have looked at that curve without aversion, blocking their consideration of what it indicates is the probable, or even inevitable, future of humanity. Instead, they continue to measure and communicate those results, but call for action in ways that do not fully take on board the implications of that data (for instance, see Mann forthcoming).

Growing anxieties can mean people cling more tenaciously to their particular world view and are less present to what is actually happening (Doppelt 2016). They might waste huge amounts of time, effort and money to concoct new confirmations of their stories of reality. That could be scientists doubling down on their preferred methodologies in order to distract themselves from what's happening outside their window, or people turning to nationalism when realizing their past story of the future no longer feels valid, or economists doubling down on theories and associated policies which clearly do not work. But it even happens when people reject mainstream narratives and become inspired by alternative stories of humanity's salvation from eco-disaster, as their supporters claim that if we believe in them more, then they will come true.

When I was completing my PhD in 2002, I became most acutely aware of the problem of aspiring to surety. I had developed a framework of concepts that I thought helped explain the moral or ethical use of influence. For my final chapter, I decided to explore all the potential limitations of my framework, and suddenly the whole edifice came crashing down. After four years of work, that realization was a bit stressful and I wrote a new ending about the inability to describe love-in-action through concepts because context and intention are always important. My friend read it and told me I was stumbling into basic Buddhist philosophy (Hagen 1998).

With that in mind, I wonder what I am doing in writing this chapter. My desire to systematize my perspective on an ideology of e-s-c-a-p-e is because I feel that it matters to have maps or models to help us understand the world and our place within it, to enable discussion and future action. In my life I have privileged seeking surety through concept and language over other ways of knowing and being in the world. I have succumbed to that ideology, despite increasingly knowing that offering models such as e-s-c-a-p-e will not help many people to understand or change. Rather, it is my experiences of loss, pain and non-ordinary states of consciousness that have helped me to know that there are different ways of interpreting experience than from within the dominant e-s-c-a-p-e ideology. If I was to suggest to myself or other people that the most important response to our predicament is to become clearer conceptually about what's wrong in our shared cultural experience, then I would be succumbing to this misplaced interest in surety. Instead, I offer the framework in this essay merely as a limited and fallible tool.

Before progressing beyond this ideological element of 'surety', I would like to give some nods to related schools of thought. The French existentialist philosophers were quite clear on the difficulty of being confident about any particular framework for understanding the world or finding meaning. For me, Simone de Beauvoir was the best in showing how our ethical frameworks will always be ambiguous, and therefore when not questioned terrible violence can occur. Like the other existentialists, she chose personal freedom as a viable foundation for meaning (Beauvoir 2015). In doing that, she was settling on a form of surety which fitted with her and others' own proclivities at the time. Theodor Adorno and the German critical theorists were good at pointing out how our concepts are socially constructed in ways that reflect and reproduce power relations in society. They also showed how the Enlightenment and subsequent emphasis on scientific rationality meant that existential angst grew to a point where humanity increased its violent destruction of others and the world (Adorno and Horkheimer 1997). However, their critique was of the Enlightenment, and then mainly of bureaucracy and capitalism, rather than of human attachment to surety. More recently, the philosopher Charles Eisenstein (2018) has offered a similar critique that we have been living in an age of separation. He does not critique surety in general, as he suggests that our stories of reality are realities themselves. Before him, the philosopher Richard Rorty (1989) was more circumspect about the ability of human thought to describe or reveal realities. Therefore, he invited people to consider a variety of ideas as well as ways of dialogue that welcome complexity and paradox. My perspective is that Gautama Siddhartha, otherwise known as the Buddha, goes further than all of these schools of thought in connecting our sense of being a separate entity with our aversion to impermanence and death as the reason why we are attracted to ideas, information and people that seem to offer a sense of stability – i.e. surety (Hagen 1998).

Control in e-s-C-a-p-e ideology

The dominant modern culture around the world, not just the West, accepts the idea that it is possible for the human, both individually and collectively, to control the environment and others, and that it is good to do so (Greer 2015). It may appear to us that this is possible and that we benefit from controlling others and nature, but that is only ever a momentary situation. As the self-reinforcing feedbacks further heat our planet, we should come to realize that although our actions influence nature, we are not in control of nature and never were. It is because of this assumption of control that humanity has not paid sufficient attention to the complex environmental home with which it is interdependent.

The assumption of control arises from a lack of attention to how our subjective experience of the world and other people is just that – our own experience that does not dictate what the outside world actually is. It is normal for us each to label what we experience, from apple to cloud to person. However, when we forget that labels are arbitrary and provisional, the complex world becomes a mere array of 'objects' on our own subjective stage, which we then seek to control for our own purposes. Therefore, we make assumptions that one person is less worthy of attention and power than others by virtue of the label we have applied to them in our minds. For instance, people become trash, the hordes, the anarchists, the fascists, the mob, or even just 'the staff', 'the confused' or 'the enemy', rather than people like you and me. It also occurs as unconscious bias related to categories of race and gender (Irigaray 1993). This othering and alienation among ourselves, or the group we identify with, are dehumanizing and allow us to ignore the plight of others or perpetuate abuses. They become people to be controlled, either actively or through exclusion.

This 'othering' process is also reflexive as we receive from culture ideas about how we should feel, think and behave. Therefore, there are aspects of our inner worlds which we are invited to see as less acceptable or likeable, especially in certain contexts and for certain 'types' of people. Therefore, on behalf of dominant culture, we seek to control our own emotions and present an appropriate version of ourselves to the world. This process is deeply problematic for the individual and those whom they relate to (Bailey 2019). However, on a collective level, it can be suicidal for a culture as we do not allow the wisdom of our emotions to become part of our collective sense-making about what our situation is and what matters. For centuries, people have been suppressing their emotional pain about the way we live and the state of the world, as they told each other that such suppression was the responsible thing. Part of this process has been the collective subjugation of women and the feminine principle, in all aspects of existence, including the sacred (Vaughan-Lee 2017).

I did it myself – and for years covered my emotional pain with faux positivity and confidence. That was because for so much of my life I was concerned about my own security, even though I was telling myself I was more interested in social justice and environmental protection than in my status, finances or personal life. I was compromising all the time to be able to work for organizations like the WWF, the UN, the UK Labour Party and corporations. I was trying to control my situation financially. When I began assessing the latest climate science from the end of 2017, my mortality became more real for me. I realized that what really mattered was that I wanted to live my truth and be more present with people without hiding my weaknesses, insecurities and doubts. That was why I wrote and released the deep adaptation paper as a pdf from my Institute, rather than rewrite it to be acceptable for an academic journal and have another publication to make my career safer. Oddly, that recklessness led to the biggest impact that I had in my life.

The categories that we apply to ourselves and 'others' do not appear from nowhere but are given to us by our culture, arising from and maintaining specific power relations (Foucault 1984). This fact reminds us that we might not be so in control of ourselves, which deserves some more elaboration.

Autonomy in e-s-c-A-p-e ideology

The dominant culture I am describing here also assumes the idea that each of us is the separate autonomous origin of our awareness, values and decisions, and that it is good to become more autonomous. This assumption is false. Instead, not only is our ability to conceptualize and communicate socially constructed and conditioned by our culture and upbringing (Fairclough 2014) but also our ability to even perceive stimuli is influenced by that conditioning (Lakoff 2002). This does not mean that there is no free will but that our will is socially conditioned. Aside from that social conditioning, the nature of our being is influenced by the biology of our physical body and brain.

I once thought I knew who I really was and that I was consciously choosing my way of life. But then I had a close relationship where my partner helped me to see how my responses to situations could be coming from emotional wounding and patterns from childhood, which I had ignored due to my experiences in our dominant culture. One lesson for me is that I can never be sure what conditionings are creating my sense of identity and influencing my choices. It means I now recognize self-construal as a constant question in my life and can never be fully confident of the answers. The idea of autonomy, however, runs deep in culture. In recent times, it is being refuelled by misreadings of the insights of quantum physics, as well as New Age spiritualities and positive psychologies, which suggest we can manifest any reality if we believe it to be so (Woodstock 2007). Being more conscious of our feelings, thoughts and contexts is important to making better-informed choices; being aware of the way culture shapes our thoughts is an important step in that process.

This delusion of autonomy is problematic when it blinds us to the ways we are being controlled and exploited. Powerful interests work tirelessly to persuade us what to want and not want (Fairclough 2014; Foucault 1984). As such, we are more likely to unconsciously follow norms of thought and behaviour, even when those norms are producing collectively insane outcomes for humanity, as they are today. People who believe themselves autonomous are less likely to question norms as societies break down and are therefore less likely to engage in creative dialogue.

Recognizing that each of us and our experiences of the world are co-produced by our natural and cultural contexts means that we can begin to engage in those contexts to help more people reconsider their values and behaviours and to recognize that our capabilities have been developed through collaboration and solidarity with others. That means we might more consciously discuss how to reduce harm, promote joy and enable meaning, while never forgetting that our ideas on that will always be relational, provisional and open to challenge.

Progress in e-s-c-a-P-e ideology

The idea that humanity is advancing from the cave to the stars, through a process of civilization without interruption, is almost total in its encompassing of the public sphere (Greer 2015). The advance of technology is dazzling, and I am a grateful beneficiary of it. However, the assumption that material progress is possible and good means that new technologies and ideas are given the benefit of the doubt, and the hidden or unforeseen costs of those ideas tend to be downplayed or fixed with even less tested ideas (ibid.). Despite some positive exceptions, typically the push for new and more correlates with more consumption of the natural world and more pollution (Dietz and O'Neill 2013). It is the assumption of progress which permits us to take huge risks, rolling out technologies which disrupt the patterns of nature, and to deprioritize preserving the original wealth that is our natural world. It has also provided motivation, or a cover story, for colonial and imperial powers to intrude and disrupt the lives and communities of peoples around the world.

Some people are so entrenched in the narrative of progress that they simply reject information that does not support it. That is deeply damaging of our public discourse at a time when we need to rethink everything. In addition, the assumption of progress has captured our moral imagination so that most people find it awkward or impossible to think about values and right action without the assumption of progress. That perspective is incredibly disabling at a time of massive disruption, accelerating degradation and forthcoming loss. For instance, some people cannot imagine becoming creative and motivated to work towards a lesser dystopia for people and planet.

The dominance of the belief in material progress is why people think they are the strange ones for not being excited about Space-X launches. In fact, it might be quite reasonable to have a gut reaction that this is a childish distraction on a planet needing an urgent channelling of resources and intelligence into its terrestrial problems. Instead of assuming that progress is inevitable and good, we could consider alternative ways of framing our human condition, such as it being an era for the conscious retreat of humanity.

Exceptionalism in e-s-c-a-p-E ideology

I'm concerned about two kinds of exceptionalism: firstly, that we and our kin are different and better, or at least more entitled than others and their kin; secondly, that humans are an exceptional species in natural history.

It appears quite normal, throughout history, for people to think, without thinking, that their lives and those of their family, their community, country, race or religion are more important than the lives of others. These assumptions have led to conflict in the past and do so today. Yet another aspect of it is that people more easily accept their participation in systems of oppression and do not feel complicit in those systems or the terrible suffering that they create. On a planet that is one indivisible whole, this sense of exceptionalism and denial of the importance of 'others' supports sustained degradation and destruction. It is one way that colonialism of the past is related to the destruction of the present (Andreotti 2014).

Another way this exceptionalism manifests is when people think that because they are different, they can escape the destiny of most of the people as humanity faces a climate catastrophe. When people think about building bunkers, moving to New Zealand, growing vegetables off-grid, and such like, they may be pretending to themselves that they can escape a situation that will ruin the lives of billions of other people. Yet people who think themselves different may be less attentive to the possibilities for shared action in solidarity with 'ordinary' humans.

This argument does not mean that there is never a place for considering there to be an exceptional circumstance for oneself or one's group. However, being exceptional or making an exception is contingent on context, provisional and not necessarily legitimate. Therefore, such views should be open to constant question from many stakeholders. For instance, if a few were special enough to be saved, who should decide who they were? Or if a few think they know what is best for the rest of us, what powers should we have to disagree and prevent them from deciding that?

In the realm of social and organizational change, we see a lot of exceptionalism. It is the origin of baseless myths of the importance of the special leader, the need for heroes, the validity of the moral judge, the character of rich businesspersons, or the saviour role of a younger generation and such like (Bendell, Sutherland and Little 2017). The problem with that exceptionalism is that it means we look in the wrong directions for how to create social change. Clearly, the possibility for narcissistic attitudes and behaviours exists in everyone, but the problem with e-s-c-a-p-e ideology is that it has been encouraged by a culture through praise and resources.

The grandest exceptionalism is our story of humanity being separate, and completely different, from the natural world. This is enshrined in some religions and also in secular cultures. Even in some New Age spiritualities, there can be an emphasis on humans being the apogee of consciousness on the planet and perhaps the universe. Assuming this to be true, rather than an interesting story, means in some cases that people are more able to disregard, desecrate and destroy other life forms and the natural world (Eisenstein 2011).

The sense of exceptionalism in most of us arises due to our beliefs in autonomy, entitlement and control, which I described earlier. It may also arise in some people to distract themselves from an inner angst that, deep down, they know their stories of surety are false. When people act from a belief in being exceptional, they may actually harbour some panic about the robustness of their world view and personal identity.

A few years ago, I came to realize my own exceptionalism, where I had needed to think I was special in some way to compensate for my insecurities and the absences in my life. I was living a hero story, working hard on activities which were not fun but which I thought would mean I had an impact on social and environmental outcomes. I was spending my life in front of text on a screen, injuring my body as a result. Those sacrifices in my past may lead me to further justify the same kind of striving in what I do now. For instance, to whom do I think I am offering an encompassing critique in this chapter? I reflected on this question and wondered whether a sense of exceptionalism might, conversely, have been holding me back from sharing my views on the causes of our predicament. I had wanted to avoid causing disagreements within the emerging community on deep adaptation. That concern is founded on an assumption that I might be seen as special. So then I realized that people in the deep adaptation field could read my views on e-s-c-a-p-e, think them mumbo jumbo and move on! What is important is that we all have an ability to reflect and express. So I invite you to think about how you, in your heart, would answer the question 'Why did humanity destroy so much life on earth?' I suggest you answer this question yourself, not to others, and express yourself in your own way – words, poems, painting, dances, prayers, songs, arguments. Not because you are exceptional but because this is a question that every person on the planet should be asking soon.

Box 5.1 The ideology of e-s-c-a-p-e

Entitlement involves thinking, 'I expect more of what I like and to be helped to feel fine.'
Surety involves thinking, 'I will define you and everything in my experience, so I feel calmer.'
Control involves thinking, 'I will try to impose on you and everything, including myself, so I feel safer.'
Autonomy involves thinking and feeling, 'I must be completely separate in my mind and being because otherwise I would not exist.'
Progress involves thinking and feeling, 'The future must contain a legacy from me, or make sense to me now, because if not, when I die, I would die even more.'
Exceptionalism means assuming, 'I am annoyed in this world because much about it upsets me and so I believe I'm better and/or needed.'

Habits of e-s-c-a-p-e in the climate change field

When humanity moves into a period of greater turbulence and breakdown, we risk continuing the injuries of the e-s-c-a-p-e ideology and thereby making matters worse. It is natural that the ideology expresses itself within the communities of people working on climate change, and unless it is identified and questioned, it could lead to a lot of counterproductive behaviours. To help avoid that, the climate profession could learn a lot from the experiences of people working on decolonization. A collective of indigenous scholars, activists and their colleagues explains it well. Due to:

> habits of being that many of us have been socialized into as subjects within modern systems and institutions, we need to attend to not only the intellectual dimensions of de/colonization, but also to its affective and relational dimensions ... It is therefore not (simply) a lack of information that leads to the reproduction of colonialism, including within efforts to decolonize, but also enduring affective

[i.e. emotional] investments in, and desires for, the continuation of its promises and pleasures. (Stein et al. 2020)

The collective, called Gesturing Towards Decolonial Futures (GTDF), identified habits of people engaged in efforts to create change that nonetheless seek to retain or restore various entitlements and desires:

> When these desires or perceived entitlements are not met, it can lead to feelings of frustration, hopelessness, and betrayal, which can in turn result in outward displays of various fragilities or even violence. When thinking educationally, if these desires are not identified, interrupted, and 'composted,' that is, transformed into something different and more generative, then decolonization itself will either be outright resisted, or else be packaged into processes, experiences, or expressions that can be readily consumed in ways that appease these desires. [S]imply garnering more 'information' about colonial power relations does not necessarily disrupt dominant frames of knowing, being, hoping, and desiring that are themselves continuously (re)made through colonial relations. (ibid.)

To help address this problem, the GTDF developed a c-i-r-c-u-l-a-r model of the habits of being within coloniality and modernity that also arise in communities of people seeking to promote positive change in society. Mapping it onto e-s-c-a-p-e demonstrates strong similarities, but c-i-r-c-u-l-a-r goes further in identifying difficulties in the habits of people engaged in social change, as you can see in Box 5.2.

I summarize these insights from the decolonialization field as they seem highly relevant to understanding a new kind of 'collapse denialism' within climatology and environmentalism. When some environmentalists and climatologists reject the view that it is too late to prevent dangerous climate change from breaking most societies, they might be e-s-c-a-p-e-ing our situation. There may be a habit of **entitlement** to avoid emotional pain like despair and to preserve their persona of an ethical agent of positive change. There may be an adherence to the project of natural science in an unsophisticated way, not admitting the fairly arbitrary socially constructed conventions that underlie

---

Box 5.2 Comparing c-i-r-c-u-l-a-r and e-s-c-a-p-e models

Continuity of the existing system (e.g. 'I want what was promised to me'). In e-s-c-a-p-e, this is both the elements of progress and entitlement.
Innocence from implication in harm (e.g. 'Because I am against violent systems, that means I am no longer complicit in them'). In e-s-c-a-p-e, this relates to entitlement but goes further by inviting reflection on complicity in harm.
Recentring the self or majority group/nation/etc. (e.g. 'How will this change benefit me?'). In e-s-c-a-p-e, this relates to entitlement and progress.
Certainty of fixed knowledge, predetermined outcomes, and guaranteed solutions (e.g. 'I need to know exactly what is going to happen, when, and where'). In e-s-c-a-p-e, this relates to surety.
Unrestricted autonomy, wherein interdependence and responsibility are optional (e.g. 'I am not accountable to anyone but myself, unless I choose to be'). In e-s-c-a-p-e, this relates to autonomy, which also involves people assuming they are not produced by their culture and have an individualistic way of looking at problems and solutions.
Leadership, whether intellectual, political and/or moral (e.g. 'Either I, or my designee, is uniquely suited to direct and determine the character of change'). In e-s-c-a-p-e, this relates to exceptionalism and control, though exceptionalism includes the justifications people make for all kinds of behaviours that we do not expect or wish for others.
Authority to arbitrate justice (e.g. 'I should be the one to determine who and what is valuable and deserving of which rights, privileges and punishments'). In e-s-c-a-p-e, this relates to surety, control and exceptionalism. It usefully brings attention to a moralizing 'better than thou' aspect of some people's thinking.
Recognition of one's righteousness and redemption (e.g. 'But don't you see that I'm one of the "good" ones?'). In e-s-c-a-p-e, this relates to entitlement, autonomy, surety and exceptionalism but goes further in identifying how a person's need for self-affirmation is driving these habits.

---

the creation of subject disciplines and the norms of statistics, for example. That may suggest a need for **surety** to an extent that can lead to stupidity. Whether explicit or implicit, there is often a story that humanity is in **control** of our destiny within a turbulent environment and that we should somehow control our own emotions and those of people who listen to us. There is also the idea that individuals have the **autonomy** to change within our current system through voting, through consuming differently or through activism, as if we did not have bills and taxes to pay, creditors breathing down our necks, children to feed and clothe, intransigent politicians, security services infiltrating our activist movements and unrecognized ideologies calling us like sirens to our collective destruction. There is also a quasi-religious attachment to the idea of material **progress** and therefore the inability to conceive of courageous creative action without guarantee of material betterment (Greer 2015). Then there are assumptions of **exceptionalism,** such as when activists ignore how it is already too late to avoid climate-driven collapse or catastrophe for many people who have experienced that already. There is also exceptionalism when some activists say that they comprise the unique few percentage of a population who will change everything or imply that the environmental predicament overrides all other considerations, including human rights and democratic accountability.

In the last couple of years, some scientists and academics that are critical of collapse anticipation have used misrepresentations, personal attacks and moral condemnation in order to suppress discussion of societal collapse (for instance, see Mann forthcoming). That indicates an academic fragility, arising because climate chaos is challenging the world view, identity, status and knowledge frameworks of some scientists and academics. One reason I have taken some pages in this book to reflect on this phenomenon is that I believe there is potential for harm to arise from unreflective, panicked action on climate change. For instance, it is increasingly popular in climate communication to speak of a 'climate war' (Mann forthcoming), to encourage authoritarian state action and encourage inter-generational blame rather than action on the systemic oppression that has caused environmental destruction.

Today, the 'hope' that many environmentalists speak of is a hope imbued with e-s-c-a-p-e ideology. Even the fact that they think they need hope at all for motivation to take meaningful action is the result of the e-s-c-a-p-e ideology shaping their thought. If a hope in hell arises from the dominant culture of our time, and therefore does not invite meaningful conversation about deep cultural change, that hope is hell itself. Instead, it would be helpful for anyone concerned about the future of humanity in a chaotic climate to consider how the destructive ideology of e-s-c-a-p-e proliferated and therefore what might be done about that in future. Which is what we will now consider.

The economic reproduction of e-s-c-a-p-e

To reject the ideology of e-s-c-a-p-e is to have little place in public discourse today. That is not by accident. The ideology of e-s-c-a-p-e has been conducive to the rise of certain power relations which are embedded in capitalism and all political systems. That ideology is reproduced and spreads through those economic and political systems. There is a relationship between material contexts and the deep rules or 'operating systems' of all societies and economies, on the one hand, and the ideologies which become widespread on the other. You may recall that Karl Marx once wrote about how the 'mode of production' of goods and services incentivizes certain ways of understanding oneself, the world and society (Cole 2007). It is clear that the 'mode of transaction and consumption' is as important as the mode of production for how we understand ourselves and the world. There is an iterative relationship between material contexts on the one hand and ideas about self and society on the other, especially when those ideas reshape what is considered (or is possible to experience as) a material resource. But what my perspective means is that some of the deepest rules or codes of our society will necessitate the maintenance of this e-s-c-a-p-e ideology, whatever happens in the world and however we feel about it. That deep code is our system of money creation. Money was never a physical thing, despite some of the inaccurate stories of some historians. Money has always been an agreement about how we transact with each other, which over time, through habit, turns into an assumption of how value is transacted and what 'money' is. To help that process, sometimes we have created stories about material objects having transferable value. Those stories can become widespread and can influence behaviours so that people begin to assume an object, such as a type of metal, has a value in its essence rather than ascribed by social convention (Graeber 2011).

Latterly, the reification of markets has led to narratives that we do not control money or the economy. A better way to view modern money is as one of a series of institutions which support commerce, alongside various laws, banks, courts, bailiffs, markets, armies, relationships and social customs. As such, money is by no means a force outside our control which dictates that the rich get richer and the poor get poorer; rather, the distribution of wealth and resources is absolutely under our collective control.

The current monetary system in nearly all countries of the world is one where banks issue new electronic money when they make deposits in current accounts after their clients (people, organizations or governments) have signed loan agreements (including the selling of bonds). In most countries of the world, that electronic money, issued in return for a debt agreement, constitutes almost all of the money in circulation (Bendell and Greco 2013). This debt-money system fuels the e-s-c-a-p-e ideology in a number of ways.

Entitlement: a debt-money system creates inequality through the payment of interest to the creditors from the debtors, maintains inequality especially when compound interest makes debts harder to pay, and therefore enables the creation of distinct cultures of consumption related to one's place on an economic ladder, which therefore shapes separate identities.

Surety: a debt-money system rewards with new credit people who adopt the mentality of mapping, planning and calculating.

Control: a debt-money system offers an experience of power not constrained by time or space. This is because the electronic money in a bank account does not rust, rot or get lost. This nature of money affects all of our perceptions of reality. People with money can control their lives without being subject to others: money buys not only material goods and services but also status, media attention, indemnity and arguably both votes and laws.

Autonomy: because every person now needs some of this money in order to live, you can find someone to do what you want for a simple transaction, without relying on social relations of solidarity. Regarding money as personal property supports the idea that each person should be responsible for himself over the idea that we are responsible for each other. Everyone must have to have something to sell in a marketplace in order to be independent of others. But this autonomy is a charade. Money only switches our dependence on family, friends and neighbours to dependence on the market, which is to say on corporations and strangers. And it is a double dependence because we must go to the market first to get the money and again to spend it.

Progress: a debt-money system requires expansion of economic activity in order to avoid economic disruption. This matter has been debated by economists, but I will show in a forthcoming paper that the arguments against a growth imperative from bank-issued debt-money are flawed. The need for expansion of transactions means we have experienced progress as material expansion that is seen as both normal and desirable.

Exceptionalism: a debt-money system requires the continual conversion of the natural world into products, and the instrumentalization of people as objects for the pursuit of profits.

Some of you might be benefiting from this process if you receive share dividends. However, it is unlikely you are gaining a net benefit, given the amount of money that we spend due to helping companies service their debts (some calculate that interest payments amount to about 40 per cent of the price of goods and services in western economies (Bendell and Greco 2013)). You may have benefited if you have cashed in on the sale of real estate to buy a cheaper home. But do not be fooled that the price of your house is a benefit if not realized through a sale where you downsized to release capital. After all, the market price of a house is merely a story of value until you access finance from it.

Modern humans, like myself, have been hypnotised by the e-s-c-a-p-e ideology to be compliant and mutually self-police as workers and consumers to systematically destroy our planetary home to provide wealth and power to people we do not know. The e-s-c-a-p-e ideology is therefore an ideology of oppression for exploitation that is producing omnicide. Therefore, our climate tragedy is the result of our oppression. Any meaningful environmentalism should be first and foremost a movement for our co-liberation from those systems of oppression that have been forcing us into the insanity of destroying the life-support system of ourselves and our families.

However, because environmentalists have been trapped within

the e-s-c-a-p-e ideology, they have framed the problem as one of side effects and accidents that need our better management and control, or even as an opportunity for more consumer self-expression and heroism – basically anything which would fit the e-s-c-a-p-e ideology rather than actually realize how that ideology is the cause of the problem. Honest environmentalism must now involve the aim and effort for humans to be freer to connect to, honour and sustain our environments. Any other environmentalism is a lie. The atmosphere tells us that it is a lie, with the fact of an atmospheric concentration of 417 ppm CO_2 in 2020.[1]

Perhaps it is because so much of the environmental movement and profession has been trapped in e-s-c-a-p-e thinking that there has not been the identification of the phenomenon that destroys life. People speak of colonialism, patriarchy, industrialism or anthropocentrism, but I have not heard a term for the concepts and practices that are destructive of ourselves, others and nature. I have emphasized above a process of the incarceration of ourselves in systems that mean we then incarcerate other life. That incarceration has been, and is, death for many people and much of the natural world. We might regard the post-Enlightenment era as the great incarceration. It appears to me to be important as modernity and coloniality in shaping our lives. So it is worthy of a name – perhaps the paradigm of 'incarcerity'. What might be gained from considering our aims as the de-incarceration of life? It might provide us more challenge and guidance than seeking to overcome separation. After all, we never were separate, but through experiencing ourselves as separate, aspects of our being were incarcerated as we joined a project of incarcerating life (Thich Nhat Hanh 1987).

Moving beyond e-s-c-a-p-e to c-o-s-m-o-s

So how do we move beyond e-s-c-a-p-e? Recognizing that this ideology exists and has been involved in enabling and spreading the attitudes and behaviours that have caused irreparable damage to life on earth, as well as our own species' experience of life and

---

[1] https://research.noaa.gov/article/ArtMID/587/ArticleID/2636/Rise-of-carbon-dioxide-unabated

future potential is a useful start. To help us all move beyond being stuck in the mere recognition of e-s-c-a-p-e ideology, I am curious about the possibility for a simple guide to the habits or qualities of mind that are the opposite of the habits of e-s-c-a-p-e. To stimulate reflection on that, I have developed a provisional guide, which I call the c-o-s-m-o-s remedy to the ideology of e-s-c-a-p-e. I describe it here by using simple statements of the perspective and how it is an opposite of the relevant element of the ideology of e-s-c-a-p-e. The c-o-s-m-o-s remedy is something I have only recently begun to use to support the design of my courses, the way I analyse and write, and the way I am in the world, so I have no 'road testing' or impacts to report on.

Whereas the habit of entitlement involves thinking 'I expect more of what I like and to be helped to feel fine . . .'
Compassion, in this context, involves sensing that 'I feel an active responsibility for any of my contribution to your suffering, without expecting to feel right, better or worse.'

Whereas the habit of surety involves thinking, 'I will define you and everything in my experience so that I feel calmer . . .'
Openness wishes 'I will keep returning to be curious about as much as I can, however unnerving.'

Whereas the habit of control involves thinking 'I will try to impose on you and everything, including myself, so I feel safer . . .'
Serenity involves allowing the feeling that 'I appreciate the dignity of you, myself and all life, however disturbing situations might seem.'

Whereas the habit of autonomy involves thinking and feeling 'I must be completely separate in my mind and being, because otherwise I would not exist . . .'
Mutuality involves remembering 'as this world has produced me and societies have shaped me, I will question all my understandings and ways of relating with others.'

Whereas the habit of progress involves thinking and feeling that 'the future must contain a legacy from me, or make sense

to me now, because if not, then when I die, I would die even more . . .'
Oneness awareness involves sensing 'what is important is how I live more lovingly right here and now, without needing to believe that I matter or am improving'.

Whereas the habit of exceptionalism means assuming 'I am annoyed in this world because much about it upsets me and so I believe I'm better and/or needed . . .'
Solidarity involves acting from the part of you that knows 'our common sadness and frustration arise from our mutual love for all life and motivate us towards fairness, justice and healing.'

In choosing c-o-s-m-o-s as the acronym, I do not mean to invoke the image of a cosmos 'out there' in space. Rather, the c-o-s-m-o-s is everything, everywhere, 'everywhen'. Experiencing oneself as an aspect of the cosmos may be both blissful and painful, as all that we consider good and bad, pain and pleasure, is within the cosmos (Macy 2020). Although the modern era reinforces e-s-c-a-p-e ideology, this c-o-s-m-o-s remedy is not 'anti-modern' or completely rejecting modernity (Versluis 2006). There will be some thoughts and feelings within each of the elements of the e-s-c-a-p-e paradigm that are useful and could remain useful. The problem is the unthinking allegiance and adherence to these elements, along with the enforced spreading of these elements through systems of economics, politics, education and cultural artefact. Rather than being anti-modern, my deconstruction of the ideology of e-s-c-a-p-e and an era of incarcerating ourselves and all life has some resonance with radical postmodernism (Atkinson 2002), which critiques the deeper assumptions of modernity (such as unidirectional progress and power-ignoring truth claims). It most closely resonates with the interests of people involved in the diverse and emerging intellectual project of 'transmodernism' (Cole 2007). Typically, adherents critique modernity from an anti-imperialism standpoint, lament the absence of a coherent political project arising from postmodernism and encourage a mixing of ideas and approaches from different cultures, including pre-modern ones.

I recognize that I am a white, middle-class, middle-aged western man with an elite education. Although I have learned from a

number of female scholars, activists and professionals working on
anti-racism, anti-patriarchy and decolonization, who are black,
indigenous and people of colour (BIPOC), anything I suggest
about a better way of thinking as we face collapse is influenced by
my experience of life as someone inhabiting a privileged identity.
Therefore, my ideas may be affected by e-s-c-a-p-e in ways I do
not yet recognize. And therefore, in addition to my offer of c-o-
s-m-o-s, it will be useful to consider others' ideas about how to
move beyond e-s-c-a-p-e (or beyond however you understand the
causes of our predicament). In particular, I encourage the consideration of the advice and tools from GTDF. They have suggested
guidance for reducing the habits of c-i-r-c-u-l-a-r and e-s-c-a-p-e
ideologies, which they call c-o-m-p-o-s-t.

In developing their c-o-m-p-o-s-t guidance, they drew on
insights from how social activists, including people working on climate, including themselves, can exhibit the habits of the ideology.
Therefore, their model may speak powerfully, and uncomforta-
bly, to people involved in any social or environmental activism or
policy work (GTDF 2020). In opposition to entitlement, C is the
Capacity for holding space for painful and difficult things without feeling irritated, overwhelmed, immobilized or wanting to
be coddled or rescue; while O is Owning up to one's complicity
and implication in harm (the harms of violence and unsustainability required to create and maintain 'the world as we know
it' with the pleasures, certainties and securities that we enjoy).
In opposition to surety, M is the Maturity to face and work on
individual and collective shit rather than denying or dumping shit
onto others, or spreading it around (their terminology, not mine,
though I am not criticizing!). Instead of control and progress, P
is the Pause of narcissistic, hedonistic and 'fixing' compulsions in
order to identify, interrupt and dis-invest from harmful desires,
entitlements, projections, fantasies and idealizations. In opposition to autonomy, another O is the Othering of our self-images
and self-narratives in order to encounter the 'self beyond the self',
including the beautiful, the ugly, the broken and the fucked up
in everything/everyone (again, the words of GTDF). In opposition to exceptionalism, S is the Stamina and sobriety to show
up differently and do what is needed rather than what is pleasurable, easy, comfortable, consumable and/or convenient; while
T is a Turning towards unlimited responsibility with humility,

compassion, serenity, openness, solidarity and mutuality, and without investments in purity, protagonism, progress and popularity. Further insights from the GTDF are offered in chapter 6. I hope that this chapter has helped to show how a critique of e-s-c-a-p-e ideology and the suggestion of a c-o-s-m-o-s remedy is aligned with anti-oppression efforts, whether people understand and pursue that in terms of anti-patriarchy, anti-imperialism, anti-racism or decolonization. In addition, I hope that it is clear that anti-oppression efforts are best pursued in a reflexive way, where we recognize how we are all oppressed and oppressing, even when choosing to be engaged for change. Therefore, I think the concept of co-liberation could be useful for future work on deep adaptation to climate chaos. For me, co-liberation describes an aspiration towards co-freeing each other from systems that differentially oppress all people within both dominant and marginalized groups in societies. Therefore, it includes co-creating our co-freedom with people in communities that seek to avoid systemic oppression.

Considerations for co-liberation from destructive ideology

If this is making sense to you, then a natural question to ask is what to do about reducing our own habits of e-s-c-a-p-e, and how to engage in co-liberation from systems of oppression and destruction. To begin with, it is useful to recognize how phobias around impermanence and death are at the root of the habits of e-s-c-a-p-e, and how those phobias mutually consolidate separative ways of experiencing and understanding ourselves and the world, thereby diminishing our affinity for all life (Jenkinson 2016). Understanding that then points to where the most powerful remedies to e-s-c-a-p-e may be found. Anything which helps us to become more aware and less reactive to our emotion of fear, while also experiencing ourselves as less separate from all life but part of a consciousness that is timeless and limitless, will support us to reduce our habits of e-s-c-a-p-e and the systems of oppression and destruction which it produces. Practices such as insight meditation, breathwork and deep relating appear useful to me (chapter 7). Also useful has been my increasing involvement in the social justice aspects of the climate crisis. That involves moving beyond a focus on my emotional coping to accepting that some emotional pain about the world and my part in it will be an unavoidable aspect of my life from now on. It involves feeling and acting in solidarity with people who suffer more than I do, a key part of my response to the predicament. That solidarity involves supporting efforts to disrupt and disengage from the economic systems that maintain oppression and incentivize e-s-c-a-p-e thinking. The allure of emancipation from my complicity and pain may be great, but that is an e-s-c-a-p-e entitlement habit to feel good and be righteous. Instead, if we become freer from our aversions to emotional pain of any kind, we can be more radically present to what is happening and respond usefully. In that sense, co-liberation must involve liberation from any expectations or desires to feel innocent, validated, righteous or absolved. Aspiring to greater equanimity while opening one's heart, in the understanding that will mean more pain as well as joy, is the only true path of co-liberation. It is also part of an engaged spiritual life (Rothberg 2006).

Efforts at co-liberation from e-s-c-a-p-e will be wise to avoid privileging a focus on one oppression over another. A particular challenge is how to bring the matter of economic justice into the ways of working together in groups of activists and community members. For instance, whereas people can learn to be more aware of their unconscious bias about gender and race, the matter of economic inequality can be even more challenging, as it is typical for people to choose to maintain their economic privilege and not consider the implications of economic disparity. Yet without addressing prejudices and oppressions involving economic class, efforts at co-liberation will likely alienate many people who are economically disadvantaged.

Perhaps the only way of sustaining oneself in this shift of being beyond e-s-c-a-p-e ideology is to participate in communities that practise other ways of living. Those communities can be both non-local and local, though it is best not to rely on non-local communities in the coming years (chapter 12 on relocalization). It will also be helpful for such communities to be engaged in social and economic justice efforts so that their focus does not become entirely inward. Involvement in 'climate justice' initiatives that seek to reduce harm where it is being experienced the most can become key to deep adaptation and co-liberation (Reyes Mason and Rigg 2019). Another reason for engagement in climate justice is the reality of the global nature of our predicament. Small groups of people escaping e-s-c-a-p-e will be a positive, particularly for them, but it probably will not have a lasting impact on a planet being destroyed by behaviour arising from a widespread destructive ideology and the economic systems it co-maintains.

Although it is important to explore ideas for alternative paradigms, I am not under any illusion that such processes will have much impact on wider society. Why? Because, for now, we will not be heard by many people. A few of us may be fortunate enough to be exposed to critical social theory like that synthesized in this chapter or to popular translators of those ideas for the general public, such as comedian and social commentator Russell Brand. However, unless the monetary system changes, the ideology of e-s-c-a-p-e will continue to be fuelled during forthcoming societal disruption and we will be marginal onlookers. It is important that while co-liberatory ways of being involve attention to moment-by-moment interactions with other people, that does not mean we do not need changes in government policies at local, national and international levels. Connecting the personal with the political-at-scale is essential (chapter 11).

The question that could therefore be asked is: would you like to hope that the e-s-c-a-p-e ideology collapses sufficiently at scale in order to help people to reduce harm, find joy and meaning, or even create more possibilities for life on earth and the human species? If so, we must consider how our monetary system might collapse and be replaced by some other forms that will not replicate its problems. Towards that aim, could we try to help disrupt the economic fuel of the e-s-c-a-p-e ideology? Should we do this in ways other than creating small alternatives that remain niche? Could there be efforts at a grand scale, even at a geopolitical level? Could there be efforts to hijack the populist backlash against the end of progress, and channel it towards a real transformation of ideology, rather than the increasing 'populist' brutalizing of the public? I would welcome more people engaging in such conversations in future, as co-editor Rupert Read attempts in chapter 11.

I have not yet considered what might be a useful framework and terminology for communicating with general publics about these deeper philosophical critiques and potential remedies. The framework I offer in this chapter is only intended for discussion between people who choose to engage in theoretical questioning. If you are interested in talking to other people about the ideas in this chapter, then I know it will be difficult! I think processes like those explained in chapter 7 on facilitation are more useful. Some people may respond that these philosophical ideas sound like leftist views being added to the climate agenda. One way to respond can be a question. Something like:

> Compared to the rest of the world, as you are a relatively well-rewarded individual of a species that has destroyed life on earth to such an extent that it is as bad as a large asteroid, and is now facing massive death of its own species as a result, are any aspects of your world view, identity or ways of knowing being shaken? Are you feeling difficult emotions and considering what they might be telling you?

If they do not accept the premise about biological annihilation, then they need to learn and then be asked the question again. Such conversations can be frustrating and so some solace may be found in remembering an even broader context. Because of its disconnect with reality, the collapse of e-s-c-a-p-e ideology will happen eventually. But after remembering that for a moment and taking a breath, it will be time to engage again with the ongoing mess as part of your 'wild love for the world' (Macy 2020).

References

Abhayananda, S. (2002) *The History of Mysticism: The Unchanging Testament*. London: Watkins Publishing.

Adorno, T. W. and Horkheimer, M. (1997) *Dialectic of Enlightenment*. London: Verso.

Andreotti, V. (2014) 'Conflicting Epistemic Demands in Poststructuralist and Postcolonial Engagements with Questions of Complicity in Systemic Harm'. *Educational Studies* 50(4): 378–97.

Atkinson, E. (2002) 'The Responsible Anarchist: Postmodernism and Social Change'. *British Journal of Sociology of Education* 23(1): 73–87.

Bailey, C. (2019) 'Teaching in Outrageous Times: Vipassana Practice and the Pedagogical Power of Anger'. *Journal of Contemplative Inquiry* 6(1). Available at: https://journal.contemplativeinquiry.org/index.php/joci/article/view/189

Bakewell, S. (2016) *At the Existentialist I: Freedom, Being, and Apricot Cocktail*. New York: Other Press.

Beauvoir, S. de (2015) *The Ethics of Ambiguity*. Translated from French by B. Frechtman. London: Philosophical Library/Open Road.

Bendell, J. and Greco, T. (2013) 'Currencies of Transition', in M. McIntosh (ed.), *The Necessary Transition*, 1st edn. Sheffield: Greenleaf Publishing.

Bendell, J., Sutherland, N. and Little, R. (2017) 'Beyond Unsustainable Leadership: Critical Social Theory for Sustainable Leadership'. *Sustainability Accounting, Management and Policy Journal* 8(4): 418–44.

Budolfson, M., McPherson, T. and Plunkett, D. (forthcoming) *Philosophy and Climate Change*. Oxford: Oxford University Press.

Ceballos, G., Ehrlich, P. R. and Dirzo, R. (2017) 'Biological Annihilation via the Ongoing Sixth Mass Extinction Signaled by Vertebrate Population Losses and Declines'. *PNAS* 114(30). Available at: https://doi.org/10.1073/pnas.1704949114

Cole, M. (2007) *Marxism and Educational Theory: Origins and Issues*. London: Routledge.

Dietz, R. and O'Neill, D. (2013) *Enough Is Enough: Building a Sustainable Economy in a World of Finite Resources*. Oakland, CA: Berrett-Koehler Publishers.

Doppelt, B. (2016) *Transformational Resilience: How Building Human Resilience to Climate Disruption Can Safeguard Society and Increase Wellbeing*. London and New York: Routledge.

Doucet, A. and Mauthner, N. (2006) 'Feminist Methodologies and Epistemology', in C. D. Bryant and D. L. Peck (eds), *21st Century Sociology: A Reference Handbook* (*Volume 2*), 1st edn. Thousand Oaks, CA: Sage Publications.

Eisenstein, C. (2011) *Sacred Economics: Money, Gift, and Society in the Age of Transition*. Berkeley, CA: Evolver Editions.

Eisenstein, C. (2018) *Climate – A New Story*. Berkeley, CA: North Atlantic Books.

Fairclough, N. (2014) *Language and Power*, 3rd edn. London: Longman.

Foucault, M. (1984) *The Foucault Reader*. London: Pantheon.

Gandhi, M. (1993) *The Story of My Experiments with Truth*. Boston, MA: Beacon Press.

Graeber, D. (2011) *Debt: The First 5000 Years*. Brooklyn, NY: Melville House.

Greer, J. M. (2015) *After Progress*. Gabriola Island, BC: New Society Publishers.

GTDF (2020) 'Preparing for the End of the World as We Know It'. Open Democracy. Available at: https://www.opendemocracy.net/en/oureconomy/preparing-end-world-we-know-it/

Hagen, S. (1998) *Buddhism Plain and Simple: The Practice of Being Aware, Right Now, Every Day*. New York: Broadway Books.

Hughes, S. and Pennington, J. (2017) *Autoethnography: Process, Product, and Possibility for Critical Social Research*. Thousand Oaks, CA: SAGE Publications.

Irigaray, L. (1993) *An Ethics of Sexual Difference*, trans. C. Burke and G. Gill. Ithaca, NY: Cornell University Press.

Jenkinson, S. (2016) *Die Wise – A Manifesto for Sanity and Soul*. Berkeley, CA: North Atlantic Books.

Lakoff, G. (2002) *Moral Politics: How Liberals and Conservatives Think*. Chicago, IL: University of Chicago Press.

Macy, J. (2020) *A Wild Love for the World: Joanna Macy and the Work of Our Time*. Boulder, CO: Shambhala Publications.

Mann, M. (forthcoming) *The New Climate War: The Fight to Take Back Our Planet*. New York: Public Affairs Books.

Menzies, R. G. and Menzies, R. E. (2019) 'Emotional Pain and Suffering: The Search for Global Solutions', in P. Rhodes (ed.), *Beyond the Psychology Industry: How Else Might We Heal?* 1st edn. New York: Springer.

Nhat Hanh, T. (1987) *Interbeing*. Berkeley, CA: Parallax Press.

Reyes Mason, L. and Rigg, J. (2019) *People and Climate Change: Vulnerability, Adaptation, and Social Justice*. Oxford: Oxford University Press.

Rorty, R. (1989) *Contingency, Irony, and Solidarity*. Cambridge: Cambridge University Press.

Rothberg, D. (2006) *The Engaged Spiritual Life: A Buddhist Approach to Transforming Ourselves and the World*. Boston, MA: Beacon Press.

Servigne, P., Stevens, R. and Chapelle, G. (2020) *Another End of the World is Possible: Living the Collapse (and Not Merely Surviving It)*. Cambridge: Polity.

Stanley, L. and Wise, S. (1993) *Breaking Out Again: Feminist Ontology and Epistemology*. London: Routledge.

Stein, S. et al. (2020) 'Gesturing Towards Decolonial Futures: Reflections on Our Learnings Thus Far'. NJCIE 2020 4(1): 43–65. Available at: https://journals.hioa.no/index.php/nordiccie/article/view/3518/3521

Vaughan-Lee, L. (2017) *The Return of the Feminine and the World Soul*. San Francisco, CA: Golden Sufi Centre.

Versluis, V. (2006) 'Antimodernism'. *Telos* 137: 96–130. Available at: http://www.arthurversluis.com/Antimodernism.pdf

Woodstock, L. (2007) 'Think about It: The Misbegotten Promise of Positive Thinking Discourse'. *Journal of Communication Inquiry* 31: 166–89.

6

Unconscious Addictions: Mapping Common Responses to Climate Change and Potential Climate Collapse

Rene Suša, Sharon Stein, Vanessa Andreotti, Tereza Čajkova, Dino Siwek and the Gesturing Towards Decolonial Futures Collective[1]

Introduction

The authors of this article are part of the Gesturing Towards Decolonial Futures (GTDF) collective, an international assemblage of researchers, artists, educators, students, social justice and environmental activists and ancestral/indigenous knowledge keepers. The work of the collective is multifaceted, but one of its key commitments lies in exploring the many conscious and unconscious layers of attachments, investments, perceived entitlements, privileges and securities that condition and frame our existence as members of modern societies and limit our ability to imagine *otherwise*.

In terms of concerns about the potential impending collapse of these societies – due to climate change, a global pandemic or any other combination of destabilizing factors – the analysis put forward in this chapter focuses on four constitutive denials that are preventing us from engaging with the multiple crises we are facing in deeper, wiser and, arguably, more sober ways. This includes the denial of: systemic violence; unsustainability; entanglement; and the magnitude/complexity of the problems we face. Through the

[1] This work was supported by Mitacs through the Mitacs Accelerate Program.

metaphor of 'the house modernity built', the text draws attention to the various degrees of our shared complicity in the reproduction of systemic harms (in terms of the house's inherent violence towards human and other-than-human beings) and the various direct and indirect benefits that accrue to us – the inhabitants of the house – as a result of violent systemic continuity and expansion. Drawing on the authors' experience of working with various social justice movements, sustainability initiatives, policy makers, advocates and activists, this chapter also maps out five prevailing types of response to the possibility of climate collapse – romantic, revolutionary, rational, reactionary and 'rehab'.

Climate collapse denial

The subject of climate-change denial and its various (visible and invisible) forms and manifestations has garnered considerable attention in different circles in recent years. Examples of the more visible forms of denial that could be observed in 2019 include, for instance, Donald Trump announcing the US withdrawal from the Paris Climate Agreement (Pompeo 2019) and the Australian government's continued commitment to investments in coal power and the proposed Carmichael coal mine (*Economist* 2019), even after experiencing months of devastating bushfires and temperatures that regularly exceeded 40°C. Sometimes the visible forms of denial can manifest themselves in almost surreal ways, such as Prime Minster Morrison's New Year's message to Australians that was delivered through almost unbreathable air in Sydney, in which he claimed that 'there is no better place in the world to raise kids anywhere on the planet' (Remeikis 2019). Similarly baffling was Brazil's president Jair Bolsonaro's address at the UN General Assembly in September 2019, in which he claimed that (regardless of decades of deforestation) the Amazon forests were 'practically untouched' (Anderson 2019) and that the 2019 fires were started by environmentalists or 'greenies' to 'bring problems to Brazil' and to 'bring attention to themselves' (Anderson 2019). Since Trump, Morrison and Bolsonaro are all well-known self-professed climate-change deniers, their statements and actions should thus not be taken as surprising because they are consistent within their respective frameworks and belief systems.

The subject of denial becomes somewhat more intricate if we consider an example from Canada, where the parliament declared a national climate emergency in June 2019, acknowledging that climate change represents a 'real and urgent crisis, driven by human activity, that impacts the environment, biodiversity, Canadians' health and the Canadian economy' (Jackson 2019). This declaration was made by the parliament of the same nation whose prime minister, Justin Trudeau, decided a year earlier to spend Canadian $4.5 billion (US$3.5 billion) to nationalize the Trans Mountain Pipeline (Chase, Cryderman and Lewis 2018), which would vastly increase the production of oil from Alberta's tar sands and thus substantially increase Canada's carbon footprint. Although he was no doubt aware that Canada is experiencing 'a national climate emergency' and a 'real and urgent crisis, driven by human activity' (Jackson 2019) when he approved the nationalization of the pipeline in 2018, Trudeau also made it explicit that 'no country would find 173 billion barrels of oil in the ground and leave them there' (CBC 2017).

In the examples from Australia, Brazil and the United States, the level of the leaders' climate denial is perhaps jarring, but it is nevertheless coherent and internally logically consistent in the sense of belonging to the same overarching narrative of denying human influence on the earth's atmosphere. By contrast, the example from Canada is indicative of a different kind of denial. If the first three cases could be considered as simply whole-scale dismissals of any climate debate, the reaction of Trudeau's government offers instead an example of strategically selective wilful ignorance. Although other authors that use the term 'wilful ignorance', or 'will-to-ignorance' (Alcoff 2007; Maldonado-Torres 2004; Tuana 2006), usually refer to the ways in which wilful ignorance works on a deeper level through unconscious suppression (i.e. we do not want to know what we do not know), the acts of wilful ignorance performed in relation to climate emergency are often quite deliberate. Responses in the form of wilful ignorance or other possible forms of conscious and unconscious strategies of denial come into play when we are forced to deal with knowledge or information that we find too difficult, too discomforting, too disturbing or too inconvenient to acknowledge (Pitt and Britzman 2003; Taylor 2013; Zembylas 2014). As such, our actions are generally not driven by our rational choices but rather by the unconscious structuring of our desires for comfort, certainty and control (Andreotti et al. 2018).

Here it is perhaps important to emphasize that the denial of climate change and the denial of a very strong likelihood of impending climate collapse are actually two very different things. In fact, one should seriously consider the possibility that accepting a certain, relatively comfortable, sanitized narrative about human-induced climate change that is unfolding in a slow, predictable, linearly progressive way is actually the first and arguably most widespread strategy that people use to safeguard themselves from entertaining a possibility of an uncontrollable and rapidly unfolding climate collapse (climate catastrophe). Relatively speaking, the number of those that engage seriously with the possibility of climate collapse can be considered as just a fraction of those that believe in climate change in general, and the number of those that consider the whole (or at least several parts of the) spectrum of modernity's false promises and constitutive violences, injustices and (self-)destructive tendencies is even smaller. The next section introduces the metaphor of the house of modernity and explores the existential dimensions of denial that set the parameters of our modern existence.

The house of modernity and its four constitutive denials

One possible way to situate the discussions about climate change and climate collapse in broader (critical) conversations is to consider them in the light of social, political, economic, affective, cognitive and relational structures that constitute what Andreotti et al. (2018) refer to as 'the house of modernity'.

Although the term 'modernity', as used here, can generally be considered as largely analogous to the concept of 'modern society', it is actually broader than that. The house of modernity contains both what we usually call the 'system' – our existing social, political, legal and economic structures that are articulated through different national/cultural variations (facades of the house), and the affective, relational and cognitive frameworks of its inhabitant – the modern (Cartesian) subject. In popular discourse, the word 'system' often refers only to selected

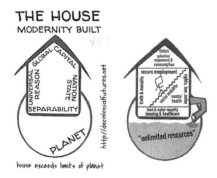

Figure 6.1 The House that Modernity Built (adapted with permission from Andreotti et al. 2018)

aspects of the house, usually in relation to a specific configuration of social, political and economic relations, such as for instance (global) capitalism. Yet capitalism is just one part of the whole house – though arguably the one that garners the most (critical) attention. Stein et al. (2017) and Andreotti et al. (2018) use the metaphor of 'the house that modernity built' to write of modernity as a way of being, seeing, desiring and relating to the world that is grounded on the foundation of separability (between humans and nature), the twin carrying walls of the nation-state and Enlightenment (humanism), all sheltered by the roof of global capitalism. There are, of course, other important characteristics of modernity, such as its singular, evolutionary, progress- and development-based hierarchical meta-narrative of (white, western/northern, cis-gendered, male, etc.) human exceptionalism. However, the metaphor of the house offers a graphic visualization of modernity's main constitutive parts that we would like to draw attention to.

Our (decolonial) analysis of the problematic aspects of modernity is informed and inspired by indigenous analyses and practices that affirm that our current global problems, of which climate change and collapse is but one important aspect, are not related to a lack of knowledge but to an inherently violent modern-colonial habit of being. This is somewhat different from other critical analyses (such as those presented under romantic, revolutionary and rationalist approaches below) that, in different ways, usually consider only the lack of knowledge and/or the influence of existing power structures and power relations as the main obstacles for (necessary) change and transformation. These analyses usually do not consider how our socialized desires, perceived entitlements, projections and attachments are exerting a deeper, more foundational influence. In recent discussions on our observable unwillingness and incapacity to deal with the possibility of climate collapse, there has been a body of scholarship (Bendell 2018; Foster 2015; Marshall 2015) that also considers the psychological (emotional and/or affective) dimension of denial-based responses, but much of this work is grounded in evolutionary psychology that assumes modern existence as the apex of evolution. This leaves us with few tools for an analysis that could examine the neurobiologically conditioned and culturally sanctioned ineffective long-term risk assessment responses that seem to be characteristic of modern existence.

Although a lot of our critique and analysis is inspired by the work and lived realities of indigenous and other communities that operate in contexts of high-intensity struggles, the majority of our daily work (as researchers and educators) engages with communities and movements in low-intensity struggles, mostly in countries of the global North. We consider communities of high-intensity struggle as those whose members' personal safety, well-being and continued existence are directly threatened by the violences needed to sustain the house of modernity. These threats can extend across a broad spectrum of possibilities, from exploitative and discriminatory to overtly genocidal. In contrast, communities and movements that operate in contexts of low-intensity struggles do not have their personal well-being and safety directly threatened by systemic violences, though they might feel some of the negative effects. When examining different strategies and approaches of how various communities, especially in the context of low-intensity struggles, engage (or not) with the problematic aspects of modernity's multiple inherent structural violences, we have observed four main (kinds of) constitutive denials. The general prevalence and, in many cases, depth of these denials have led us to suggest that we may count them amongst the structural elements of the modern/colonial habit of being. These four denials are:

- the denial of systemic violence and complicity in harm (the fact that our comforts, securities and enjoyments are subsidized by expropriation and exploitation somewhere else);
- the denial of the limits of the planet (the fact that the planet cannot sustain exponential growth and consumption);
- the denial of entanglement (our insistence in seeing ourselves as separate from each other and the land, rather than 'entangled' within a living wider metabolism that is bio-intelligent); and
- the denial of the depth and magnitude of the problems that we face. (Andreotti et al. 2018; Stein 2019)

Although these denials are each present to various degrees in different contexts, we have thus far not encountered any initiatives (popular or otherwise), especially in the context of low-intensity struggles, that would seriously engage with all four of them. In the context of discussions on climate change and potential climate collapse, we have been able to observe some conversations and initiatives that are mindful of one or two of these denials, but never all four. Usually the observable engaged denials are those related to the carrying capacity of the planet, with occasional (but very frail) gestures towards acknowledgement of (selected aspects of) systemic violence and complicity in harm. Further, the initiatives that are taking seriously the magnitude of the problem usually frame this magnitude exclusively as the potentially catastrophic outcome of impending climate collapse. Although these initiatives acknowledge the climate-related threats to continued human existence, they remain largely oblivious of the magnitude of historically inherited and socially sanctioned and encouraged continuity of multifaceted violences (cognitive, affective, relational, economic, environmental). These violences have been threatening the continuity of human (and other-than-human) beings' life on a (comparably) massive scale in places that have been 'out of sight and out of mind' for a very long time.

Particularly problematic seems to be our (modern/colonial) incapacity to engage generatively with the denial of separability. Given that the European Enlightenment-based idea of (atomistic, individualistic) separability, not just between humans and (the rest of) nature but also between humans and other humans, may be considered as foundational to the modern habit of being, this is

perhaps to be expected. As destructive as the results of this notion
are in themselves, equally worrisome seem to be the outcomes of
our attempts at re-sensing entanglement (connectivity) with the
earth's larger metabolism. Embodied practices, such as various
forms of meditation, trance-inducing, ecstatic and entheogenic
practices, that enable a (temporary) suspense of the experience
of oneself as merely the 'skin-encapsulated ego' more often than
not take the form of spiritual escapism or spiritual bypassing that
ends up upholding the very same problematic habits (of strengthening the egoic self) they aim to dissolve.

The escapist tendencies and refusals to engage with our complicity in harm are not particular to various spiritual and other
related practices. Jem Bendell's contribution to this book introduces the problematic pervasiveness of 'e-s-c-a-p-e' ideology, an
acronym that stands for continued investments in entitlements,
surety, control, autonomy, progress and exceptionalism (chapter
5). Elsewhere (GTDF 2020), our collective has suggested that e-s-
c-a-p-e is not simply an ideology but a harmful and even violent
habit of being that foregrounds our thinking. This habit of being
encompasses deeper affective, relational and neurobiological
dimensions, including hopes, desires and unconscious attachments, compulsions and projections that cannot be interrupted
by the intellect alone. When these investments, and our positive
self-image, are threatened, the fragilities that we embody due to
our socialization tend to prevent us from mustering the necessary
stamina and sobriety to deal with the challenges and critiques of
these investments in generative and non-defensive ways. When
critiques are delivered in ways that are considered threatening to
our perceived (benevolent) self-image, the emotional labour and
the affective, relational, even physical danger is borne by those
that have voiced the critique. This is especially common in situations where critiques to modern-colonial entitlements come from
racialized bodies and marginalized communities.

Systemic violence is complex and multi-layered, and climate
change (or collapse) and our responses to it represent merely one
of its many aspects. One thing that cuts across layers is the dis-
proportionate amount of labour that indigenous, black and other
racialized people bear when they are expected to teach other
people about systemic colonial and racial violence. The excerpts
below, taken from a poem written by indigenous artist Elwood

Jimmy (2019) and other racialized members of the GTDF collective, list the reasons why it is emotionally and physically costly for indigenous, black and racialized people to hold spaces for other people to learn about their complicity in systemic harm. The poem hopefully also explains why softening the critique to appease multiple fragilities translates into more emotional labour for members of these communities. We hope that by reading the poem, readers will understand better why the responsibility to deal with the affective responses to the critiques, presented in the next section, should not be externalized onto others. We suggest you read the poem once and pay attention to the different kinds of emotional responses it evokes. We also suggest that, in case the poem elicits very strong (negative) responses, readers should perhaps take a pause before proceeding or even skip reading the final section of this chapter altogether. Alternatively, those who may wish to engage with the poem in deeper ways can find accompanying exercises on the GTDF website (Jimmy 2019).

Do You Really Want to Know Why I Can't Hold Space for You Anymore?

Because
You see my body as an extension of your entitlements

Because
I have held space for you before
and every time, the same thing happens
You take up all the space
and expect me to use my time,
energy and emotion in service of fulfilling your desires:
to validate you as someone who is good and innocent
to be the appreciative audience for your self-expression
to provide the content of a transformative learning experience
to perform my trauma
to affirm your innocence
to celebrate your self-image
to centre your feelings
to absolve you from guilt
to be always generous and generative
to filter what I say in order not to make you feel uncomfortable

to make you feel loved, important, special and safe
and you don't even realize you are doing it

Because your support is always conditional
On whether it aligns with your agenda
On whether it is requested in a gentle way
On whether I perform a politics that is convenient for you
On whether it fits your personal brand
On whether it contributes to your legacy
On whether you will get rewarded for doing it
On whether it feels good
Or makes you look good
Or gives you the sense that we are 'moving forward'

Because when you 'give' me space to speak
It comes with strings attached about
what I can and cannot say
and about how I can say it

You want an easy way out
A quick checklist or one-day workshop
on how to avoid being criticized
while you carry out business as usual

And even when I say what I want to say anyway
You can't hear it
Or you listen selectively
And when you think you hear it
You consume it
You look for a way to say 'that's not me'
'I'm one of the good ones'
and use what I say to criticize someone else

Your learning
your self-actualization
your credibility
your security
and your sense of 'loving kindness'
always come at my expense.
That is why I can't hold space for you anymore.

The next section looks more specifically into different groups of responses to climate change and potential climate collapse and explores what kind of imaginative possibilities and constitutive denials are observable in these responses and how those map onto the four denials that this section identified in relation to the house of modernity.

Responses to the possibility of climate collapse

This section introduces four observable groups or types of responses (romantic, revolutionary, rationalist, reactionary) to climate change and the possibility of climate collapse that we have been able to identify through our work with various environmentally and socially engaged communities and initiatives, mostly in the countries of the global North. This mapping was developed using social cartography (Andreotti et al. 2016; Paulston and Liebman 1994; Suša and Andreotti 2019), a methodology for mapping discursive, intellectual, affective and existential orientations in different communities. The purpose of this cartography is not to claim that the options presented here are exhaustive of all possible positions and that this mapping is the definitive representation of the broad spectrum of responses to climate change and potential climate collapse. Rather, the idea is to outline some of the prevailing (problematic) patterns that are observable in the four main groups of responses, identify some key absences (denials) and mobilize further conversations and reflections.[2]

The romantic

Romantic responses emphasize the role and importance of individual self-realization and self-expression, based on an idealized notion of an inherently good, virtuous and just humanity, as well as intentional community building and pre-packaged solutions. We find the romantic approaches to be the most prevalent in

---

[2] Elsewhere (Stein et al. forthcoming), a modified version of the cartography of romantic, revolutionary, rationalist, reactionary and 'rehab' has been used in ways that address the challenges and paradoxes of education for sustainable development.

initiatives and communities that share a strong commitment to developing and nurturing locally oriented sustainable practices that seek to create micro-utopias that often in different ways attempt to develop some up-to-date version of a 'pastoral idyll' of times past. Desires for simple, less stressful and more personally fulfilling lifestyles are the ones that could be seen as largely operating in the romantic imaginary. With often idealistic readings of the past, the majority of these initiatives remain largely wilfully ignorant of (not engaging with) systemic violences outside of the negative aspects of global capitalism on their personal lives (diminished well-being) or the lives of their (local) communities. Romantic communities and initiatives also operate from desires for (personal) innocence that are seen as being achievable through reduced and more sustainable personal consumption. While climate change is of (main) concern for the majority of romantic approaches, these movements in principle do not engage robustly (or at all) with the potential reality of climate collapse that would likely render their seemingly sustainable alternatives unviable. In terms of 'the house of modernity' metaphor, romantic approaches seem to be mindful of some of the negative aspects of global capitalism, but they largely do not question the role of the nation-state as the mediator (and warrant) of existing social relations. Their questioning of the role of Enlightenment humanism (and Cartesian rationality) and separability often manifests itself through individuals' interest in various, mostly eastern, meditative and other spiritual practices. These practices are usually not directed towards deeper explorations of personal and collective investments and complicity in historically sanctioned violences and systemic harm but are instead geared towards personal elevation above it by focusing on experiencing the beauty, bliss and vitality of being part of the collective whole and suppressing the sensation of pain, death and disease that is likewise felt by the collective body.

The revolutionary

Unlike romantic movements that are oriented at small-scale personal or local transformation, initiatives that claim revolutionary potential and momentum see themselves as speaking either as legitimate representatives of various oppressed groups or as legitimate representatives of the universalized notion of 'the people'. Targeting either the existing political structures or specific large polluters (big corporations) or both, these movements also often operate from desires for innocence and virtue that seek fulfilment through externalizations and projections of responsibility (exclusively) onto others, specifically onto those in positions of power or others considered insufficiently 'woke'. In general, the level of critique is deeper and more complex than in romantic approaches, and revolutionary movements are more inclined to take seriously the possibility of climate collapse.

Revolutionary approaches usually exhibit a fairly strong critique of global capitalism and some aspects of dysfunctionality of the modern nation-states. Largely depending on whether they emerge from high- or low-intensity struggles, they may or may not challenge other constitutive frameworks of modern states, such as the existing legal system and the kind of personal, institutional and property relations it engenders. Revolutionary approaches in general do not challenge Enlightenment humanism/Cartesian rationality and the notion of separability; in fact they would often consider those (for instance, from the romantic approaches) that are interested in exploring other existential possibilities to be engaged in navel gazing, distracting practices that are focusing their attention away from pressing issues and politicized action.

The rationalist

Rationalist responses emphasize critical thinking and a need for more and better analysis that would lead to better informed decisions. This group of responses places its faith in the power of rational deliberation (either as individuals, collectives or humanity at large) to either (adequately) prepare us for the impending collapse or to give us the required tools to avert it. It would be possible to argue that there exist at least two (mainstream) strands of rationalist approaches, both of which emphasize the importance of informed analysis and scientific data for development of practical collective measures. Despite their many commonalities, these two strands differ significantly in their overarching goals. The first (mainstream) strand is focusing on mitigating or assuaging the effects of climate change through measures that resemble a large-scale, state- and business-supported version of romantic approaches that seeks to avert (or ignore) the possibility of climate collapse. Given the subject of this book, the text here will focus more on the second, much less visible and much less numerous, strand that operates from the assumption that climate collapse is unavoidable and seeks to develop measures of adapting to the post-collapse world. Both rationalist approaches, but especially the second strand, often look with suspicion at the energy invested (and seen as potentially wasted) in romantic and revolutionary approaches. Being more aware of both the urgency of the problem and of systemic inertia, rationalist approaches take the possibility of climate collapse not merely as very realistic, but also potentially as a fait accompli. Rationalist approaches also tend to operate less from desires for personal virtue and innocence and to ignore personal complicity less. However, the depth of environmental or climate-related reflection is not necessarily complemented with corresponding depth of critical (self-)reflection along the other lines of modernity's constitutive violences. Due to strong investments in knowledge and knowing as guiding mechanisms for action and deliberation, rationalist responses tend to resist challenges to the dominating rule of Enlightenment-based Cartesian rationality and the foundation of separability. The concerns and arguments that challenge rationality and separability are viewed by rationalist responses as distracting and irrelevant, likely motivated by underlying fears of loss of control and orientation that different kinds of reasoning and sensing the world can bring about. What separates the second strand of rationalist approaches from the romantic and revolutionary ones are above all their relation to the question of hope and acceptance (of climate collapse), where rationalist approaches are much less keen on investing their energies into measures that would avert (or ignore) the possibility of collapse but are more interested in exploring options of adaptation to existing and future threats.

The reactionary

Reactionary responses perceive the potential climate collapse as a serious and imminent threat to their livelihoods and personal safety. Similar to romantic responses, they are usually focused on small-scale (personal) survival techniques that would enable people to 'weather' the coming collapse, often in enclosed and – depending on the context – heavily protected, even militarized locations. Although the emphasis on security and protection of personal property sets them apart from romantic approaches, future developments may lead to a convergence of these two approaches. Driven by fears of scarcity and desires for continuity and control, the adherents of the reactionary group tend to manipulate fears and rationalize the protection of property, security and entitlements at all costs. Not all preparatory measures are necessarily or inherently violent, but when security and protection of personal property and existing entitlements are prioritized at the expense of collective well-being, reactive dispositions are the ones most easily mobilized towards harm. Depending on personal circumstances and the level of resources (and legislative frameworks) available, such responses may range from small-scale family preparations of stocking up on food and other supplies to whole-community-sized projects that feature their own closed-loop systems of food production, together with health, education and entertainment services, backed up by heavy military protection (Koenig 2017; Stamp 2019). The spectrum of reactionary responses is very broad, and although currently the securitized reactionary responses occupy a margin in climate-related discussions and actions, we could potentially soon witness a rise in these kind of responses on a much larger scale, driven either by state intervention or by interests of various groups, based either on class privilege, ethnic, religious, political or any other type of identity-based differentiation.

The rehab

We conclude this chapter by sketching a 'rehab', or rehabilitation, approach as an imperfect gesture towards developing new possibilities, not just for showing up to the unprecedented challenges of our time but also to owning up to the violence and destructiveness that underwrite our current existence. Very differently from the four approaches presented above, the rehab approach seeks to explore ways to wean us off the neurophysiological (neurochemical) addictions and attachments to our current (modern/colonial) unsustainable habits of being. Grounded in a wide spectrum of different indigenous cosmologies that, although diverse, do not share modernity's ontological foundation of separability, these approaches seek to reorient and restructure our desires away from historically inherited problematic and harmful patterns. Since our desires can be considered to be hard-wired into our neural networks and their corresponding neurochemical reward mechanisms, their proposition is that we not only have to change our 'software' (our thinking and doing) but also our 'hardware' – the ways in which our bodies allow us to think and act. Elsewhere (Andreotti 2019), these approaches have been described as attempts at neuro- or onto-genesis, which can be translated as (re)generating new or forgotten possibilities and habits of thinking, doing, hoping, relating and being.

It is highly problematic and controversial to speak of ourselves in terms of our neurobiology – especially given the ways in which this discourse has been used in the past to justify various kinds of discriminatory practices and policies. However, if we use the language of neuroscience in speculative and metaphorical ways, we can bring attention to the fact that the differences in our responses to the perils of climate collapse, or any other aspects of the multifaceted crisis that we are facing, are not merely derived from conflicting ideological positions but also from the differences in the ways we sense ourselves to be (part of) in this world. For this purpose, we will use metaphorically, serotonin – the neurotransmitter mainly responsible for our sense of interconnectivity and well-being – to represent a neurochemical configuration that enables the sense of entanglement with and metabolic responsibility towards the world. We will also use figuratively the neurochemicals dopamine, oxytocin, endorphins and adrenalin to represent the neurobiological configuration that supports our sense of separability and mode of insatiable consumption in our relationship with the planet. Each configuration prompts a different kind of neuro-functionality and neuroplasticity, generating different capacities and possibilities in terms of desires and modes of engagement with the world.

Speaking figuratively, the process of rehab – that is, of reorienting our harmful desires – would thus entail finding alternative sources for our depleted levels of serotonin. When our sense of connection to the world around us is cut, and when our sense of individuation, individualism and self-absorption increases, our levels of serotonin drop, potentially causing feelings of depression, hopelessness and loss of direction and purpose. In recent literature (Kraus et al. 2017; Liu et al. 2017), serotonin is described as one of the key modulators of neuroplasticity – our brains' ability to adapt and grow new neural networks that correspond to the changing contexts of our external environment. The lower our capacity to adapt and accept the uncomfortable realities that we are facing, the more we seek to hold on to our pre-established (harmful) patterns of behaviour and problematic desires that underwrite them. Given the increasingly precarious state of global mental health, especially among young people, it is not surprising that an overwhelming part of our collective and individual behaviour, also visible in various responses to climate change and/or collapse, is geared towards seeking to substitute our serotonin deficiencies with other, temporarily effective, surrogates. In this sense, the vast majority of our engagements are based upon constantly increasing our levels of dopamine (reward-based behaviour, such as Facebook 'likes' or YouTube subscriptions), endorphins (pain-relief behaviour, such as blaming, shaming and externalizing responsibility onto others), oxytocin (exclusivity-based social bonding, such as joining intentional communities and movements) or adrenalin (joining protests or collecting arrest records). Our addiction to these kinds of behaviours arguably makes us ill fit for sober and grounded decision making that will be much needed, if only a small fraction of the direst predictions will come true.

In this sense, rehab does not mean a return to the usual or normal state of affairs after a program of detoxification – a return to 'the house of modernity' – our 'old home'; it rather seeks to abolish the need for a predefined normality, especially for one that is grounded on the continuous externalization of the costs of our privileges and comforts onto others. While critical systemic thinking and self-reflexive work are indispensable, if unpleasant, components of the rehab process, they are also unfortunately by themselves insufficient. Much deeper work on the unconscious levels of our psyche, which is often difficult to access and more difficult to re-code, is needed if we are to break with the harmful patterns that we are often not even aware we inhabit. And, in spite of anyone's potential best intentions, relapses are part and parcel of this process. We need both courage and stamina to navigate our way through them, and for this we will have to sit comfortably with the discomfort at the edge of a form of existence that is dying. In this grieving process, if we learn well, we may find the seeds of something that is struggling to be born and that runs the risk of being suffocated with our projections. Between death and birth, hospicing and assisting with midwifery, lies a space where individual and collective shit needs to be composted so that new soil can be created.

References

Alcoff, L. M. (2007) 'Epistemologies of Ignorance: Three Types', in N. Tuana (ed.), *Race and Epistemologies of Ignorance*. Albany, NY: SUNY Press, pp. 39–57.

Anderson, J. L. (2019) 'At the U.N., Jair Bolsonaro Presents a Surreal Defense of His Amazon Policies'. *New Yorker*. Available at: https://www.newyorker.com/news/daily-comment/at-the-united-nations-jair-bolsonaro-presents-a-surreal-defense-of-his-amazon-policies

Andreotti, V. (2019) 'The Enduring Challenges of Collective Onto-(and Neuro-)Genesis'. *LÁPIZ* (4): 61–78.

Andreotti, V., Stein, S., Pashby, K. and Nicolson, M. (2016) 'Social Cartographies as Performative Devices in Research on Higher Education'. *Higher Education Research & Development* 35(1): 84–99.

Andreotti, V., Stein, S., Sutherland, A., Pashby, K., Suša, R. and Amsler, S. (2018) 'Mobilising Different Conversations about Global Justice in Education: Toward Alternative Futures in Uncertain Times'. *Policy & Practice: A Development Education Review* 26: 9–41.

Bendell, J. (2018) *Deep Adaptation: A Map for Navigating Climate Tragedy. IFLAS Occasional Paper 2*. Available at: http://www.lifeworth.com/deepadaptation.pdf

CBC (2017) 'Trudeau: "No country would find 173 billion barrels of oil in the ground and leave them there"'. CBC News. Available at: https://www.cbc.ca/news/world/trudeau-no-country-would-find-173-billion-barrels-of-oil-in-the-ground-and-leave-them-there-1.4019321

Chase, S., Cryderman, K. and Lewis, J. (2018) 'Trudeau Government to Buy Kinder Morgan's Trans Mountain for $4.5-Billion'. *The Globe and Mail*. Available at: https://www.theglobeandmail.com/politics/article-trudeau-government-to-buy-kinder-morgans-trans-mountain-pipeline/

Economist (2019) 'Black in Business. Adani's Giant Australian Coal Mine Gets the Go-Ahead'. Available at: https://www.economist.com/asia/2019/06/29/adanis-giant-australian-coal-mine-gets-the-go-ahead

Foster, J. (2015) *After Sustainability*. Abingdon, UK: Earthscan/ Routledge.

GTDF (2020) *Preparing for the End of the World as We Know It*. Open Democracy. Available at: https://www.opendemocracy.net/en/our economy/preparing-end-world-we-know-it/

Jackson, H. (2019) 'National Climate Emergency Declared by House of Commons'. Global News. Available at: https://globalnews.ca/ news/5401586/canada-national-climate-emergency/

Jimmy, E. (2019) 'Why I Can't Hold Space for You Anymore'. Available at: https://decolonialfutures.net/portfolio/why-i-cant-hold -space-for-you-anymore/

Koenig, N. (2017) 'The Nuclear Bunkers Designed for Luxury Living'. BBC. Available at: https://www.bbc.com/news/business-38795967

Kraus, C., Castrén, E., Kasper, S. and Lanzenberger, R. (2017) 'Serotonin and Neuroplasticity – Links between Molecular, Functional and Structural Pathophysiology in Depression'. *Neuroscience & Biobehavioral Reviews* 77: 317–26.

Liu, B., Liu, J., Wang, M., Zhang, Y. and Li, L. (2017) 'From Serotonin to Neuroplasticity: Evolvement of Theories for Major Depressive Disorder'. *Frontiers in Cellular Neuroscience* 11, Article 305. DOI: 10.3389/fncel.2017.00305

Maldonado-Torres, N. (2004) 'The Topology of Being and the Geopolitics of Knowledge: Modernity, Empire, Coloniality'. *City* 8(1): 29–56.

Marshall, G. (2015) *Don't Even Think about It: Why Our Brains are Wired to Ignore Climate Change*. New York: Bloomsbury Publishing.

Paulston, R. G. and Liebman, M. (1994) 'An Invitation to Postmodern Social Cartography'. *Comparative Education Review* 38(2): 215–32.

Pitt, A. and Britzman, D. (2003) 'Speculations on Qualities of Difficult Knowledge in Teaching and Learning: An Experiment in Psychoanalytic Research'. *Qualitative Studies in Education* 16(6): 755–76.

Pompeo, M. (2019) 'On the US Withdrawal from the Paris Agreement'. Press statement. Available at: https://www.state.gov/on -the-u-s-withdrawal-from-the-paris-agreement/

Remeikis, A. (2019) '"No Better Place to Raise Kids": Scott Morrison's New Year Message to a Burning Australia'. *Guardian*. Available at: https://www.theguardian.com/australia-news/2020/jan/01/no-bett er-place-to-raise-kids-scott-morrison-new-year-message-burning-aust ralia

Stamp, E. (2019) 'Billionaire Bunkers: How the 1% Are Preparing for the Apocalypse'. CNN. Available at: https://www.cnn.com/style/arti cle/doomsday-luxury-bunkers/index.html

174 SHIFTS IN BEING

Stein, S. (2019) 'The Ethical and Ecological Limits of Sustainability: A Decolonial Approach to Climate Change in Higher Education'. *Australian Journal of Environmental Education* 35(3): 198–212.

Stein, S., Andreotti, V., Suša, R. and Čajkova, T. (forthcoming) 'From "Education for Sustainable Development" to "Education for the End of the World as We Know It": Interrupting Denial and Inviting Otherwise Possibilities'. *Educational Philosophy and Theory*.

Stein, S., Hunt, D., Suša, R. and Andreotti, V. (2017) 'The Educational Challenge of Unravelling the Fantasies of Ontological Security'. *Diaspora, Indigenous, and Minority Education* 11(2): 69–79.

Suša, R. and Andreotti, V. (2019) 'Social Cartography in Educational Research'. *Oxford Research Encyclopedia of Education*. Avalable at: https://oxfordre.com/view/10.1093/acrefore/9780190264093.001.0001/acrefore-9780190264093-e-528

Taylor, L. K. (2013) 'Against the Tide: Working with and against the Affective Flows of Resistance in Social and Global Justice Learning'. *Critical Literacy: Theories & Practices* 7(2): 58–68.

Tuana, N. (2006) 'The Speculum of Ignorance: The Women's Health Movement and Epistemologies of Ignorance'. *Hypatia* 21(3): 1–19.

Zembylas, M. (2014) 'Theorizing "Difficult Knowledge" in the Aftermath of the "Affective Turn": Implications for Curriculum and Pedagogy in Handling Traumatic Representations'. *Curriculum Inquiry* 44(3): 390–412.

7

Facilitating Deep Adaptation: Enabling More Loving Conversations about Our Predicament

Katie Carr and Jem Bendell

The importance of facilitating groups in the face of collapse

Upon reflection, deep adaptation (DA) is not actually a 'map for navigating climate tragedy', as the subtitle of the original paper suggested. When framing DA in that paper as a series of questions (Bendell 2018), it was an invitation for a global conversation. Rather than offering a map, DA is more an invitation into *maplessness*, where all of the landmarks that we've previously relied on are found to be a mirage. Those landmarks include mainstream science, assumptions of progress and the superiority of humankind on earth. Instead of scientific certainty, little seems certain any more. The triumph of scientific empiricist discourse over all other ways of being and knowing, which took root in Europe during the Age of Enlightenment and has become well-nigh ubiquitous since, has begun to lose its power in orienting people in their world (Rabkin and Minakov 2018). Stories of progress, in which it is assumed that tomorrow will be better than today, are also losing their dominance (Greer 2015). Even the belief in the superiority of humankind amongst all other life, expressed in our self-labelling as *homo sapiens* (which in Latin means 'wise man'), seems a narcissistic conjecture that ignores our driving of mass extinction of life on earth (Diaz et al. 2019), including a growing risk even to our own species (Xu and Ramanathan 2017).

By *maplessness*, we mean that we cannot rely on previous 'perceived certainties' – including our stories of progress, meaning, purpose and identity. Maps can be a useful tool but are neither true to the complexity of any landscape, nor without an assumed intention of how one engages with a landscape. They can create an illusion of safety through the sense of being in 'chartered territory'. They condition us to take notice of certain features and ignore others. Road, footpaths, streams and boundaries are included, but not the smells, sounds and emotional responses to a landscape. They focus on unchanging landscape features, not the seasonal migration of birds, changing colours, or the life and death that inhabit every place. Although a map is never the territory, and a model not the reality, the implicit suggestion of both maps and models is that to map is to measure and name in order to know, and to know is to control. The trend towards ever greater mapping and detailed measuring of our infinitely complex and changing world reflects the aim, since the Enlightenment, of attaining a sense of safety from the mysterious. The mapping impulse is therefore an expression of the ideology of e-s-c-a-p-e, with its attachment to the illusion of surety, control and progress, as described in chapter 5.

In the 2020s, as we witness both ecosystems and societies increasingly break down, so the processes of mapping and modelling are challenged. That is not only because those breakdowns reveal that we are neither 'safe' nor in control. Rather, the breakdowns are occurring because sufficient numbers of people, over centuries, have used the power of mapping life to exert a destructive power and have not been able to understand our living world so as to avert its destruction. The anticipation of societal collapse is therefore to acknowledge a crisis of epistemology and a collapse of the hitherto dominant ways of seeking to know the world. That anticipation invites us to explore other ways of understanding life and our places within it. It means people become interested in relinquishing reliance on redundant and harmful mental 'maps' of who we are, who we are not and how the world is, and rediscover or restore forgotten ways of being and knowing. This means bringing the somatic, the affective and the relational – the wisdom of our bodies, hearts and communities – wholly to bear on how we face the unfolding predicament. DA is primarily a container for dialogue that begins with an invitation to unlearn, to let go of our maps and models of the world and to not prematurely grasp at any new ones. That can be difficult because a habit of needing fact, certainty and right answers means people are often uncomfortable being with uncertainty or 'not knowingness'. It is for that reason that alternative ways of relating in groups on all aspects of our predicament is so important, which is why facilitation of group processes is so central to DA.

Unfortunately, the difficulties of late capitalism, as more of us are pressured to compete with each other in distorted markets while we increasingly perceive the turbulence both around and ahead of us, means that anxieties are on the rise in many parts of the world and for many age groups (chapter 4). One indicator of this process is the increasingly damaging approaches to young people's education in many countries. Katie worked with schools for many years and witnessed an increasing tendency towards measurable knowledge. She saw a shift in the way children would respond to open questions from teachers, to which there are no right or wrong answers. Where there used to be creative expression of multiple ideas, there is increasing hesitancy because of a belief that there should be a memorizable or logically calculable correct answer to any question. The impact of a classroom with walls covered with correct answers and, particularly, a weekly testing regime from a very early age is one reason for this shift (Carr and Bindewald 2019). As adults, within our modern cultures, we have also been schooled to feel fearful of not knowing. A growing sense of vulnerability, due to increasingly precarious personal circumstances and perception of a more turbulent world, means we can grasp for 'correct' answers rather than allow for more 'not knowing' and more 'maplessness'. Providing spaces for each other where we can build our resilience for experiencing difficult emotions, such as the fear associated with uncertainty without grasping at quick and simple answers, is therefore an important activity.

The aim of people we know involved in DA is to reduce harm in the face of societal collapse. To pursue that aim, there must be an understanding of the sociocultural mechanisms that have led to humanity's failure to live in a way that is harmonious with the wider system of life on earth, of which we are part, and to understand the ways in which these mechanisms are not 'out there'. Rather, we exist as part of a culture, the fabric of which is socially constructed. We are products of that culture, and we constantly reproduce it through our actions. It is this culture and the ideologies within it, as described in chapter 5, which will prevent us from reducing harm. A central part of that culture and ideology is what can be described as alienation: the imagined separation of ourselves (or large parts of ourselves), from each other and the wider web of life.

For a few years, we have been facilitating dialogue about these issues, and witnessing and experiencing the intensity that comes from an anticipation of societal collapse in our own lifetimes. From that experience, we discovered that facilitation for deep adaptation can help participants to experience ways of relating that can bring awareness to the unconscious patterns we have just described. Group processes can be an opportunity for us to experience a different way of relating to difficult information, difficult emotions and to each other. We can help each other learn how to be with our difficult emotions without suppressing them and consequently reacting by unconsciously grasping for habituated ideas or stories that might offer relief or distraction. Our intention is that more of us will avoid adopting simplistic narratives of blame or salvation and the unhelpful actions that might then arise. More of us may discover alternative ways of responding to our feelings of anxiety than blaming the Chinese for coronavirus, or voting for a proto-fascist government, or building walls around our vegetable gardens or countries. To help with that process, facilitation needs to be effective in providing a container for radical uncertainty, a 'liminal space' in which people can build stamina for being with insoluble dilemmas and the challenging emotions surrounding them through developing skills of self- and co-regulation. It needs to invite ongoing courageous self-inquiry and a willingness to let go within a wider container of compassion, acceptance, forgiveness, humility and accepting mistakes (our own and those of others).

Understanding 'othering' and its remedy with facilitation

As people engage in inquiry and dialogue about the reasons for such oppression and destruction, we have been on a journey to consider the deepest reasons and how they can be practically addressed. We recognize there are various theories about how this predicament has arisen. We also sense that as the anticipation or experience of societal collapse spreads, so people will offer explanations that align with their pre-existing world views, or to seek to justify their future actions. In our inquiry, we have sought to be neither strategic nor defensive in our exploration of causes and lessons. That has led to an exploration of the way our own mental and relational habits maintain an ideology that is oppressive and destructive of ourselves, others and nature (chapter 5). Looking more closely at those habits, we conclude that they all relate to a seemingly innate process of imagining separation.

The 'Other', as a philosophical concept and psychological phenomenon, was first introduced by Hegel in the eighteenth century to describe the necessary counter-image to the 'self'; in order to hold a sense of self, we must construct a 'constitutive [individual or collective] Other' which we define as different from, and 'less than' or 'inferior to', oneself or from the group to which one identifies as belonging. Othering is a psycho-social process which is implicated in discrimination of all kinds (race, gender, class, age, etc.). It is closely connected to Marx's concept of 'alienation' ('workers' are alienated from aspects of their humanity through being reduced to an economic entity in service of capitalism) and has been influential in the evolution of feminist theory and subaltern and critical race studies. The process of 'othering' makes it easier to dehumanize people or groups and to conclude that they are unworthy of respect or dignity, and scholars are increasingly incorporating an analysis of 'othering' in theorizing about genocide and nationalist ideologies (Murray 2015). 'Othering' can also be seen at the root of the imagined separation between humans and non-human life and of the desacralization of nature. A 'deep ecology' perspective invites a non-anthropocentric account of the relationship between 'humans' and nature (Naess 1977). The cultural assumption of humanity's assumed superiority to all non-human life – and therefore our entitlement to manage and consume – is central to the western world view, and it is often traced to the Judeo-Christian tradition and translations of the Bible that give man dominion over the earth.

If we valued all other life, human and non-human, as much as we value ourselves, or that with which we identify, could we participate in systems of oppression and destruction? We do not know because we are all immersed in our internal processes of 'othering'.

'Othering' occurs because our self-construal is predicated on identifying that which is not ourselves – whether that is other views, other behaviours, other people and even other life at large. 'Othering' is, fundamentally, a process of objectification; by naming and defining something, someone, or a group of someones, we are subtly separating ourselves – as the agentic subject – from the other, as the passive object upon which we act. The modern world view considers a person as the subject who observes everything else that 'he' encounters, which involves the objectification of whatever is encountered. Martha Nussbaum (1995) distinguishes seven features of objectification: instrumentality, denial of autonomy, inertness, fungibility, violability, ownership, and denial of subjectivity. We use the masculine pronoun purposefully here, referring to the feminist critique of rational objectivity as being inherently patriarchal (see, for example, Beauvoir 2011). Because this world view is embedded in the very building blocks of the way we communicate – our language of subjects acting upon objects – we can call this a 'grammar of being' which both reflects and enables 'othering'.

The process of self-construal that requires 'othering' is accentuated if we assume or wish for a fixed and unchanging self, rather than a fluid and uncertain phenomenon. It is also accentuated if we assume or wish for that self to be the autonomous author of our lives, rather than the expression of complex relations – more so if we assume or wish for our self to be good and better than others. Therefore, any attachment in us to the idea of a self that is whole, sovereign and good makes 'othering' more compulsive. Paradoxically, this means that the belief that one can become a self-actualized good human being can be a contributor to further oppression and violence.

The rise of the ideology of e-s-c-a-p-e in the modern era (chapter 5) is predicated upon, and further galvanizes, our inner processes of 'othering'. For the mental habit of Entitlement, we must consider ourselves differentially worthy of good experiences. For the mental habit of Surety (another word for certainty), we must consider the rest of life to exist meaningfully only in ways that we choose as mattering to us. For the mental habit of seeking

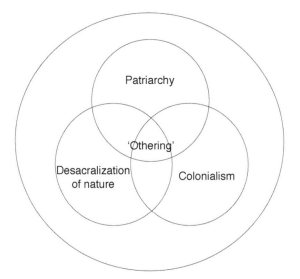

Figure 7.1 Interrelated forms and drivers of othering

to Control, we must objectify and reduce the subjectivity of that which we seek to control. For the mental habit of assuming our Autonomy, we must reduce the significance of all which influences and creates who we are. For the mental habit of assuming Progress, we must consider the world primarily as material to be shaped. For the mental habit of Exceptionalism, we must consider ourselves to be better than other people. Therefore, if we wish to become less unconsciously oppressed by this ideology, and less involved in reproducing it in society, it is useful to become more aware of our inner processes of 'othering'.

The figure above illustrates how the ideologies that are commonly cited as being instrumental in the destructiveness of the modern western culture, and which have brought the planet to its knees, can each be viewed as cultural manifestations of a subtle but catastrophic process of institutionalized 'othering'.

When we became aware of how 'othering' is at the root of both oppression and destruction, we wondered what could be useful in our work as educators and facilitators. We learned that 'othering' is constituted relationally when people interact (Frosh 2018), and so an approach which enables people to 'notice' this widespread phenomenon as it arises within them and find ways of making choices that are less driven from that impulse will be essential to the cause of reducing the potential for future harm. We found insights from critical theory and Buddhism, and the connections between the two (Hattam 2004), to be particularly helpful, alongside experiences of sitting in circles with the intention of unusually transparent and vulnerable sharing of thoughts and emotions.

Critical theory is useful as it brings attention to how processes of 'othering', and the ideology of e-s-c-a-p-e, are expressed through language and culture in ways that crystallize unequal power relations. Critical theory is a movement in social and political philosophy which seeks not only to understand those processes but to dismantle them in order to reduce inequality and oppression (Sim and van Loon 2004). Such theory invites us to become more aware of the language, symbols and behaviours that we use and that surround us, and how they are all involved in reproducing power relations. For instance, a newspaper headline, an advert, a form of speech or a manner of dressing can all be stimuli that convey meanings with normative or power-laden dimensions (Fairclough 2001). By becoming more aware of such processes, we develop what is described as critical consciousness or criticality (Freire 2005). That is a way of interpreting the world and oneself, where attention is given to possible normative or power-laden dimensions of any meanings intended or received from any stimuli so one can choose to either disengage or disrupt. Although there are modalities suited to classrooms, such as the 'critical reading' of texts, our climate predicament invites modalities for the development and everyday application of critical consciousness, particularly in group settings. We therefore concluded that it would be useful that facilitation for DA includes efforts to invite critical reflection on any cultural norms, often as expressed in language.

Another source of insight for us on how facilitated processes could bring attention to, and hopefully overcome, processes of 'othering' has been Buddhist philosophy and practice. One of the basic tenets of Buddhist teachings is the realization of impermanence. The perspective that the self is an unchanging, separate and coherent phenomenon is not accepted in Buddhism. Instead, we are invited to consider, and through insight meditation to experience, the self as a moving assembly of sensations, emotions and thoughts (Hagen 1998). The potential of experiencing self in that way is that we become less attached to the processes of self-construal, as described above, and therefore less engaged in unconscious 'othering'. In such meditation, we are also invited to notice how we are either averse to or desirous of certain thoughts and emotions in ways that can influence our decisions about what to focus on or what to believe to be true. That level of detailed attention to our inner thoughts and emotions can help reveal the moments when we label and judge stimuli of any kind, and whether we accept an idea or not. If people can bring that greater awareness into the moment of interpersonal interactions, to maintain an orientation towards inter-subjectivity in their relations with others (Irigaray 1985) and a more 'critical' interpretation of everyday culture, then there is greater opportunity for disengaging or disrupting systems of oppression and destruction.

Aspects of facilitating deep adaptation

The role of a facilitator is to support the empowerment of individuals to learn collaboratively and experientially in a group, and the legitimacy of this role is consented to voluntarily by members of the group (Heron 1999). The specific context for facilitation of DA (above) is relevant for all kinds of groups, whether concerned with 'inner' deep adaptation (the psycho-social, the emotional or the spiritual aspects of integrating collapse awareness) or 'outer' deep adaptation (the practical aspects, e.g. exploring and putting into practice realistic measures for addressing food security at community or country level). Throughout several years of working with people in groups on this seemingly all-encompassing topic, we have observed how easily people can move into practical conversations from a place of urgency or a felt need for productivity or usefulness. What we have realized, over time, is that people who have been socialized in a modern, western culture do not need encouragement or practice to activate their impulse to 'get busy', valuing productivity and outcomes above connection and process, and this impulse can easily become a distraction or a means of escape. Fortunately, there are many approaches that exist to support more democratic, participatory, practical collaboration. Ingredients and practices from sociocracy,[1] micro-solidarity[2] and liberating structures[3] are all being used to support collaborative working by members of the Deep Adaptation Forum (DAF). But without hosts and participants giving adequate attention to the ways in which dominant cultural ideas are transmitted and enacted discursively, these approaches, in themselves, are not immune to enabling the reproduction of harmful assumptions. Spaces can still be dominated by the same confident voices, and even the language of 'agility', 'producing better results' and 'social benefit' can confer subtle assumptions of patriarchy, colonialism and anthropocentrism. That is why our focus in the next two sections is on ways to cultivate critical awareness of 'how we are' when we show up, rather than 'what we do', underpinned by the belief that meaningful, engaged collaborative action can arise from empowered acceptance of our predicament.

What follows is a summary of some key aspects of facilitation for deep adaptation, which have emerged from the engagement of a lively community of practice of facilitators for deep adaptation, who bring together a wide range of relevant backgrounds, from psychotherapy and counselling to somatics, mindfulness, social work and community development, psycho-spiritual development, as well as expertise in distributed and collaborative leadership and participatory decision making.

Containment

A fundamental element of the process of group facilitation is to provide containment, described by Ringer (1998) as 'group members having the conscious and unconscious sense of being firmly held in the group and its task'. Containment, in the context of DA, is creating a space – and conditions – in which people feel *safe enough* to feel and express their most difficult emotions relating to collapse, or to reveal the ways in which the discursive foundations of the micro-violences of 'othering' are internalized and unconsciously enacted in our interactions with each other.

---

[1] See, for example, https://sociocracy30.org
[2] https://www.microsolidarity.cc
[3] http://www.liberatingstructures.com

Containment is a fundamental aspect of facilitation practice and paramount to facilitation of deep adaptation.

Smit (2014) proposes two aspects of containment: external ('hard') containment (or the structures that form the context in which the facilitation is taking place); and internal ('soft') containment (or the qualities of presence that the facilitator brings to their role). External containment begins well before the gathering takes place and includes the clarity of the 'call' or invitation (will people experience what they are expecting to experience?), administrative arrangements for participation and joining instructions. It also includes (in face-to-face gatherings) giving intention to the space, accessibility and comfort, as well as ensuring that the physical needs of the participants and facilitators are met. Internal containment includes such qualities of the facilitator as a non-judgemental presence, trustworthiness, support, empathy and consistency, and practices that enable these.

Drawing on influence from deep ecology (Naess 1977), we suggest including a non-anthropocentric, non-western empiricist paradigm in creating a sense of containment. For some, this may mean inviting and giving thanks to ancestors (human and non-human), or invoking the feeling of being held by and in service to the earth. For others, it means connecting with a higher power (implicitly or explicitly), connecting with our own teachers and honouring the presence of collective wisdom rather than individual approaches.

Containment is often understood as the facilitator creating a 'safe space'; however, this is problematic for a number of reasons. First, the context of facilitation for deep adaptation is not only inherently unsafe (considering the implications of the loss of security, sustenance and meaning; Bendell 2018), but also predicated on the fact that much of our harmful action throughout history has arisen from a felt or perceived need for safety and security. Second, a sense of safety is a subjective experience; for example, what feels like a safe space for a male participant who is white may be experienced as very unsafe by a woman of colour, or anyone else who is a member of a group which has been systematically marginalized by dominant culture. Thirdly, the facilitator is not unaffected by what is being explored so it is appropriate to positively acknowledge that emotional involvement to themselves and the participants. For these reasons, we recommend that spaces are always co-hosted by two or more people, and that careful and honest attention is given to the relationship between and amongst co-facilitators. In any group situation, our own boundaries as facilitators can begin to collapse; each of us has our own unconscious patterns and beliefs, which, when triggered, mean we may begin to lose a sense of integrity, and consequently our ability to 'hold space' energetically can be compromised. The concept of accompaniment in psychotherapy offers a useful metaphor: the collapse of stories of self, of previous architecture of meaning, requires the possibility of letting go into a liminal space:

> There is a river, it is in flow and unpredictable. The people in your group might be in that river, or it might be part of your intention for them to be able to explore that river. So you need to have one foot in the river and one foot on the bank. Working with co-facilitators means that one person can always have two feet on the bank.

Given that the context of deep adaptation to societal collapse is a topic that is experienced as inherently unsafe, and that safety is relative and subjectively experienced, the aim of giving attention to containment and boundaries challenges the myth that it is possible to create a safe space. Instead, we give attention to holding a space that is *safe enough*, and inherent in that process is increasing our capabilities for self- and co-regulation. Facilitating for deep adaptation is about becoming more resilient, by building our stamina for tolerating difficult emotions, and about the sobriety to be able to take considered generative action, rather than turn towards what feels more pleasurable, easy or comfortable. Creating a safe enough space doesn't make what happens inside the container more comfortable; it makes it more possible for us to hold ourselves and each other in discomfort (see chapter 6).

Denial and radical uncertainty

These are unprecedented times, challenging people's sense of self, security and agency, with the fear of societal collapse and even human extinction, triggering fear responses (chapter 4). As people from all walks of life, including climatologists and policy makers, feel anxiety, this can encourage habitual responses which will be unhelpful for wise action. Of particular concern here is an overemphasis on ever more detailed measurement, along with an aversion to diverse ways of knowing, holistic analysis and consequent inhibited ability for wise discernment within ambiguity.

If we take the exponential increase of human-caused carbon emissions as our indicator, many decades of climate science have not had an impact in reducing the unsustainability of society (chapter 1). We have become better at measuring and at producing more measurements. Stepping back from the specific researchers and their research, our society's emphasis on measurements can be regarded as a manifestation of contemporary discomfort with living in a state of uncertainty. That reflects the modern culture that has developed over hundreds of years since the scientific revolution. Within the culture of modernity, 'man imagines himself free from fear when there is no longer anything unknown' (Adorno and Horkheimer 1997: 16).

This emphasis on a positivist-scientific response to perceived threats is unhelpful when it maligns the more diverse forms of insight as well as the state of not-knowing. In the worst manifestations of this ideology, people can condemn more holistic analyses and suppress anything uncertain and threatening. In addition, rather than remain in a state of uncertainty, people may unconsciously choose to adopt simplistic stories of blame and safety, such as political narratives characterized by racism, nationalism and authoritarianism (chapters 5 and 6).

With its emphasis on the social construction of our ways of knowing the world, critical theory teaches us that certainty is an illusion (Rorty 1989). That view echoes many spiritual traditions. Taoism, Buddhism, Hinduism and indigenous world views suggest that human agency is not central; rather, humans are understood as being *in relation* with other forces within a reality we cannot fully comprehend. These sources of wisdom recognize the possibilities for a felt sense of inter-being, humble appreciation of our interdependence, and openness to integrate insights from multiple ways of knowing our world (Abhayananda 2002).

Reducing culturally produced resistance in all of us to letting go of our previously assumed certainties about the world, knowledge and personal identity is therefore at the heart of facilitation for deep adaptation. Enabling people to feel more equanimity with uncertainty and ambiguity, within a context of people perceiving increasing vulnerability and change, is therefore a key aim of holding space for deep adaptation.

Grief

The affective dimension of experience has been repressed in the western modern world view, or relegated to a domestic and feminine sphere outside of dominant discourse. That dominant discourse suppresses emotionality of any kind, but fear, and fear of death in particular, has been a key factor in the denial of our predicament with dangerous climate change. As the implications of that predicament are becoming more widely acknowledged, the field of psychology has been exploring the phenomenon of 'eco-distress' (chapter 4). Within that field of expertise, the general agreement is that western culture is grief phobic, meaning that unpleasant emotions associated with grieving are problematized and framed as needing to be relieved and overcome. A critical-theoretical perspective on this phenomenon suggests that 'the social rules that govern the expression of grief, the role of attachment, social pain, and shame [are] potent forces that promote compliance with social rules' (Harris 2010: 241). Suppression of different aspects of grief can result in becoming stuck in denial (Kübler-Ross 1969). Collective acceptance of our predicament, by becoming enabled to move through all of the difficult emotional experiences, is one way of finding loving equanimity in collapse (Cunsolo and Landman 2017).

To write about the emotion of grief by discussing expert analysis risks repeating the deadening patterns we have criticized so far in this chapter. So we will take a moment to share with you in a different way. We know that grief decimates and destroys us. In the depth of the grieving process, we lose connection with our sense of self and everything that previously seemed certain about the world, the familiar landmarks of our person, our relationships and our social context. It feels unbearable, and in fact the self that encounters it cannot bear it because that self is not big enough to comprehend it. The boundaries of our self are broken down and expanded in order to become big enough (or to have an increased capacity) for integrating the experience of loss. A new self emerges, one that is created during the journey of integrating the incomprehensible. In the depths of grieving, all becomes lost. There is no stable ground from which to orient. In order to locate ourselves and navigate, we need at least two known coordinates: where we are, and something else on the horizon to use a reference point. Without those, we become lost in a continually shifting landscape.

In a culture which is 'death denying' and in which there is a paucity of death-related rituals (Thieleman 2015), there is an important role to be played by providing spaces where the complex and challenging emotions involved in grieving can be shared and collectively witnessed. Experiences and expressions of grief and loss are not individual but form an important part of community collective experience, and examples of such practices as grief tending, death cafes and the Work that Reconnects offer insights into what is possible (chapter 8).

Examples of deep adaptation modalities and facilitated processes

The Deep Adaptation Forum is an international space to connect people, online and in person, to foster mutual support, collaboration and professional development in the process of facing societal collapse. It was established as an emergent online community in early 2019 in response to the unexpected scale of the impact of the original 'Deep Adaptation' paper, published in July 2018. A community of practice of volunteer facilitators, with expertise in group facilitation, training, psychotherapy, eco-therapy, mindfulness, somatics and a host of other associated fields relevant to DA, has been creating and offering regular online gatherings for DAF members. There follows a description of three 'modalities' or facilitated processes that have emerged, informed by the context described above.[4]

---

[4] For detailed advice on organizing and facilitating these processes, see the relevant guides at http://jembendell.com/facilitate

Deep listening

These small group gatherings are a space in which participants are invited to share honestly and openly how they are feeling and what they are experiencing, as they grapple with the implications of the unfolding climate tragedy. Crucially, they are not dialogic. Rather, in small groups of four to six, each person has equal time to share, while the others bear witness without comment or judgement. (In this respect, the container has something in common with the firm boundaries established in an AA meeting, where there is no cross-talk allowed, positive or negative.) As listeners, participants are encouraged to suspend their own process of self-referential sense-making or judging and instead to practise empathy, through active listening and bringing curiosity. These are not intended as therapeutic spaces, although this practice of active, attentive and non-judgemental listening is an aspect of therapeutic practice. This space for sharing emotions that may have felt unbearable or unspeakable (particularly as many people in the Deep Adaptation Forum have joined because they feel isolated in their world view) can be a powerful and healing experience. The modality is central to DA because it is a space where the affective dimension of experience is foregrounded, and negative or difficult emotions are not framed as problems to be solved. Many participants share their experiences of grieving aspects of the natural world that have already been destroyed or devastated, or grieving as they relinquish hopes they may have had for the future. This can play an important role in substituting for the lack of collective grief rituals in modern society.

Deep relating

Deep relating is a relational meditation practice, or an approach to being in relationship with another person, or group of people, in a way that is grounded in a deep and detailed awareness of present-moment experience. Participants are invited to speak from and of only what is arising in the 'here and now', which can include physical sensations (including what is seen and heard), emotions and thoughts, then trying to articulate what is experienced as clearly as possible with the intention of inviting the other into your world for deeper connection. People are invited to notice when the impulse to 'tell stories' arises, that is, to explain, justify or evaluate experience by referencing past or future, or prior assumptions or frameworks of meaning. In this respect, it has some association with 'experiential' compared with 'narrative' modes of being, as described in research into the impacts of meditation (see, for example, Farb et al. 2007). The focus becomes increasingly towards the minutiae – our impulses and judgements that may have previously passed under the radar of awareness.

There are generally no instructions as such but a set of principles that guide emergent dialogue:

- **commitment to connection** with ourselves, each other and everything that arises in the present moment;
- **staying with sensations** – noticing the sensations and emotions as they arise in the body in the present moment, and allowing them to be expressed and acknowledged;
- **welcome anything** – we trust that whatever emotions and sensations are being triggered by our interactions are here to enable us and the group to shift into higher awareness and acceptance;
- **owning our experience** by returning back to the independent observer within and examining closely the source of our experiences, especially when triggered by others;
- **being with the other in their world** – while others are sharing, we explore what it's like to be this person, what sensations, emotions and thoughts arise as we listen to them, and we ask questions that allow us to understand their present experience better.

This practice is similar to, and has evolved from, other modalities know as authentic relating,[5] circling,[6] 'focusing' in psychotherapy, and also the modern Buddhist practice of insight dialogue (Kramer 2007). It is also influenced by Bohmian dialogue, so it is not goal-oriented but invites 'a stream of meaning flowing among and through us and between us . . . [which makes] possible a flow of meaning in the whole group, out of which will emerge some new understanding . . . this shared meaning is the "glue" or "cement" that holds people and societies together' (Bohm 1996).

One of the ways in which deep relating is distinct from these practices is that 'collapse awareness' is explicitly present in the space and is named by facilitators. The intention is to remove any barriers to full expression around this topic; it doesn't mean that there is necessarily intention that this topic will arise.

The principles and practice of deep relating offer potential for exploring and surfacing the unconscious patterns of dominant western discourse described earlier that are important for addressing the mental habits that can result in othering, denial and escape (chapter 5), and so the practice of deep relating can be an invaluable approach for deep adaptation. There is an emphasis on somatic and affective dimensions being as important as the cognitive or narrative; dialogue is emergent and not outcome-oriented; and that (ostensibly at least) anything is welcomed rather than there being rule-governed modes of participation. However, the presence of these ingredients is not sufficient to ensure critically conscious engagement. We have witnessed similar modalities which are framed as a way of revealing one's 'true' or 'authentic' self, a narrative which can amplify, rather than lessen, a sense of exceptionalism and entitlement, typical of what Foucault (1984) called the *California Cult of the Self*. That can be particularly attractive for some people whose anticipation of personal mortality and a loss of past identity in the face of collapse leads them to choose narratives, experiences and communities that offer to support them in the least complicated (or most enjoyable) manner. If a 'spiritual bypass' response to lessening one's conformity with society drives people's response, then there may even be a suppression of attention to questions of complicity and solidarity. Not only would that reduce opportunities for them to learn, engage and reduce contributions to unnecessary harm, it is an exclusionary narrative that might therefore align with the tendencies towards repressive politics that are occurring in many countries.

In the past, we have witnessed hosts of similar processes embodying, enabling and legitimizing subtle enactments of power-laden discourse. Therefore, if facilitators are not holding space with some of the 'critical consciousness' we described earlier, there is a risk of allowing or inadvertently reinforcing dominant narratives – about power, domination, entitlement and progress – which will hinder the deep adaptation process. Therefore some attention to how we, as facilitators, can better avoid ideologies of e-s-c-a-p-e will be useful. A useful moment of reflection, either by an individual facilitator or within a group, is to ask: 'what might culture be producing, or reducing, in us right now?' Whether this aspect of deep relating needs to be developed into an additional principle to 'ponder culture' is something we are exploring through practice.

Death cafes

Death cafes were set up by Jon Underwood in 2011 to provide a safe, confidential setting for people to come together to talk about death and dying, 'to increase awareness of death with a view to helping people make the most of their (finite) lives'.[7] Underwood was inspired by the work of Bernard Crettaz, a sociologist and anthropologist, who recognized the need, within cultures which are generally death-phobic, for a space where people could explore their relationship with death and mortality (Crettaz 2010). Online 'DA Death Cafes' have been held during 2020, offering an opportunity for people to engage with death and mortality against the backdrop of cataclysmic climate change. They have offered a space in which people share and explore their experiences as they are coming to terms with the global predicament, species extinction and possible collapse of societies. It is clear that people find great comfort and support as they share and deeply listen to others; they are also open and willing to talk about what these immense challenges mean to them.

Aversion to acknowledging our mortality can be understood as implicated in subtle as well as obvious forms of climate denial (discussed in chapter 2), and in the e-s-c-a-p-e ideology (see chapter 5).

Conclusion

In concluding our discussion of facilitation for deep adaptation, we wish to point out that the theoretical frameworks, ideas and

---

[7] https://deathcafe.com/

modalities proposed here, in the conventions of academic written form, may serve to drain this topic of its vibrancy. Facilitation of groups towards deep adaptation to the unfolding effects of climate chaos, in line with the principles and context that we have expounded in this chapter, is at once a crucial, challenging and rewarding endeavour. As much as it is an honour to support people as they share in painful processes of personal and collective relinquishment, and build the resilience together that is required to face courageously the sometimes overwhelming feelings of uncertainty, disorientation or fear associated with looming crisis, there is commensurate joy in accompanying people as they discover new ways of experiencing deeper connection with each other, renewed appreciation for life, restored capacities for playfulness, creativity and motivation founded in solidarity, and determination to 'extend the glide and soften the crash' (Bendell 2019).

Our hope and intention is that the facilitated group experiences we outline in this chapter, and others occurring in the DA field, will support us all in reconnecting with our sense of interbeing and active solidarity with all life. As well as feeling uplifting, it will necessarily and rightly continue to be messy and painful (chapter 6). We agree with critical theorist and philosopher Richard Rorty's (1989) view that the only chance to eradicate exclusion and oppression is to expand the conception of 'we' until no one is excluded. The possibility of this realization for supporting groups in deep adaptation could be significant in terms of finding ways to avoid the continuing emergence of parochial, exclusionary or nationalist narratives in mainstream cultures as people sense greater uncertainty and vulnerability.

References

Abhayananda, S. (2002) *The History of Mysticism: The Unchanging Testament*. London: Watkins Publishing.

Adorno, T. W. and Horkheimer, M. (1997) *Dialectic of Enlightenment*. London: Verso.

Beauvoir, S. de (2011) *The Second Sex*. London: Vintage Books.

Bendell, J. (2018) 'Deep Adaptation: A Map for Navigating Climate Tragedy'. IFLAS Occasional Paper 2. Available at: http://www.life worth.com/deepadaptation.pdf

Bendell, J. (2019) 'The Love in Deep Adaptation – A Philosophy for the Forum'. JemBendell.com. Available at: https://jembendell.com/2 019/03/17/the-love-in-deep-adaptation-a-philosophy-for-the-forum/

Bohm, D. (1996). *On Dialogue*. London and New York: Routledge Classics.

Carr, K. and Bindewald, L. (2019) '"Zero Is Where the Real Fun Starts" – Evaluation for Value(s) Co-Production', in P. Bamber (ed.), *Teacher Education for Sustainable Development and Global Citizenship: Critical Perspectives on Values, Curriculum and Assessment*, 1st edn. Abingdon: Routledge.

Crettaz, B. (2010) *Cafés mortels: sortir la mort du silence*. Geneva: Labor et fides.

Cunsolo, A. and Landman, K. (eds) (2017) *Mourning Nature: Hope at the Heart of Ecological Loss and Grief*, 1st edn. London: McGill-Queen's University Press.

Díaz, S., Settele, J., Brondízio, E., et al. (2019) *Summary for Policymakers of the Global Assessment Report on Biodiversity and Ecosystem Services of the Intergovernmental Science-Policy Platform on Biodiversity and Ecosystem Services*. Bonn: IPBES Secretariat. Available at: https://ipbes.net/sites/default/files/2020-02/ipbes_global_assessment_report_summary_for_policymakers_en.pdf

Fairclough, N. (2001) *Language and Power*. Harlow: Longman.

Farb, N. A. S. et al. (2007) 'Attending to the Present: Mindfulness Meditation Reveals Distinct Neural Modes of Self-Reference'. *Social Cognitive and Affective Neuroscience* 2(4): 313–22.

Foucault, M. (1984) 'On the Genealogy of Ethics: An Overview of Work in Progress', in P. Rabinow (ed.), *The Foucault Reader: An Introduction to Foucault's Thought*, 1st edn. London: Penguin.

Freire, P. (2005) *Education for Critical Consciousness*. New York: Continuum International Publishing Group.

Frosh, S. (2018) 'Rethinking Psychoanalysis in the Psychosocial'. *Psychoanalysis, Culture and Society* 23(1): 5–14.

Greer, J. M. (2015) *After Progress*. Gabriola Island, BC: New Society Publishers.

Hagen, S. (1998) *Buddhism Plain and Simple: The Practice of Being Aware, Right Now, Every Day*. New York: Broadway Books.

Harris, D. (2010) 'Oppression of the Bereaved: A Critical Analysis of Grief in Western Society'. *Journal of Death and Dying* 60(3): 241–53.

Hattam, R. (2004) *Awakening-Struggle: Towards a Buddhist Critical Social Theory*. Flaxton: PostPressed.

Heron, J. (1999) *The Complete Facilitator's Handbook*. London: Kogan Page.

Irigaray, L. (1985) *Speculum of the Other Woman*, trans. G. C. Gill. Ithaca, NY: Cornell University Press.

Kramer, G. (2007) *Insight Dialogue: The Interpersonal Path to Freedom*. Boulder, CO: Shambhala Publications.

Kübler-Ross, E. (1969) *On Death and Dying*. New York: Macmillan.

Murray, E. (2015) *Disrupting Pathways to Genocide*. Basingstoke: Palgrave Macmillan.

Naess, A. (1977) 'Spinoza and Ecology'. *Philosophia* 7: 45–54.

Nussbaum, M. (1995) 'Objectification'. *Philosophy and Public Affairs* 24(4): 249–91.

Rabkin, Y. and Minakov, M. (eds) (2018) *Demodernization: A Future in the Past*. New York: Ibidem Press.

Ringer, M. (1998) 'Two Vital Aspects in the Facilitation of Groups: Connections and Containment'. *Australian Journal of Outdoor Education* 4(1): 5–11.

Rorty, R. (1989) *Contingency, Irony, and Solidarity*. Cambridge: Cambridge University Press.

Sim, S. and van Loon, B. (2004) *Introducing Critical Theory*. Royston: Icon Books.

Smit, H. (2014) *The Depth Facilitator's Handbook: Transforming Group Dynamics*. The Depth Leadership Trust.

Thieleman, K. (2015) 'Epilogue: Grief, Bereavement, and Ritual across Cultures', in J. Cacciatore and J. DeFrain (eds), *The World of Bereavement Cultural Perspectives on Death in Families*, 1st edn. Cham: Springer.

Xu, Y. and Ramanathan, V. (2017) 'Well below 2°C: Mitigation Strategies for Avoiding Dangerous to Catastrophic Climate Changes'. *Proceedings of the National Academy of Sciences* 114(39): 10315–23. Available at: https://www.pnas.org/content/114/39/10315

8

The Great Turning: Reconnecting through Collapse

Sean Kelly and Joanna Macy

Natural allies

When we first encountered the fundamental premises of the deep adaptation movement – that (civilizational) collapse is likely, inevitable or already unfolding; that (ecological) catastrophe is likely; and that human extinction is possible – the effect was like a tonic. There is something vitalizing about speaking the truth. Failure to speak truth reinforces a major affliction of our times: a generalized deadening of feeling and psychic numbing. This numbing, moreover, leads to an impairment of sorely needed cognitive capacities. The ability to perceive, understand and respond intelligently to our accelerating planetary emergency requires that we raise to conscious awareness the anxiety and other forms of emotional distress which in fact are normal and healthy responses to a sense of vital threat.[1] This awareness

---

[1] In this connection, see the comprehensive multidisciplinary article by anthropologists Syme and Hagen which argues that:

> [a]group of disorders, such as anxiety, depression and PTSD, have low heritability, are caused by adversity and involve symptoms that seem to be adaptive responses to adversity. Because they are relatively common throughout adult life, they account for a substantial fraction of disease-burden attributable to mental illness. These might not be disorders at all, however, but instead aversive yet adaptive responses to adversity. If so, this has several important

cannot arise, however, without putting words to what is never-theless felt, however indirectly or unconsciously and despite the formidable defences against such awareness. It is therefore with a sense of gratitude that we have witnessed the growth of the deep adaptation movement. We consider it a powerful ally in the work we and many others have been engaged in on behalf of life and the wider earth community.

The ideas of climate grief and ecological anxiety have recently entered the mainstream (see, for instance, Mendosa 2019). This is a good thing, as it is encouraging many people to name what they have been feeling. So far, recommendations on the part of health professionals include such common-sense strategies as staying well informed while knowing when to disengage from the onslaught of bad news; seeking out like-minded people with whom to discuss both information and concerns; staying physi-cally healthy through regular exercise and a good diet; spending time in nature; and taking concrete steps towards making a difference, including lifestyle choices and getting involved in organizations devoted to addressing threats to the natural world. Though recognizing the value of cultivating relationships with like-minded people, most recommendations for dealing with eco-anxiety or climate grief tend to focus on the individual, with an emphasis on coping strategies. By contrast, the Work that Reconnects was developed to allow people to work together in groups with the explicit intention of not only expressing blocked emotions but of catalyzing a deeper sense of identity as active participants in what we and others call the Great Turning toward a life-sustaining society. The suite of practices included in the Work have been developed over the past several decades, and there is now a growing network of many hundreds of facilitators throughout the world (workthatreconects.org; Macy and Young Brown 2014).

The idea of the Great Turning, which serves as the orienting framework for the Work, includes three dimensions, all of which can be considered as forms of activism, though the first dimension – 'Holding Actions' in defence of the greater earth community

---

implications. First, these conditions would largely indicate social problems, not medical ones, and therefore call for social, not medical, solutions. (Syme and Hagen 2019)

– is what most people associate with the notion of activism. Such actions aim to hold back and slow down the damage being caused by the political economy of 'Business as Usual' and can take political, legislative and legal form, along with direct actions. We can think of the massive climate marches, the youth-led climate strikes or the many actions of Extinction Rebellion (XR) as emblematic of this kind of activism. The second dimension – 'Life-Sustaining Systems and Practices' – has two complementary sides, a critical and a constructive. The critical side takes the form of analysis of the structural causes of our planetary predicament, and an uncovering of the dynamics of industrial-growth society and its plagues: ecospheric devastation, social injustice, psycho-social and spiritual malaise. The constructive side involves the creation of alternatives to current social, economic, political, legal and educational arrangements – including renewable energy, regenerative design, permaculture, earth law, local currencies, co-ops and too many more to list here.

The third dimension – 'Shift in Consciousness' – is generally implicit in the first two dimensions but must be made explicit for them to be fully coherent and sustainable. We come to see ourselves as participants in a grand evolutionary adventure and as vehicles for an emerging planetary, or Gaian, consciousness. It embraces multiple ways of knowing – holistic, systemic and complex; imaginal and poetic; emotional and embodied. It involves waking up to, and celebrating, our radical inter-being, our inseverable participation in the sacred web of life, affirming and enacting our solidarity with all members of the earth community. The Work that Reconnects is devoted to catalyzing this shift in consciousness.

Facing collapse

As with 'probable catastrophe' among the fundamental premises of deep adaptation, the idea of the Great Turning has always been paired with the recognition that we are in the accelerating phase of the Great Unravelling of the web of life. Deep adaptation has added a critical element to our work in the Great Turning with its emphasis on the likelihood of civilizational collapse. Until relatively recently, in presenting the idea of the Great Turning and in practising the Work, it was assumed by most that there was still a fighting chance to halt the Great Unravelling and to transition to a life-sustaining society without having to pass through a phase of collapse. While we recognize an inescapable uncertainty in such assessments, we have come to expect the inevitability of collapse. This expectation is based on the fact that the industrial-growth society which has brought us to the threshold of ecological catastrophe is inherently unsustainable and shows signs of ever-increasing fragility. As an indication of the proximity of this threshold, we can note that at least four of nine identified planetary boundaries have already been crossed (climate change, loss of biosphere integrity, land-system change and altered biogeochemical cycles [phosphorus and nitrogen]; ocean acidification is sure to be added soon). We are already witnessing wars catalyzed by climate change, waves of climate refugees, increased mortality, disruptions and distress due to extreme weather, and now the crippling effects of a global pandemic. We have become acutely aware of the destabilizing potential of global pandemics with the quick spread of the Covid-19 virus, which is among the so-called zoonotic diseases (that is, diseases which can be transmitted from animals to people) that cause 70 per cent of human infections. Commenting on the relation between the Covid-19 virus and environmental degradation, the UN Environment Programme notes that 'it is important to address the multiple and often interacting threats to ecosystems and wildlife to prevent zoonoses from emerging, including habitat loss and fragmentation, illegal trade, pollution, invasive species and, increasingly, climate change'.[2] Jem Bendell, for his part, has warned of the particular risk of food shortages and disruption of supply chains as a likely catalyst of more widespread collapse (Bendell 2019b).

Despite the delusional conviction to the contrary on the part of the partisans of Business as Usual, the stability of the political economy is intimately dependent upon the benign functioning of our Gaian systems. Collapsologists Pablo Servigne and Raphaël Stevens summarize our planetary predicament with the following observations: (1) 'the engine of thermo-industrial civilization – the energy-finance dynamo – is on the verge of shutdown. Limits

---

[2] https://www.unep.org/cep/news/editorial/coronavirus-outbreak-highlights-need -address-threats-ecosystems-and-wildlife

have been reached'; (2) 'the exponential material expansion of our civilization has irremediably disrupted the complex natural systems on which it rested'; (3) 'the ever more complex systems which provide food, water and energy, and which enable politics, finance and the virtual sphere to function, require increasing energy inputs'. They conclude by noting that, 'These three states (approaching the limits, exceeding boundaries and increasing complexity) are irreversible and, when combined, they can lead to only one outcome' (Servigne and Stevens 2020: 178–9).

Of course, collapse is already happening to varying degrees across the planet. As collapse intensifies and becomes more widespread, we can expect a corresponding intensification of human suffering, not only through hunger, homelessness, extreme weather-related disasters and more prevalent zoonotic diseases but through the spread of what Buddhist teachings refer to as the 'three poisons': greed, hatred and delusion. While these poisons have always been with us, any sufficiently 'deep' adaptive strategy to collapse and catastrophe will include means to counter them with their traditional antidotes: generosity, compassion and wisdom. The beginning of wisdom in the present context might include the realization that the collapse of industrial-growth society is not only likely or inevitable but in some sense necessary. It is necessary because industrial growth society is the main driver of climate chaos and the Great Unravelling. We realize that many still envision the possibility of a smooth transition to a sustainable form of civilization. We are not banking on such a possibility. Our expectation of the increasing likelihood or inevitability of collapse is not merely a matter of rational calculation of the odds, however. It involves as well an equal measure of intuition, a 'feeling-into' the complex of factors under consideration with the full participation of the heart-mind. In purely pragmatic terms, as Servigne and Stevens remind us, it may very well be that such expectation will promote optimal readiness for adapting to what is to come, minimizing the extent and rapidity of catastrophic fallout, if not also, against all odds, increasing the likelihood of seizing whatever chance there might be to avoid the expected collapse (Servigne and Stevens 2020: 99–100; on the place of intuition, see pp. 8 and 98). In any case, regardless of expectations, we affirm the ethical imperative to do what we can to ensure a softer landing, to minimize suffering, to save what can be saved and to prepare the ground for the possibility, at least, of life-sustaining societies that might not only survive but flourish on the other side of collapse.

Doing the work

Jem has proposed four 'Rs' (the call to resilience, relinquishment, restoration and reconciliation) as guidelines for a (deep) adaptive response to the prospect of collapse. The first three Rs have some resonance with the first three stations in the Spiral of the Work that Reconnects (*Coming from Gratitude*, *Honouring our Pain for the World* and *Seeing with New Eyes*). All four Rs can also be seen as guiding values for how we enter into the phase of *Going Forth*, the last station in the Spiral of the Work.

The first station – *Coming from Gratitude* – honours the universal practice among indigenous communities (and of most religious traditions) by affirming 'the words that come before all else'. These words acknowledge our interdependence with all that is, the gratuitous gift of existence itself, and all that sustains us and makes for a meaningful life. Starting from gratitude is itself a powerful form of resistance to the scarcity and competition at the core of Business as Usual. It uncovers a stable and nourishing ground upon which we can proceed to the next station – *Honouring our Pain for the World*. Here we give voice to the suffering of the earth community, to the Great Unravelling and signs of collapse that we already know and feel in our bodies and heart-minds, despite the distractions of Business as Usual. A simple but highly effective practice here and throughout the Spiral of the Work involves participants sitting across from one another in pairs. The facilitator offers a series of *open sentences* which each person repeats and completes, speaking freely for a couple of minutes while their partner listens attentively in silence. An example of an open sentence used at this point is: 'When I imagine the world we are leaving our children, I feel . . .' As we commented on above, opening to our pain for the world is a sign of psychological, social and spiritual health. It is an expression of our vital connection with the web of life and our solidarity with the wider earth community. It raises to consciousness and empowers our deeper identities as living members of the living earth.

One of the most powerful practices in this station of the Spiral is that of the *Truth Mandala*. Here participants are convened around a sacred circle and invited, as the spirit moves them, to enter into one or more of the quadrants where, assisted by a ritual object (dry leaves for grief, a stone for fear, a stick for anger and an empty bowl for the sense of deprivation and need), they can speak their pain for the world. We use elemental forms of ritual (such as sitting in a circle, intoning, bowing) in this and some other practices of the Work to free participants to speak not only as themselves but more archetypally and on behalf of life itself in this planetary moment. This ritual is not merely cathartic since what emerges in the end is the insight that this pain is an expression of a deeper love and solidarity with the greater Life in which we are embedded.

With the second station – *Seeing with New Eyes* – we enter more directly into the story of the Great Turning, making explicit what was already implied and enacted in the previous two stations of the Spiral. In contrast to the alienating individualism promoted by the story of Business as Usual, here we allow for the experience of a wider and deeper sense of self, one that is defined in terms of relations, connections, mutuality and synergy. This goes hand in hand with a more organic and vital sense of kinship that extends horizontally to include the totality of this living earth. A particularly rich practice for enacting this sense of kinship is a group ritual known as the Council of all Beings in which participants take on the face of an other-than-human being and speak on their behalf, giving voice to their suffering and to their unique perspectives on our shared world in peril. This practice can liberate the imagination from the deadening grip of a mutilated, and mutilating, anthropocentrism. It allows for an embodied experience of the deeper, and more complex, ecological or Gaian Self as a 'communion of subjects' (rather than a mere 'collection of objects', as 'geologian' Thomas Berry puts it; and see Swimme and Berry 1992: 243). The ecological or Gaian Self not only transcends but includes the human. This inclusion is enacted later in the ritual when each of the participants, after having spoken on behalf of an other-than-human being, sets aside their mask and enters the centre of the circle to be addressed directly by members of the wider earth community and to receive their gifts as a means of reclaiming their authentic Gaian identity.

204 SHIFTS IN BEING

The expanded sense of kinship extends vertically as well since we now know that earth is the expression of an ongoing 4.6 billion-year evolutionary journey, whose story we carry in each of our cells and the major phases of which we rehearse in our mother's womb. We know too that our present actions will co-determine the fate of the entire earth community for many generations to come. In contrast to the compressed and flattened time-sense that dominates industrial growth societies, practices of the Work from this station of the Spiral (such as *Harvesting the Gifts of the Ancestors* or *The Seventh Generation*) allow participants to access an experience of *deep* time. We enter into this experience through the exercise of our moral imagination, and in so doing we reclaim our solidarity with all of our ancestors – human, other-than-human and cosmic – as well as with the future beings, whose subtle support we can call upon in our time of need. Learning to see and feel into this expanded sense of self and community, to open to this deeper sense of time, reveals previously hidden sources of strength and courage to face the prospect of collapse and participate creatively in the unfolding story of the Great Turning.

The Great Turning is as much a form of activism as it is a new story. In fact, the story itself is a form of activism insofar as it involves identifying and amplifying values, perspectives and choices which resist and seek to transform the ways of Business as Usual. In the last station of the Spiral – *Going Forth* – participants commit to bringing the fruits of their journey through the first three stations to their daily lives and aspirations for the future. Especially now in the shadow of collapse, even as we cultivate visions of a desired future, we stress that participating in the story of the Great Turning does not require belief in the likelihood of success. Regardless of imagined outcomes, the values that inform this story are held as intrinsically good. Choosing life, affirming our indissoluble inter-being, and thinking, feeling and acting in solidarity with all members of the earth community are not means but rather ends in themselves. Whatever chances we might have to emerge from the ruins of industrial growth society to a life-sustaining culture will doubtless rest on the expression of these values. Their expression, however, brings its own immediate reward in the here and now, reconnecting us to the sense of gratitude with which we began.

Meaning and hope in a time of collapse

The prospect of collapse, catastrophe and extinction cannot help but activate a sense of fundamental insecurity and existential dread. While some might prefer to focus on pragmatic strategies for avoiding the worst, on psychotherapeutic techniques for reducing stress, or simply on finding effective distractions, throughout human history it is the world's religious and spiritual traditions that have been tasked with coming to terms with the inevitability of suffering and death. From its inception, the Work that Reconnects has had a special relation to Buddhist teachings on the nature and causes of suffering, wisdom and compassion, and the Bodhisattva ideal of universal liberation. It has also drawn inspiration from certain strands of the Abrahamic religions and from many indigenous spiritualities. Apart from any specific teachings, however, the Work has preserved some core elements of the religious or spiritual dimension which, in part at least, help account for its effectiveness as a form of group process for working with such strong emotions and with matters of deep existential import.

To begin with, the orienting framework of the Great Turning acts as a potent living symbol of our times, as depth psychologist C. G. Jung might put it. Living symbols facilitate the vital connection between individual consciousness and the numinous realm of the archetypes of the collective unconscious, which act as carriers and catalyzers of existential meaning. The image-concept of the Great Turning evokes the archetypal journey of transformation as well as the universal symbol of the mandala, the sacred circle of wholeness and integration, which Jung understands as a universal symbol of the true Self. The Spiral of the Work participates in the same archetypal symbol. We have already seen how some of the practices take on the explicit form of a ritual (the *Truth Mandala*, the Council of All Beings). In general, those facilitating the Work should do their best to create the sense of working within a safe and sacred container. At a more overarching level, the stations of the Spiral reproduce the fundamental structure of rites of initiation, a structure which Joseph Campbell also identified with the most widely diffused mythological motif (the 'hero's journey') having to do with the quest for meaning.

Even if not pointed to explicitly, when properly facilitated, those who do the Work will travel along well-worn psycho-spiritual paths.

The practices of the Work that Reconnects facilitate a reconnection with the experience of our deeper selves as continuous with the living body of Gaia and the greater cosmos that birthed her. They reconnect our minds, hearts and bodies, opening to the Great Mystery of our unknown origins and destiny, to the creative powers that have lured the journey of the universe to the production of life, consciousness, wisdom, compassion and love. While this spirit of reconnection complements and empowers all four Rs of deep adaptation, the naturally potent psycho-spiritual dimensions of the Work recommend it as a particularly powerful ally for those wishing to explore the path of reconciliation.

In his proposal for the fourth R – reconciliation – Jem offers the idea of 'radical hope' as an alternative to more common forms of 'passive' or 'magical' hope, where the emphasis is on maintaining confidence in our ability to avoid collapse and on cultivating visions of a positive future. By contrast, Jem reminds us that, 'We can no longer stop disruptive climate change.'

We might be able to slow it. We can try to reduce the harm coming from it. We can explore how to live and die lovingly because of it. But all of that we can do because we have a faith or sense that this is the right way to be alive, not because it will work. Most calls for hope that we're hearing are from, or for, those fearful of living with death in their awareness . . . It is time to drop all hopes and visions that arise from an inability to accept impermanence and non-control and instead describe a radical hope of how we respond in these times. We believe it's possible and necessary, through mutual inquiry and support, for our fears, beliefs or certainties of collapse to be brought to a place of peaceful inner and outer resourcefulness. Ours is a time for reconciliation with mortality, nature and each other (Bendell 2019a).

In a similar vein, Joanna and Chris Johnstone have proposed the idea and practice of *active* hope. Rather than trying to sustain activism through the expectation of a successful transition to a life-sustaining society or 'ecological civilization', active hope involves an affirmation of the liberating power of intention and choice in the present and in the near term of what is always possible to achieve: a life guided by wisdom, compassion and generosity. Addressing those for whom the idea of hope, however radical or active, no longer appeals, Sean has explored the related idea of a different kind of *faith*. Not a faith in otherworldly salvation or in the promise of endless 'progress', but faith as a trusting in, and unconditional affirmation of, our mutual solidarity and common destiny as earthly or Gaian beings (see Kelly 2020).

Conclusion: People of the Passage

Though collapse may seem inevitable, and indeed is already happening in places, there remains the possibility of some form of human culture, if not civilization, on the other side of the threshold. At the same time, to slow and limit the Great Unravelling, while adapting to collapse, calls for the most compassionate and effective engagement with our world. The Great Turning to a life-sustaining culture can serve as vision and compass for this engagement. The Great Turning is not an alternative to collapse but a passage *through*. As an evolving vision and commitment, it shapes and ripens us as we make our way through the rubble of industrial-growth society. This passage can be seen as a kind of planetary initiation, a collective rite of passage to the possibility, at least, of a human culture in harmony with the greater life of Gaia, in and through whom we have our being. We do not – cannot – know how well we might navigate collapse or how successful we will be in halting, slowing or mitigating the Great Unravelling. Complexity and living systems theory alert us to the creative potential of emergent properties, themselves typically manifested in times of greatest stress. They also school us in accepting and working with the inescapable uncertainty surrounding the fate of individual consciousness and the future of life on earth. Perhaps all we can say with confidence is that, on the other side of the threshold of our collective initiation, as Joachim of Fiore wrote almost a millennium ago, 'We shall not be what we have been, but we shall begin to be other.'

The wisdom, compassion and generosity called for in this time of the Great Turning answer to a quickening in the heart-mind, the opening of gifts from all our ancestors and a stirring of future life already inhabiting us, waiting and wanting to be born. This new life is not other than the life that lives in us now. The love it summons blesses it in return; it is not conditional upon a guaranteed or even likely tomorrow but knows its truth and goodness and beauty in the pulsing mystery of the here and now. This life and love is the only terra firma in a time of collapse. It is the only clear path for we people of the passage.

References

Bendell, J. (2019a) 'Hope and Vision in the Face of Collapse – The 4th R of Deep Adaptation'. Available at: https://jembendell. com/2019/01/09/hope-and-vision-in-the-face-of-collapse-the-4th-r-of -deep-adaptation/

Bendell, J. (2019b) 'Notes on Hunger and Collapse'. Available at: https:// jembendell.com/2019/03/28/notes-on-hunger-and-collapse/

Kelly, S. (2020) *Living in End Times: On the Threshold of Planetary Initiation*. Revelore Press. Available at: https://revelore.press/public ations/living-in-end-times/

Macy, J. and Young Brown, M. (2014) *Coming Back to Life: The Updated Guide to the Work That Reconnects*, rev. edn. Gabriola Island, BC: New Society Publishers.

Mendosa, M. A. (2019) 'Climate Grief: Is It Real? Solastalgia and Mourning the Loss of the Environment'. *Psychology Today*. Available at: https://www.psychologytoday.com/us/blog/understanding-grief/2 01912/climate-grief-is-it-real

Servigne, P. and Stevens, R. (2020) *How Everything Can Collapse*. Cambridge, UK: Polity Press, pp. 8, 98, 178–9.

Swimme, B. and Berry, T. (1992) *The Universe Story: From the Primordial Flaring Forth to the Ecozoic Era: A Celebration of the Unfolding of the Cosmos*. New York: Harper.

Syme, K. L. and Hagen, E. H. (2019) 'Mental Health is Biological Health: Why Tackling "Diseases of the Mind" is an Imperative for Biological Anthropology in the 21st Century'. *American Journal of Physical Anthropology* 171: 87–117.

Part III

Shifts in Doing

9

Leadership and Management in a Context of Deep Adaptation

Jonathan Gosling

Introduction

In this chapter, my main concern is how to sustain a capacity for leadership to contribute to organizing in ways that remain kind and inclusive while also being effective and appreciated as socially legitimate. Leadership and management are aspects of 'organizing' that traditionally place a special emphasis on the authority of one or a few people. Many other organizing processes are required for productive work and wholesome community life (such as cooperation, peer pressure, self-authorization and coercion: Alvesson and Blom 2019), and all come under pressure when things start to fall apart. These pressures tend to give rise to deep-seated responses to anxiety in individuals, groups and whole societies. Leading deep adaptation in periods of collapsing social structures requires the maturity to tolerate, contain and 'turn' these responses in constructive ways. This can be accomplished through individual initiative as well as through enabling behaviours and structures that allow leadership (along with other membership contributions) from many people.

What we know about leadership in times of collapse

Societies and ways of life have collapsed – many have seen their worlds fall apart. They have been overrun by sudden attack, suffered disease and slow depletion of resources or become riven by internal strife (Cohn 1957). Facing these challenges, people in charge may tend to do 'more of the same', deepening their commitment to existing ways of leading and managing (Diamond 2005).

This is not surprising because they operate through established institutions and make choices according to the values that are admired in that culture and generally to preserve existing power relations. It's rare for an elite to undermine its own privilege, and usually the virtues that are admired in leaders do not include 'willing to give up on our way of life'. As Jonathan Lear puts it:

> By and large a culture will not teach its young: 'These are ways in which you can succeed, and these are ways in which you will fail; these are dangers you might face and here are opportunities; these acts are shameful, and these are worthy of honor – and, oh yes, one more thing, this entire structure of evaluating the world might cease to make sense.' (Lear 2006: 83)

While some aspects of adaptation are about giving up irretrievable aspects of our way of life, others are about discovering new or restoring older ways. This is led not only through the acts and influence of one person or a few people (Bendell, Sutherland and Little 2017). Leadership is an outcome of complex socio-psychological ascriptions of authority drawing on imagination and belief; but also on skilful tactics of people (individuals or groups) who want to get things done, to bolster their identity or to feel themselves part of the force of history. Let's not assume, therefore, that the romantic image of heroic leaders is sufficient to explain leadership, any more than the equally romantic ideal of the consensual community.

Disruptions caused by effects of climate change, biodiversity loss and even a global pandemic such as Covid-19 may be an opportunity to reset the economy – but for most they are a disruption of security and continuity. This reveals a stark and important truth: though we may speak of leaders as bringers of change, mostly they are called on to ensure continuity. Climate change is a huge bundle of threats to continuity, so it's not surprising that established leaders find themselves in the glare of anxious projections from their constituents.

Faced with a shock to the whole system, toughing it out and resisting all but minor reform might work if the turbulence is patchy (perhaps replacing one strong-armed boss with another); but ability to adapt and change is enhanced by flexibility and open-mindedness – by a plurality of perspectives. So much is obvious. But what if the shock is so great that it really shakes the whole structure apart – as might happen if climate-related disaster wipes out staple crops, raises outlandish storms and burns much of the habitable land?

The basis of legitimate authority, once self-evident, is shaken by such disruptions. Some societies have more diverse responses to draw on, so not all are destroyed by crisis: usually those that are already sufficiently pluralistic to accommodate multiple criteria of respect and status. All kinds of people take up leadership of all kinds of activities, including political and community activism to shape the emerging culture.

As social identity theory shows, leaders tend to be the people who best represent the most salient features of a shared identity – who stand for a valued 'us' (Haslam, Reicher and Platow 2011). The more plural and varied the 'us-es', the more diverse the leadership in a society. Cultures that accommodate this kind of plurality have been remarkably robust in the face of existential threats from war, colonization, famine and disease – for example, the countries of the Indian subcontinent. Societies find resilience to existential crises if they already have a diversity of organizing modes. Hierarchies, collectives, enterprising individuals and many who are not ambitious for power or impact yet contribute much to the bonds of love and commitment that actually make up 'society'. They are, as it were, the warp through which the distinctive patterns of culture and institutions are woven (Taylor 2019; Thompson 1997; Thompson, Ellis and Wildavsky 1990).

Nonetheless, uncertainty about imminent collapse prompts emotional responses; while some of these tend to open-heartedness and unselfishness, some can undermine the ability to trust others, tolerate differences, recognize new realities, reassess values and change behaviours (Stein 2004). Leadership can easily promote these less helpful responses, as if the work that people require of their leaders is to deny the reality of the situation or to save them from it. With care and thoughtfulness – one of the aims of this book – a third kind of leadership may emerge: leadership of adaptation. These three may be summarized as follows.

Leadership of denial

This expresses a deep-seated wish for things 'not to be so'. It can be intentional and explicit but can also appear through unconscious acts that veer away from facing up to challenging realities. Climate-change denial has long been actively and consciously led by the oil and coal companies; and unconsciously by many who celebrate unfettered consumerism.

Denial can persist amongst those who admit there is a problem but avoid giving expression to the powerful emotions this evokes. Knowing about the severity of climate change and its likely impacts on lives and livelihoods, perhaps intuiting a turmoil of disturbing emotions, many resort to a cognitive simplification, as if they have to choose between optimism and despair. Leaders may be tempted to assert that 'we must be optimistic' but, if too hasty and absolute, it is a way to deny the full range of emotions and therefore to limit creative, agentic responses.

Still more obscurely, many remain unaware of their own feelings of grief and fear, sublimating the emotional energy towards hatred and despair (Eisenstein 2020). Hence virulent conspiracy theories arise, accusing various 'others' of forcing the problems into view. The leadership methods used in these conspiracy theories may not be that different to the methods of denial promoted by the oil industry – purposeful, tactical and carefully managed. But the appeal is to more visceral drives, directly mobilizing fight (hatred) and flight (despair).

Leadership of salvation

Many people are motivated to take up leadership because they hope to rescue the situation (or at least their community). The desire for rescue is manifest in the way we invest hope in solutions such as carbon capture, hydrogen fuel cells, migration into space and the miraculous effects of mindfulness and prayer.

That we hope to be rescued expresses a profound desire for salvation from the threats around us and from the guilt we feel about our complicity in the crisis. Leadership of salvation is likely to have a religious or apocalyptic character because its energy derives from the intuition that there is another reality, less complex and compromised than this, just behind a veil of misunderstanding and ignorance. It can also make use of professional mystique – the scientists have it in hand, the algorithms will give us warning, the economists have a model, the guru has a mantra. Tangible sources of salvation from climate angst are inclusive social movements such as Extinction Rebellion (XR). The psychological wellness derived from solidarity and activism is undeniable: not all salvation is delusional (at least in the short term); and its motive force may be crucial in overcoming denial and shifting towards creative adaptation.

Leadership of adaptation

This is diverse and sometimes hardly recognizable as leadership. It may be found in counter-cultural experiments, in some protest and some policing, and is often persistent and undemonstrative in the sustaining institutions of society (schools, churches, professions, etc.). It helps us reconcile with the situation, measure the appreciation of risks, grieve when we suffer loss, weigh with discretion when our options seem narrowed and choose pragmatic and courageous change.

Sustained adaptation is not the same as crisis management, but there are similarities and relevant lessons. In a review of critical incidents in atomic power stations, Stein (2004) concludes that:

> [I]n general, a helpful response to the critical period is likely to be one that steers a course between the absence of anxiety (denial) and excessive anxiety (panic). While we should have considerable sympathy for those who ... veer towards one or other of these extremes, those who experience and tolerate an appropriate degree of realistic anxiety have a greater chance of coping and maximizing their chances of surviving the critical period. (Stein 2004: 1253)

Enabling equanimity in anxiety-provoking circumstances is an important function of leadership, whether performed by a designated leader or others in a community. This is true for short-lived crises such as a reactor meltdown, wildfire or flood; and in longer-lasting periods of turmoil. This capacity might be understood as a matter of individual competence (e.g. through practices of mindfulness, self-awareness and self-control) or of collective competence (e.g. practices for inclusive gatherings, psychological containment, collective decision making) (Gosling and Grodecki 2020; Raelin 2011).

I will address some of these competencies and practices below; a summative concept for leadership of adaptation might be that of 'sense-making' and 'sense-giving', particularly important during 'cosmology episodes' when points of orientation are lost and a sense of *vuja dé* ensues – a sense of 'I've never been here before, I have no idea where I am, and I have no idea who can help me' (Weick 1993: 633–4).

Sustaining the capacity for sense-giving over long periods of anxiety, disorientation and worsening conditions is inevitably tenuous, liable to be overrun by political forces for whom denial and salvation are more expedient (Chace, Lynerd and DeSantis 2020).

In practice, the leadership of denial, salvation and adaptation are seldom so clearly separated. The urge to deny a problem exists alongside a wish to be saved from it. Leaders committed to adaptation find themselves called on to offer reassurances and hope of salvation. So what we might call 'the politics of adaptation' involves a complex of conscious and unconscious dynamics, often contradictory. In fact, far from leading adaptation, those who are not swept up in the work of denial or salvation may just be pragmatically reacting to events, trying to sustain operations and keep their organization or community in one piece as anxious colleagues pressure them for certainty and reassurance. This might turn out to be 'adaptation', but it might just as easily be an increasingly desperate attempt to keep all the plates spinning. Leadership could well be something we recognize only in retrospect (if we are granted that opportunity).

But sometimes the differences are clear between leadership of denial, salvation and adaptation. There are prominent leaders today who unashamedly act out the impulses of denial and the fantasy of salvation with no perceptible capacity to lead the work of adaptation. Why is this?

It may be to do with distinctive ways in which we each grow up to process our desires and fears. These become so engrained as to become personality characteristics and a tendency to defend oneself against anxiety in typical ways. Freud (1961 [1931]) posits three types of personality, each associated with distinctive defences towards anxiety-creating situations. Narcissistic defences tend towards denial of external realities that challenge one's self-image; dependent ('erotic' in Freud's initial terminology) defences seek salvation from powerful sources of faith, reason or technology; obsessive defences focus on controlling what can be controlled – ignoring or denigrating what can't (Freud 1961 [1931]; Maccoby 2000). Leaders (like everyone) have a valency towards one or other of these, and their popular appeal derives partly from their ability to represent them in the social and political sphere. Leadership of adaptation requires action that overarches these common defences for, although there are few kinds of human behaviour that are void of ego defence, there are many ways in which it may be transcended.

Social functions performed by leadership

The three kinds of leadership work described above – denial, salvation and adaptation – may express personality types (narcissistic, dependent and obsessive); they also perform important social functions.

A feature of narcissism is the belief that what is good for oneself is good for the whole world: it's why narcissistic leaders impose their vision of 'the way things should be' on entire organizations; and why they like 'transcendent goals', encompassing all within the bounds of their own imagination. Protecting the vision of 'who we are and what is good about us' (as if it's the only reality that counts) could be a crucial aspect of deep adaptation, which is so much about protecting what is precious. Because denial is a perverse expression of the (narcissistic) desire for protection, this could be an axis for leadership development – an idea explored towards the conclusion of this chapter.

Denial becomes such a potent force because it offers to

protect personal self-image and collective culture. For example, admitting the atmospheric impact of coal would so threaten the self-image of Australian politicians and some publics, and the extractive industries are so significant in sustaining the economy that denying their contribution to climate change seems to be the only pragmatic policy. But sooner or later denial will become implausible, and narcissistic defences of personal and collective identities will come in a different form. Though the economic power of extractive industries currently dominates Australian politics, the costs of protecting these industries will be revealed as counterproductive when ecosystems succumb to fire and flood. Some will double-down on denial, but not all. Political and commercial leadership will emerge – with struggle – as this flourishing society evolves a new self-image more adaptive to radical change, which is where the more positive aspect of narcissism comes into play.

In the same way, people following the promise of salvation are expressing their appetite for hope. Crowding into carbon markets and electric vehicles is like craving indulgences in a medieval cathedral that we might be forgiven our sinful ways and be set straight again. The troubles that beset us are so relentless and complex and beyond fixing, no wonder people hope that a *deus ex machina* (or a new learning-machine that will create faultless algorithms) might convert the whole mess into something positive and right. We are familiar with promises of cure-all medicines for coronavirus or any other ailment, but success in saving the world from disease is (almost) always more piecemeal and partial. After 30 years of well-funded research, there is still no vaccine against HIV. But anti-retroviral therapies combined with behavioural changes and significant managerial effort add up to more or less sufficient adaptation to the persistent presence of HIV/AIDS – an adaptation that is more successful in rich countries, though still contingent on many complex aspects of public and personal health. The same limitations will apply to hope vested in other technological fixes: carbon capture, biodiversity reserves and geoengineering. Their effectiveness depends on continuous management and investment.

It's worth noting that leadership of salvation sometimes takes a more apocalyptic trajectory, finding a sense of justice and balance in the collapse of our corrupt and polluting culture. There's an element of this, arguably, in many strands of environmental activism including 'deep adaptation', where contemplating the collapse of industrial colonial capitalism reveals possibilities (which are also necessities) for more authentic and better selves. Current livelihoods cannot be saved from collapse, but we (or our souls) might be saved through it.

In a gentler version of this, communities drawn together by recognition of unfolding collapse (inter alia, deep adaptation, Collapsologie, Dark Mountain, etc.) find that as members give up hope of being saved, they discover something else in the recognition that we are dependent on others – and that 'something else' includes connectedness, curiosity and activism (Bendell and Cave 2020).

Leadership of salvation, in this analysis, has something of the spiritual about it; it can be challenging for leaders to stave off the dependent fantasies projected onto them, however determined they may be to emphasize their limitations and to share leadership. While some may succeed in stepping away, the real leadership challenge is to provide the containment that might enable members of a community to discover their interdependence. We might call this post-salvation leadership that expresses and enables the liberating admission of interdependency, what in Buddhism is referred to as contingent arising – *Pratītyasamutpāda* (Thanisaro Bhikku 1997).

We have linked denial with narcissism, salvation with dependency; and we have indicated how the same personal and interpersonal dynamics can contribute to the work of adaptation when they cease to be dedicated to defending the ego (and associated social identities). The third personality characteristic described by Freud (1961 [1931]) is obsession, a profound identification with an object of attention. In management, it might be associated with the desire to measure and control everything – even with control-freakery. It is therefore a defence much mobilized in the pursuit of more data, more research and constant updating on events. The desire for more certainty can restrict creativity and diversity, restrain progressing into more ambiguous situations. Adaptation arises as the pragmatic attempt to control our fate in the face of uncontrollable change. Flood defence schemes are an example, requiring both engineering ingenuity and subtle, complex negotiations about priorities because protecting one village or habitat usually comes at the cost of sacrificing another.

So although leadership of adaptation draws on the will to control, it also reaches beyond the controllable into matters of negotiation, where differing interests – even contradictory needs – seek resolution. There is space for the energy of the (moderate) narcissist, the dependent and the obsessive. Because the conditions of collapse brought about by severe climate change will excite all these ego defences, leadership of adaptation will mostly fall to those able to balance their energies and bring them to bear on the work . . . which now raises the question: what is the work of adaptation, and what part might be played by leadership?

What it takes to sustain kind, inclusive, effective and legitimate leadership

In an influential paper on deep adaptation to the possibility of societal collapse, Jem Bendell (2018) outlines '4 Rs', which constitute a neat summary of the kinds of work to which leaders could contribute:

1. Resilience, through stewardship of psychological, cultural, natural and material resources.
2. Relinquish habits and possessions that can no longer be sustained.
3. Restore trust, confidence, shared values and other social goods.
4. Reconcile with those who we have fallen out with in recognition of our interdependence and that life is much enhanced by amity and good will.

With this job description, leadership of adaptation is likely to be distributed through the community, much of it 'close up and personal'.

The close and personal work of deep adaptation will need more than leadership: other modes of organizing, such as collaboration, partnering and sharing, will be at the forefront. This is likely to be the work of people who enjoy having an influence on the quality of and outcomes of social life but are not overly anxious about their own identity or status. It will be (it is already) hard to relinquish so much that we enjoy in life, so we will need the promise of happiness, righteousness or mere survival, and that promise is likely to be offered by leadership of sorts – perhaps less strident than the evangelists of hi-tech but nonetheless evocative and bewitching, resonating with our intuitions of higher goods. The leadership of salvation will have its place after all.

But it is also necessary that political, media and business leaders enable policies and strategies to support deep adaptation. The greatest challenge is to stay focused on it. Leaders must contend with social defences against anxiety, as well as their own ego defences. These social defences have similarly energetic and destructive tendencies: to stereotype and attack outsiders, polarize the world into good and bad, us and them, victims and perpetrators. Maintaining an inclusive and generous approach can be politically unpopular even in the best of times; it may be unrealistic to expect it, but there is ample evidence that it is rooted and woven in society far more integrally than is often acknowledged (Bregman 2020); so we should organize for it anyway. It will be evident that everyone is dependent on the same ecosystemic resources – so, as the coronavirus has taught us, no one is secure unless we are all secure; collapsing ecosystems will reduce physical security for all, but perhaps by then we will have strengthened social bonds to compensate. Maybe these will even extend to renewal of the UN or similar instruments of international governance.

What can be done to generate the more desirable modes of leadership and management

This account has focused on individual and social factors that divert leadership towards denial or salvation. People who come to the fore in taking initiative and representing collective work are likely to be those with a valency for specific tasks, including both conscious and unconscious aspects. That valency will be related to their perceived social identity as well as internal factors (such as personality or ego-defences). As we get more into the work of resilience, relinquishment, restoration and reconciliation, and as these become ever more the focus of policy and practice throughout social life, leadership of adaptation will need support and development.

Leadership development should therefore avoid reinforcing the fantastical extremes of denial, salvation and control. There is no comprehensive list of traits that make a great leader for any circumstances, but from the foregoing we can see that a degree of maturity, self-awareness and self-control will increase the chances of ameliorating the more perverse extremes of ego-defence. This will be enhanced by opportunities for reflective and sometimes critical conversations with peers and coaches. Equally important is that others – appreciative of good leadership – become active supporters, critics and contributors. We can contribute to leadership of adaptation by noting and calling out denial, salvation and obsessive control but also by appreciating their obverse: narcissistic visions of an ideal to be protected, the dependent impulse to interact and the obsessive desire for understanding.

Leadership of deep adaptation will be a collective accomplishment, and it is best developed as a collaborative, reflective effort.

References

Alvesson, M. and Blom, M. (2019) 'Beyond Leadership and Followership: Working with a Variety of Modes of Organizing'. *Organizational Dynamics* 48(1): 28–37.

Bendell, J. (2018) 'Deep Adaptation: A Map for Navigating the Climate Tragedy'. *Occasional Paper 2, Initiative for Leadership and Sustainability, University of Cumbria*. Available at: https://iflas.blogspot.com/2018/07/new-paper-on-deep-adaptation-to-climate.html

Bendell, J. and Cave, D. (2020) 'Does Anticipating Societal Collapse Motivate Pro-social Behaviours?' *Initiative for Leadership and Sustainability, University of Cumbria*. Available at: http://iflas.blogspot.com/2020/06/does-anticipating-societal-collapse.html

Bendell, J., Sutherland, N. and Little, R. (2017) 'Beyond Unsustainable Leadership: Critical Social Theory for Sustainable Leadership'. *Sustainability Accounting, Management and Policy Journal* 8(4): 418–44.

Bregman, R. (2020). *Humankind*. London: Bloomsbury.

Chace, S., Lynerd, B. T. and DeSantis, A. (2020) '"A Distant Mirror": Sensemaking in the Era of Trump'. *Leadership*. September.

Cohn, N. (1957) *The Pursuit of the Millennium: Revolutionary Millenarians and Mystical Anarchists of the Middle Ages*. Oxford: Oxford University Press.

Diamond, J. (2005) *Collapse: How Societies Choose to Fail or Succeed*. London: Penguin.
Eisenstein, C. (2020) *The Coronation*. Available at: https://charleseisenstein.org/essays/the-coronation/
Freud, S. (1961 [1931]) 'Libidinal Types', *The Standard Edition of the Complete Psychological Works of Sigmund Freud* 21: 215–20.
Gosling, J. and Grodecki, A. (2020) 'Competencies for Responsible Management (and Leadership) Education', in D. Moosemayer, O. Laasch, C. Parkes and A. Brown (eds), *Responsible Management Leadership and Education*. London: Sage.
Haslam, S. A., Reicher, S. and Platow, M. (2011) *A New Psychology of Leadership: Identity, Influence and Power*. Hove: Psychology Press.
Lear, J. (2006) *Radical Hope: Ethics in the Face of Cultural Devastation*. Cambridge, MA: Harvard University Press.
Maccoby, M. (2000) 'Narcissistic Leaders: The Incredible Pros, the Inevitable Cons'. *Harvard Business Review* (Sept.)
Raelin J. (2011) 'From Leadership-as-Practice to Leaderful Practice'. *Leadership* 7(2): 195–211.
Stein, M. (2004) 'The Critical Period of Disasters: Insights from Sensemaking and Psychoanalytic Theory'. *Human Relations* 57(10): 1243–61.
Taylor, M. (2019) 'Why Balance is the Key to Success'. London: Royal Society of the Arts. Available at: https://www.thersa.org/blog/matthew-taylor/2019/05/balance
Thānissaro Bhikku (1997) *The Great Causes Discourse Mahā Nidāna Sutta* (DN15). Available at: https://www.dhammatalks.org/suttas/DN/DN 15.html
Thompson, M. (1997) 'Security and Solidarity: An Anti-Reductionist Framework for Thinking about the Relationship between Us and the Rest of Nature'. *Geographical Journal* 163(2): 141–9.
Thompson, M., Ellis, R. and Wildavsky, A. (1990) *Cultural Theory*. Boulder, CO: Westview Press.
Weick, K. E. (1993) 'The Collapse of Sensemaking in Organizations: The Mann Gulch Disaster'. *Administrative Science Quarterly* 38(4): 628–52.

10

What Matters Most: Deep Education Conversations in a Climate of Change and Complexity

Charlotte von Bülow and Charlotte Simpson

'Perhaps figuring out what matters most matters most.'

Redefine School 2020

As a global community, we are facing unprecedented levels of uncertainty. Today's children are born into a world in which old narratives are being deconstructed at great speed – society no longer holds a promise of security, and education systems around the world can no longer defend the certitude we used to associate with a schooling in the knowledge economy (Lauder 2012; Macdonald 2005). In the midst of it all, we are facing a crisis of values (Crawford 2015) in which it is becoming ever more challenging to discern what matters most. As personal and professional lives are increasingly lived online, our attentional behaviours are being tracked and traded in an *attention economy* we did not all knowingly elect to join (Williams 2017; Zuboff 2019). This extraordinary situation is unfolding against the backdrop of a global pandemic and a likely near-term climate-induced societal collapse (Bendell 2018; Harmer, Leetz and Eder 2020; Orr 2009), the magnitude of which has given voice to some but silenced many.

In this chapter, we instigate a conversation about the future of education in this context of uncertainty and intensifying complexity; our conception of a *deep education* is a direct response to the call for *deep adaptation* (Bendell 2018). By putting an emphasis on the importance of *conversation*, we are suggesting that education, in the spirit of deep adaptation, needs to be co-created and situated rather than centralized, overly systematized and replicated. Our proposition for a deep education is not a new syllabus, nor is it a system. Replicated practices can become dislocated practices (Bülow 2020) and we cannot afford to repeat the failures of the past (Biesta 2006; Robinson 2007). Instead, we are putting forward another way of thinking about education that can inspire all those who feel responsible for it to make bold decisions. We agree with Tochon, who says, 'Deep education is something people want to live and work for. It is never fully achieved, it is always in the making, and depends upon situations' (2010: 2).

No one can predict exactly how the disruptions to our way of life will unfold, but it is clear that the pace of change is outstripping old ways of being. When we consider education in the context of potential societal collapse, we need to recognize that conditions may arise that will eventually challenge the existence of education as we know it. Individual schools may be faced with urgent decisions about how to engage with their communities in order to prepare for hitherto unimagined events. The 'curriculum, campus, community, culture' model (Jones, Selby and Sterling 2010) is an example of a helpful framework for educators, leaders and wider stakeholders in education to begin to address *what matters most* and take action during this period of relative stability, where it still exists.

In order to prepare children and young people for the more disruptive impacts they may face beyond our lifetimes, we stress the need to become role models for how to think, feel and act in new ways – we need to discover how to respond, intentionally and in cooperation, to the uncertainty and complexity we are facing. Instead of assuming knowledge or easing our fear of uncertainty by reaching for outdated or inappropriate solutions (Bülow and Simpson 2020), we propose that it is in open, honest conversations about *what matters most* that we may find the courage to take the next important steps. This is a theme we return to below.

After years in education at all levels and two decades of working within the sector, we embrace the absence of ready answers and set out to explore instead what lives in the hearts and minds of others who are concerned with the education question today.

In what follows, we are reporting on an inquiry in which the 'Deep Adaptation Framework' (Bendell 2018) was adopted as a springboard for a series of conversations with different groups of people engaged in education. The substance of this chapter is a distillation of findings from these conversations, accompanied by observations and reflections. We conclude with a discussion of key themes and end by signposting two examples of innovative practice among the many that are emerging across the globe.

The distillations of a deep adaptation inquiry

In the early part of 2020, we set out to establish what questions and concerns live among people who are directly involved in education today, focusing on the United Kingdom for our study. We articulated a set of questions based on the four keystones (the Rs) of the deep adaptation agenda, as articulated by Bendell (2019). Over a period of eight weeks, we facilitated a series of gatherings with groups of young people currently in education, pre-school parents and aspiring parents, schoolteachers and students in higher education. This inquiry succeeded a wider consultation with educators and educational entrepreneurs from around the world in which examples of innovative approaches and practices were explored.

The four questions posed to participating groups were as follows:

Resilience
What aspects of education as we know it would we want to develop and learn from in a climate of change and complexity?

Relinquishment
What aspects of education as we know it would we want to let go of?

Restoration
What would we want to reintroduce into education?

Reconciliation
How can education facilitate acceptance as well as agency?

We acknowledge the specificity of these questions and stress that the intention here was to instigate conversations and sow seeds for further exploration rather than to find solutions. Accompanied by observations and reflections, we present in what follows key themes emerging from these conversations.

Resilience: what aspects of education as we know it would we want to develop and learn from in a climate of change and complexity?

We noted with interest that none of the participating groups proposed a complete or even partial adoption of current education systems. Most participants were sceptical about the future of conventional education in a context of uncertainty and potential societal collapse. Yet two specific, interrelated themes stood out in all conversations, and these are worth drawing attention to.

Firstly, participants agreed that early years educators and pre-schools that keep the focus on play and discovery are supporting developmental processes that are not only positive but essential. Participants highlighted that spaces where children can socialize and experience their emotions without formal evaluation or testing are crucial in order to foster self-confidence and a sense of agency. It was suggested that the short period in our lives where play and discovery come naturally to us is a time that fosters capabilities that help us cope with emotional challenges and ambiguities later in life. Play, it was noted, is a powerful way of developing emotional resilience, and participants were concerned that early testing undermines conducive environments free of judgement. It was pointed out that whilst certain pre-schools remain deeply committed to the promotion of play, exploration and discovery without assessment, the pressure on such places to conform to a more test-driven pedagogy (Garvis, Harju-Luukkainen and Yngvesson 2019) has increased in several countries in recent years. It was suggested that this move to evaluate very young children creates an underlying performance anxiety that slowly undermines the development of individual agency.

The other prevalent theme that emerged in these conversations was concerned with the developmental role of positive teacher–pupil relationships. Participants shared stories about

inspirational teachers who had affected their educational journeys in powerful ways. Despite the increasing pressure to meet
academic targets and take on larger class numbers, it was agreed
that there are still teachers who are committed to going beyond
the *teaching to the test* approach (Firestone, Schorr and Monfils
2004) and who strive to create learning environments that inspire
meaningful relational processes. Stories that were shared revealed
the power of stimulating, inspirational teacher–pupil relationships and how such experiences contributed to the development
of self-confidence and trust in later life. Participants emphasized that positive role models in the formative years help the
child develop the capacities needed to navigate in a complex and
unpredictable world. Certain groups shared a deep concern about
educational contexts that seek to equalize the relationship of
pupils and teachers, thus posing a risk to the power of a formative connection based on differences (Biesta 2006, 2020). Whilst
recognizing both challenges and risks associated with the issue, it
was suggested that positive experiences of authority and mastery
nurture emerging moral ideals and aspirations (Crawford 2015;
Sennett 2003), and these inform our values, decisions and actions
throughout life.

Where these two themes intersect, we hear a call to safeguard
two powerful cornerstones of childhood: firstly, the experience
of play and discovery in an environment that is liberated from
formal testing; and secondly, the power of positive relationships with adults that can engender aspirations towards mastery.
Reasons for preserving these particular cornerstones were concerned with the links to the development of capacities that
participants considered vital for a life that involves increasing
levels of felt ambiguity and complexity.

Relinquishment: what aspects of education as we know it would we want to let go of?

First and foremost, participants were eager to let go of the passive
learning style that dominates so many current education systems
around the world. There was a strong consensus that sitting in
a classroom and memorizing information is not conducive to a
stimulating learning experience. There were calls instead for processes that prepare pupils for life beyond exams and, in general,

grades were found to be an unnecessary source of stress and anxiety. This was felt particularly strongly by young adults currently in education and teachers who lamented the stress induced on all parties by regular testing. A learning space that is punctuated with fear of judgement leaves little room for independent thought, and participants felt that there was no opportunity for creativity where the main aim was to score highly on a standardized test.

Young adults and students in higher education complained about the repetitive and competitive nature of schooling and proposed a more cooperative framework. It was noted that the sense of individualism and competition within school communities today perpetuate the same values that are accelerating us into climate-induced collapse. Teachers explained how the pressure to 'hit targets' leaves little time to innovate, and this has led to the contentious 'one-size-fits-all' classroom experience that does not 'fit all'.

Young adults stated that they felt stifled by a system that imposed certain subjects on them and prioritized academic intelligence above all else. This left those with different gifts feeling unstimulated, disconnected and with a sense of failure. Teachers and students in higher education focused particularly on the problematic nature of traditional curricula that separate disciplines without a sense of how they connect, and they proposed that education needs to recognize interconnectedness rather than ignore or deny it (Tochon 2010). They emphasized that humanities subjects largely still promote the idea that humans are separate from nature, and this mindset at the heart of education leads us to see nature as a resource to be exploited. Instead, they suggested, we need focus on developing a sense of belonging to what one person called the 'community of life'.

It was suggested that conventional school education should urgently let go of the notion that objective, scientific knowledge is superior to all other kinds of knowledge. By prioritizing rational, disinterested, technical observation, said some, traditional education is at risk of casting the human being in the role of disconnected bystanders, as opposed to teaching us about our connection with the natural environment.

These conversations invite a review of the pervasive use of common measurements in education (for a thorough critique, see Biesta 2010), and if we consider the possibility of societal collapse, we need to urgently revisit why we are placing such emphasis on testing in schools and what we are testing for. Conversations with participants further validated that the crisis of values we are facing, and the resultant confusion about what to care about (Bülow 2020; Crawford 2015), might be rooted partly in an education that has promoted a mindset of separation and disconnect, rather than a sense of belonging (Orr 2009). If we are conditioned to experience the world as spectators, rather than participants, we are at risk of simply replacing one set of reductive values with another. The conversations we need to have about education must go deeper and reach the core of what it means to be human. Only then might we discover 'our place in the family of things' (Oliver 2004: 110).

Restoration: what would we want to reintroduce into education?

Conversations about education in the context of increasing uncertainty and complexity inspired participants to explore how capacities to re-imagine new ways of living are developed. In one group, the power of play was felt to be one of the most effective ways to connect with others and the natural environment. Others emphasized how low-intensity social opportunities without judgement inspired connection and sense of belonging. There was deep concern about education that is largely facilitated online or indoors, and this was felt to widen the gap between children and the natural world. Teachers called for a more situated, village-style schooling, where people of all ages would interact with each other and the local environment and in which children would have the opportunity to learn from their elders and vice versa. There was a sense that our horizontal school system, where classes consist of students of the same age, misses out on the wisdom that can be passed across generations.

Participants wanted a reintroduction of life skills. Students in higher education felt that it was important for children and young people to learn how to grow their own food. They argued that not only would this have practical benefits as they gained knowledge and experience of sustaining themselves, but it might also help them to cultivate a deeper appreciation of nature. This could also play a part in addressing the food waste crisis, it was suggested. Furthermore, a reintroduction of life skills, making and mending was considered valuable – this would reduce reliance on external suppliers and mitigate the perpetuation of consumer culture. These types of skills are empowering and allow children and young people to develop a sense of self-reliance and capability.

All conversations expressed a longing to re-engage with the physicality of matter and a deep need for learning that empowers. In Crawford (2015), Gordon and Bülow (2012), Robinson (2007) and Sennett (2003) among others, we find the call for an education that offers both facilitated and spontaneous opportunities for a meeting with resistance in the way that only engagement in practical skills activities provides. This is the counter-gesture we need to adopt to avoid the disempowering experiences created by the digital treadmill of incompetence (Williams 2017). A continual state of ignorance is imposed upon us by the attention economy with its updates to our digital technology that leave us ever the beginners and never the masters of gadgets we now completely rely on. This absence of mastery leads to resignation and lethargy, which undermine our natural sense of agency. The encounter with matter and the natural authority that it offers fosters determination and flow experiences that empower (Nakamura and Csikszentmihalyi 2009) – not through short-lived gratification but through hard-won, lasting competence.

Reconciliation: how can education facilitate acceptance as well as agency?

In response to this question, the dominant theme that emerged was concerned with the importance of honesty and the impact of its absence. Participants felt that educators today must endeavour to communicate, as truthfully and accurately as is possible, the reality of our global situation and to promote acceptance of the uncertainty we are facing as a result. Education should aim to facilitate meaningful discussions where children and young people can speak openly about their feelings in order to process them effectively and arrive at a place of acceptance and empowerment. Teachers found that one of the biggest obstacles to facilitating meaningful discussions about climate change and its impact was the lack of time and opportunity, leading to difficult questions being left behind. All participants recognized that the issue of climate-induced societal collapse is a topic that preoccupies young people today and often has them feeling anxious and helpless. It was suggested that the creation of a 'safe space' that is not constrained to a timetable window would be helpful in allowing pupils to voice their concerns and work through the issue with a sense of togetherness.

Some groups proposed that the development of agency would be better facilitated if young people were given more opportunities to engage in meaningful decision making and experience instances of failure and success in a space that embraces the value of both. This would inspire independent thinking, self-confidence and a heightened sense of responsibility for self and others, they suggested.

Storytelling was proposed as another powerful way of exploring and developing agency (an example can be found in Hull and Katz 2006). Teachers in particular were concerned that the story being told to young people today is one that undermines the agentive self – it promotes a future in which young people are cast as cogs in an industrial machine that will have broken down by the time they leave school. We need a new story to tell young people, they suggested, and education should encourage that we never perpetuate an old narrative without scrutiny.

Finally, participants discussed the power of gratitude. Some argued that this attitude has the power to override the story of anthropocentric entitlement to nature's resources and inspire us to rewrite a narrative of reciprocity. Resisting stories of wealth creation is an impossible task unless new and more powerful stories about what matters can be co-created. Education, they noted, is the right context for exploring new stories – it is the foundation from which we begin to determine what we value and what we care about.

The deep education conversation

As we consider the findings from these conversations, we observe with interest that all groups were silent on the subject of educating for the knowledge economy (Lauder 2012) and there may be several reasons for that. Two questions are worth asking here: firstly, are we so deeply embedded in the knowledge economy that we take it for granted and forget to question, or indeed mention it, when given the opportunity to explore the future of education? Or are we not concerned with knowledge-focused education anymore? Are we disillusioned – has it simply not delivered? These questions notwithstanding, we are unconvinced that the acquisition of knowledge plays no significant role for the groups we consulted; instead, we assume that what is in focus now is the conception of new educational practices that include the acquisition of knowledge as part of widening curricula that equally promote the development of inner attitudes, such as individual and collective resilience, cooperation and personal agency.

In our conversations about 'resilience' and what we would want to maintain in an education of the future, we heard the call to early childhood educators and schools to maintain the cornerstones of childhood with the promotion of unassessed play and discovery. The other important insight was about the importance of forming adult–child relationships (Biesta 2006, 2020) that inspire trust and self-confidence. On the question of 'relinquishment', we learnt that the schools need to dial down the emphasis on standardized testing and refocus education on cooperation, rather than competition (Biesta 2006; Firestone, Schorr and Monfils 2004; Garvis, Harju-Luukkainen and Yngvesson 2019). It was suggested that transdisciplinary and inter-generational approaches would be a means of addressing this. On the question of what we wish to let go of, we also heard that the prevalent mindset that still informs conventional curricula is at risk of widening the gap between humans and nature. The call was for a situated education with a focus on our interconnectedness with the natural environment (Orr 2009; Stone 2005; Tochon 2010). Conversations about 'restoration' yielded the need to reintroduce in education a focus on the development of mastery through meaningful practical activities (Crawford 2015; Sennet 2003). The absence of the kind of flow experiences afforded by such activities deprives children and young people from healthy absorption and stifles the development of self-discipline and the agentive self (Nakamura and Csikszentmihalyi 2009). As we opened up the conversation about 'reconciliation', groups responded with a deep-felt call for safe spaces where children and young people can learn to *be with* and *language* their emotions – spaces for truth and honesty where trust and confidence can grow. Groups stressed the significance of developing gratitude and reciprocity and issued an invitation to explore how education can *go deeper* and take us *beyond ourselves* (Orr 2009).

So on the premise that most current education systems are created in the image of a world that no longer exists (if it ever did), our findings suggest, as do others (especially Biesta 2006, 2020; Egan 2008; Robinson 2007), that the idea of a one-size-fits-all education system was always going to fall short. In the context of uncertainty and the potential of societal collapse, we agree that education must be co-created, situated in the current global context but conceived in creative dialogue with the immediate natural, social and cultural environments in which the educational journeys unfold.

The deep challenge

At this point, we will sketch out the deep challenge facing us in an endeavour to re-imagine education at this time. We do this not to discourage action but to anchor our findings in the reality as we perceive it and bring into awareness some of the major obstacles to change.

In recent years, regular reports have raised awareness of the impact of education as an *industry* (Biesta 2020), and this is linked to the effects on children and young people of living and learning in the *attention economy* (Bülow 2020; OECD 2018). Educational research confirms that it is not too late to change educational approach but that we need to create consensus about *what matters most* in the context of radical global change (Stone 2005). Indeed, the question, 'What matters most?', should be easy to answer – if we know what we care most about then, presumably, we also know what matters most to us. It is far from simple, however – whilst this question offers opportunities for discourse and discovery among us, it generates ever more discontent, disharmony and disruption in our world. When we try to collaborate and find consensus about what we value or how value is measured, we find that what matters most to some, matters less – or not at all – to others. We suggest with Crawford (2015) that this points to a widespread confusion about what we should give attention to and what to care about.

We observe how recent events have split communities into political tribes that tell very different stories about what matters: in one tribe, a global pandemic might be framed as a catastrophic distraction from a climate emergency we should be giving our undivided attention to; in another tribe, the climate crisis is a distraction from giving attention to individual wealth creation. In the context of recent global events, the coronavirus challenge is a good example. Its arrival among us has highlighted that a dominating narrative, holding large parts of the world in its grip, is one that focuses in on our inherent fear of endings and death. Death represents the ultimate ending for some, but it is the promise of a new beginning for others. Western culture in particular suffers from a widespread resistance to endings (Wong and Tomer 2011) – this was also the issue that informed the hitherto most frequent response to the proposition that we are likely facing near-term climate-induced societal collapse. When faced with the potential dissolution of old ways of being, the prevailing tendency we have witnessed is best described as a head-in-the-sand approach – the unspoken rationale is that if we give attention to something else, perhaps the problem ceases to exist or goes away.

What these stories all have in common, we propose, is that '*it matters what we pay attention to* and *what we pay attention to becomes what matters*' (Bülow 2020: 167). There are two aspects to this that are worth exploring in the context of the education question. Firstly, the choices we make with our attention signal to our environment *what matters to us*. This becomes evident in a normal social encounter when, for example, the person one is having a conversation with attends to their phone instead of the conversation – the result of this attentional action may evoke a feeling of being unimportant. Secondly, our attention is frequently captured by *what matters to others*, and this is a perfectly common experience that can also be positive. Yet, if we are subjected to an increasing volume of unchosen external stimuli, our level of *attentional agency* is under threat. In such an environment, we are at risk of losing the self-discipline required to resist clicking on an advert that promises something we do not in fact care about – and in that moment, we relinquish a level of attentional freedom.

The notion of *freedom* in the attention economy is most

commonly framed as *freedom to* or *freedom from* (see also MacCallum 1967). When our experience of freedom is positioned as a relative state in this way, it is at risk of being reduced to a pursuit of basic desires. We desire to *be where we are not*, to *have what we have not* – or we long for liberation from what we do have. The power of the advertising industry enhances these desires and the message that we can *have more* is everywhere – it does not discriminate in the way it targets children, young people and adults.

As circumstances beyond our immediate control increasingly force us to live our lives online, we need to recognize how the liberation from attentional capture may become one of the deepest challenges in the endeavour to prepare children and young people for a very different future. If we continue to ignore the impact of the current prevalent lifestyle and remain captured in a state of flux between the fulfilment of basic desires, we are in danger of going to sleep with our heads still in the sand.

If instead we invite children and young people to co-create new, situated ways of learning with us, we may restore their faith in the value of education and, at the same time, challenge the idea that what matters most to some matters to us all.

The call to action

We suggest that deep education goes to the core of what it means to be human and that it comes with an invitation to have honest and open conversations that explore how we may coexist across differences and cease to live by a single story about what matters most. As educators, we are storytellers and, in this role, we have both power and influence when it comes to the narratives that children and young people grow up to live by. The transformation of education relies on a transformation of educators, and we may start today by practising acceptance, gratitude and reciprocity. We agree with Tochon, who says, 'Deep Education promotes a philosophy of curriculum that explains and addresses the current stakes and that requires a deep transformation of humans and human society in the direction of greater harmony' (2010: 5).

With our inquiry, we issue an invitation to those who feel co-responsible for re-imagining education to learn and discern, with the children and young people of today and tomorrow, what matters now. We propose that *deep education conversations* are crucial if we want to inform new stories and ways of being as we enter ever deeper into a climate of radical global and societal change and complexity.

Emerging global practices

Finally, we wish to bring attention to a couple of examples of the many emerging global practices that help renew the conversation about education. We encourage those seeking inspiration to connect with each other and establish supporting networks so that conversations can be had and action taken. Lastly, our deep thanks go to all the people who participated in this study and to the courageous educators around the world who dare to do things differently.

Workshops on climate breakdown: Simona Vaitkute, Lithuania

This initiative runs camps, courses and workshops that facilitate a space where honest conversation and authentic connection can take place. The workshops allow children and young people to express their feelings about climate breakdown and societal collapse in a safe and supportive environment. The workshops also present an opportunity for children and young people to explore ideas and solutions to engage with the climate crisis. Using an open-space discussion format, participants become very animated and engaged when they are allowed to contribute and collaborate on something meaningful together. This experience of open sharing and authentic, passionate involvement helps us process feelings of helplessness and arrive at a place of agency.

Self-directed education (SDE) and full human rights-experience education (FHREE): Je'anna Clements, Riverstone Village, South Africa

SDE is consent-based learning that is based on life experience and self-chosen activities – it is learning carried out by young people and for young people. Adult assistance is readily available when it is desired but, importantly, young people have the same amount of agency over their learning as adults do in their adult education. At FHREE SDE, young people are completely in charge of how they spend their time and what they give their energy and attention to. Therefore, most learning occurs through innate curiosity and their choices are personally meaningful. SDE FHREE helps to inspire creativity, joy, critical thinking, confidence, adaptability and agency in the face of change and challenge. It maintains life's natural flow of change and complexity and allows the young people to embrace their innate sense of initiative and empowerment.

References

Bendell, J. (2018) 'Deep Adaptation: A Map for Navigating Climate Tragedy'. Available at: www.iflas.info

Bendell, J. (2019, March 17) 'The Love in Deep Adaptation – A Philosophy for the Forum'. Available at: https://jembendell.com/2019/03/17/the-love-in-deep-adaptation-a-philosophy-for-the-forum/

Biesta, G. J. (2006) *Beyond Learning: Democratic Education for a Human Future*. Boulder, CO: Paradigm Publishers.

Biesta, G. (2010) *Good Education in an Age of Measurement: Ethics, Politics, Democracy*. New York: Routledge.

Biesta, G. (2020) 'Perfect Education, But Not for Everyone: On Society's Need for Inequality and the Rise of Surrogate Education'. *Zeitschrift für Pädagogik* 66(1): 8–14.

Bülow, C. von (2020) 'The Practice of Attention in the Workplace – Phenomenological Accounts of Lived Experience'. (Thesis). Bristol: University of the West of England Research Repository.

Bülow, C. von and Simpson, P. (forthcoming) 'Managing in Uncertainty: Contributions of Negative Capability'.

Crawford, M. (2015) *The World Beyond Your Head: How to Flourish in an Age of Distraction*. (Kindle edn). London: Penguin.

Egan, K. (2008) *The Future of Education: Reimagining Our Schools from the Ground Up*. London: Yale University Press.

Firestone, A., Schorr, L. and Monfils, L. (2004) *The Ambiguity of Teaching to the Test: Standards, Assessment, and Educational Reform*. London: Routledge.

Garvis, S., Harju-Luukkainen, H. and Yngvesson, T. (2019) 'Towards a Test-Driven Early Childhood Education: Alternative Practices to Testing Children', in G. Barton and S. Garvis (eds), *Compassion and Empathy in Educational Contexts*. Cham: Palgrave Macmillan.

Gordon, A. and Bülow, C. von (2012) 'Re-Imagining Potential: A Collaborative Action Inquiry'. Cotswolds, UK: RSUC.

Harmer, A., Leetz, A. and Eder, B. (2020) 'Time for WHO to Declare Climate Breakdown a PHEIC?' *Lancet* 396(10243): 23–4.

Hull, G. and Katz, M.-L. (2006) 'Crafting an Agentive Self: Case Studies of Digital Storytelling'. *Research in the Teaching of English* 41(1): 43–81.

Jones, P., Selby, S. and Sterling, S. (2010) *Sustainability Education: Perspectives and Practice across Higher Education*. London: Earthscan.

Lauder, H. (2012) *Educating for the Knowledge Economy: Critical Perspectives*. London: Routledge.

MacCallum, G. C. (1967) 'Negative and Positive Freedom'. *Philosophical Review* 76(3): 312–34.

Macdonald, H. (2005) 'Schools for a Knowledge Economy'. *Policy Futures in Education* 3(1).

Nakamura, J. and Csikszentmihalyi, M. (2009) 'Flow Theory and Research', in C. R. Snyder and S. J. Lopez (eds), *Oxford Handbook of Positive Psychology*, 2nd edn. Oxford: Oxford University Press, pp. 89–105.

OECD (2018) 'Children and Young People's Mental Health in the Digital Age Shaping the Future'. Available at: http://www.oecd.org/health/health-systems/Children-and-Young-People-Mental-Health-in-the-Digital-Age.pdf

Oliver, M. (2004) *New and Selected Poems, Vol. 1*. Boston, MA: Beacon Press.

Orr, D. (2009) *Down to the Wire: Confronting Climate Collapse*. New York: Oxford University Press.

Redefine School (2020) 'be you. a quiet revolution'. Redefine School. Available at: https://redefineschool.com

Robinson, S. K. (2007) 'Do Schools Kill Creativity?' TED. Available at: http://youtu.be/iG9CE55wbtY

Sennett, R. (2003) *Respect: The Formation of Character in an Age of Inequality*. London: Penguin Books.

Stone, M. K. (2005) *Ecological Literacy: Educating Our Children for a Sustainable World*. Berkeley, CA: California University Press.

Tochon, F. V. (2010) 'Deep Education'. *Journal for Educators, Teachers and Trainers* 1: 1–12.

Williams, J. (2017) 'The Attention Economy'. Available at: https://www.youtube.com/watch?v=xxyRf3hfRXg

Wong, P. E. and Tomer, A. (2011) 'Beyond Terror and Denial: The Positive Psychology of Death Acceptance'. *Death Studies* 35(2): 99–106.

Zuboff, S. (2019) *The Age of Surveillance Capitalism: The Fight for a Human Future at the New Frontier of Power*. London: Profile Books.

11

Riding Two Horses:
The Future of Politics and Activism,
as We Face Potential Eco-driven
Societal Collapse

Rupert Read

You don't have to believe that the uneven ending – the collapse – of our civilization is inevitable in order to believe in the profound importance of deep adaptation. It is enough to believe that it is definitely *possible*: because the precautionary principle then dictates the need for an 'insurance policy', given our exposure to such profound damage. I believe that this civilization is without doubt *coming to an end*,[1] and that that ending is likely going to take the form, not only possibly but probably, of collapse. Only: *not* inevitably, not certainly.[2]

This belief changes everything in politics; it means that *the politics of 'sustainability' is over* (because one can no longer take for granted that we are going to be able to sustain anything even remotely like our current arrangements),[3] and that instead *our*

---

[1] i.e. *This Civilisation is Finished*, as the title of my recent book of that name directly insists (Read and Alexander 2019).

[2] For detail on this point of disagreement between myself and Jem, see chapter 4 of my book, *Extinction Rebellion: Insights from the Inside* (Read 2020a). See also chapters 8, 9 and 11 in that book for relevant discussion. Jem and I explain how nevertheless there is by and large a rapprochement between our views in the conclusion to the present work; and this important point is also developed in the remainder of the present chapter.

[3] See John Foster's book, *After Sustainability* (2015). What is also of course overcome by this profound change is the fantasy of 'sustainable development'. See

politics becomes a sphere for frankly desperate efforts (which should be centred in transformative adaptation[4]*) to bring about a 'compassionate revolution' in time conceivably still to head off collapse, AND of profound efforts to begin the process of deep adaptation.* (I shall explain shortly why it is necessary simultaneously to pursue both – and why doing so is highly synergistic.)

Our politics, despite the burgeoning awakening of the last few years, are still very far from this condition. Most people (including most in the 'environmental' movement) are still not ready to accept that the politics of sustainability is over, let alone to accept that it now makes sense to put considerable energy into deep adaptation or even (in many cases) into adaptation at all (Phillips, Bridewell and Richards 2019; The Glacier Trust).

But there is no alternative. Anything less than the acceptance of the two points emphasized above is simply a soft denialism. A desperate Pollyanna-ism.

Moreover, the main reason why such soft denialism is still rife is that there remains a widespread dogma that assumes that unless we all keep pretending that there is a strong likelihood of our being able to effect a green transition at scale and in time to head off collapse, then we will lose faith, burn out, demoralize our followers and guarantee failure. Call this dogma 'the necessity for environmental Pollyanna-ism' (NFEP, for short).

The truth is the *reverse* of the NFEP. Extinction Rebellion (XR) has shown this very clearly indeed. XR has been a successful refutation of the dogma that one has to put on a happy face and pretend that everything is going to be fine if one is to have

Helena Norberg-Hodge's book, *Ancient Futures* (1991); and my plenary Mahbub ul-Haq lecture (Read 2019a).

[4] My conception of transformative adaptation (TrAd) – for which, see *Transformative Adaptation: A Declaration* (Read unpublished(a)) – is more radical than that found in most of the academic literature. It is based in the plain acknowledgement, first encapsulated in Green House's book *Facing Up to Climate Reality* (Foster 2019), that dangerous climate change and a rising tide of climate disasters are definitely coming, and that it is too late for only a 'mitigation'-centric approach to these, and it encompasses a scepticism that there will be an adequate 'top-down' approach to this dire situation, and thus it embraces the need inter alia for non-violent direct action, a benign form of taking matters into our own hands.

a successful 'environmental' social movement.[5] The very name 'Extinction Rebellion' brings forth possible/likely/near-certain 'apocalyptic' visions of the future against which we are rebelling (albeit that much of that rebelling takes place in a spirit of love, even joy). If the NFEP dogma were true, then XR should have been an abject failure, rather than (as it actually has done) transforming UK discourse and consciousness around climate (Todd 2019) and echoing strongly around the world.

Moreover, the assumption that without NFEP we are more likely as activists to burn out is again the reverse of the truth. It turns out that a number of XR activists, including some leaders of the movement, were influenced by deep adaptation. It fuelled their rage and resolve.[6] It turns out that burnout for most of us is *less* likely if we are given a broadly truthful picture of the darkness of our time as opposed to if we keep being surprised that (e.g.) the Conference of the Parties (COP) process is failing us utterly.[7] And it turns out that XR, while very much an imperfect human artefact, has at least tried to wisely design an anti-burnout 'regenerative culture' into its DNA; it is the first 'environmental' movement that is actually premised on its activists being helped

[5] Though let me be clear: XR has not of course succeeded in its aims; nowhere near. In the main text of this chapter (and in my book), I emphasize mainly the successes of XR; but its story is also a painfully sad one in that the substance of its demands remains almost as remote as ever, and it appears to no longer be growing, to be far short of the size that would be needed for it to tip the balance of power in society, and to have become pretty stuck in unpopularity. XR is not, it turns out, going to be the *agent*, if there is one at all, that intervenes successfully to prevent collapse. This implies looking to different flanks, either radical or (much more likely) 'vanilla', to become (or to midwife) that agent: which is how I envisage the movement that my next book, *Parents for a Future* (Read 2021), hopes to seed. But as I shall discuss below, the meaning of this brutal truth about the limitations to which XR is subject crucially includes also a need to emphasize non-shallow adaptation much more.

[6] As, in parallel, did my own starkly realistic vision in the run-up to the launch of XR, 'This Civilization is Finished' (Read 2018a), a Cambridge University public lecture which went viral and has been viewed more than 100,000 times on YouTube. Many XRebels have told me it was the reason they got involved. The sequel, 'Climate Catastrophe: The Case for Rebellion' (Read 2019b), has been viewed in total over 300,000 times.

[7] Conference of the Parties is an international body of the United Nations Framework Convention on Climate Change. It meets yearly to discuss international action on climate breakdown.

not to burn out. (The temporal cycle of rebellions is only the most obvious aspect of this anti-burnout 'regen culture'.)

It is true that there is moral hazard in holding that we can count on collapse. This is why I have expressed concerns about the deep adaptation project in *the particular form in which Jem originally expressed it*: as a felt certainty about our trajectory (Read 2018b). It is attractive to take collapse as an inevitability because that then provides one with the kind of psychical certainty that humans crave, and in particular it absolves one from having to make any further effort to hope against hope that collapse can be prevented.

It is plain false, however, to claim that a deep adaptational perspective, even of the kind expressed in the 'deep adaptation' paper, absolves one from having to make efforts at all: on the contrary, the locus of those efforts will simply, obviously, shift and (as one might put it) deepen in ways I will outline below. (And again: it would be plain weird that deep adaptation has been influential *within XR*, if deep adaptation were perceived as some kind of quietism encouraging an attitude of fatalistic passivity.) There is always work to be done to soften the blow of our likely descent; there is psychical adjustment but also there is concrete policy work (e.g. it becomes more important to take care now of nuclear waste, to make nuclear power stations safe, etc.)[8] and concrete local work (e.g. of course community building).

In sum: the NFEP picture that has held 'environmental' activism captive for far too long is dying. The time is ripe for a politics of truth telling which does not look away, which dares to look down at the abyss into which, in truth, we have begun descending.

Therefore, activism needs to change, in the kinds of ways XR – and the school climate strikers, and emerging ideas and activities around transformative adaptation (Read unpublished(a); Read 2020b), 'Climate Emergency Centres' and 'Parents for a Future'

---

[8] See the article, 'Dozens of US Nuclear Power Plants at Risk Due to Climate Change: Moody's' (Dolley 2020) for a stark mainstream assessment of one set of these risks, without even contemplating societal collapse. Touching more directly on the potential societal collapse aspect, see also Energyskeptic 2014 and Hester 2018.

(Read forthcoming)[9] – has sought and will seek to embody. Our activism needs to seek to shift society in the direction of being able to ride two horses simultaneously; two horses that most people still don't much want to ride, but that are coming into clarity more and more, and that have been pivotal to the extraordinary success of XR:

1   that of rising up to instantiate an emergency programme of 'mitigation' integrated into plans for transformative adaptation;[10]
    and
2   that of deep adaptation as the ultimate insurance policy.

The longer the debacle of humanity's current failure adequately to address the ecological emergency goes on, the more both, but especially the latter, are likely to have to take the form of bottom-up action to build local resilience. (I return to explore this point further below.)

This 'two horses' approach is obviously a complex and uncomfortable 'ask'. It lacks the easy simplicity of traditional 'environmental' activism which assumes that we can reform our way to 'sustainability' or the easy simplicity of assuming that 'we are doomed'.

But this complexity is, I argue, simply a necessary one. For we cannot know the future. Traditional 'environmental' activism

---

[9] This is a book that imagines a movement a little like XR but much larger, and somewhat less 'full-on'. The kernel of this new movement is: the necessity for parents to struggle for a better world, if they want their kids to have a future; and 'contrariwise' the impossibility any longer of providing one's kids a good future through focusing narrowly on them. The work of real mitigation of and non-shallow adaptation to climate breakdown just can no longer be plausibly 'outsourced' to politicians, scientists, etc.: as more parents wake up to this terrible truth, then we can expect to see the climate movement itself transformed and greatly expanded.

[10] As laid out in 'An Introduction to Transformative Adaptation' (Read unpublished(b)). Transformative adaptation as I reframe it is mitigation in its true sense: making the wicked problem with which we are landed less catastrophic. It is absurd any longer not to include roughly such adaptation as a priority in one's plans and demands; it is absurd, because it is too late to continue to focus, as some governments and campaigners still do, near-exclusively on a so-called 'mitigation' (i.e. emission-reduction) programme alone.

holds onto the forlorn hope that there is any realistic possibility of saving our civilization roughly as-is (i.e. reformed, rather than transformed). Such activism acts as if it is certain that such salvation is feasible, or even certain (if we do the right thing). Deep adaptation (DA) tends to sound like a kind of polar opposite of this: taking it as certain that civilization will collapse. My argument is that we have to live instead in the space of negative capability that a precautionary approach demands, and ensure that DA is framed in that space, so as to appeal to the vast majority who are not 'doomers' and so as to avoid the psychological, moral and political hazards of doomerism.

The one thing I've insisted in my work to date that we can be certain of is that to continue as we are doing, even given a solid agenda of eco-reformism, is impossible. Sooner or later, that way will lead to collapse. There is no future for this civilization, no future under even a reformed version of capitalism; the growth 'imperative' will see to that. That is what I *mean* by saying that this civilization is finished: the only way we can conceivably now perhaps prevent collapse is by looking the looming catastrophe in the face, taking it as a real and *present* danger that cannot any longer be dismissed as merely a possibility but should be understood as precisely where we are at present fast heading,[11] and so then acting finally with sufficiently great resolve and speed to change everything, such that what results will in no meaningful sense be the same civilization as the one we currently inhabit. Key to this prospect – that we might still stave off collapse – is a thorough embrace of transformative adaptation. We need to seek to adapt to the change that is coming not shallowly in a way that (self-defeatingly) tries to keep the show of this civilization on the road a bit longer, but instead transformatively, simultaneously drawing down carbon, building resilience and starting to 'model' the new society that could last. (An example of such adaptation: restoration of wetlands and no longer living on them as if we were earth's overlords.)

It is often thought that if you envisage collapse as inevitable,

---

[11] My thinking here is broadly aligned to the paradoxical thinking of the collapsologists (as manifested in chapter 3 in this volume), who in turn lean on the philosopher Jean-Pierre Dupuy (who was an influence on me in developing my philosophy of precaution).

you guarantee that it will become inevitable because you proba-bilify a 'giving-up' response. That only if we give up all hope does the chance of a different outcome die. Plainly, there is some potential validity to this worry. But what I am suggesting is that virtually the *opposite* is also potentially valid: that only if we envis-age the approaching catastrophe as utterly real – only if we see it staring *us* in the face – is there any possibility of us acting with sufficient determination to prevent its arrival. Only if we give up ordinary hope, only if we stop looking away, only if we turn our full attention to the trajectory of the juggernaut, is there any chance at all of our making it the case that the juggernaut does not end up running us down.

But given how unlikely we are to achieve that goal – given how unlikely we are to succeed in transforming everything to head off collapse – we *also* need to embrace DA fairly fast and very thor-oughly. We need to be prepared for what is coming, including focally the likelihood of an uneven ending of our current ways of sustaining ourselves; and here I have in mind especially food inse-curity[12] and the need to build towards food sovereignty.[13] The politics of food will be much more central to the coming genera-tion than it has been in the recent past.

Only if we have engaged in sufficiently serious efforts to (trans-formatively and) deeply adapt will we be even remotely prepared

---

[12] See e.g. my warning to the British public five minutes into my appearance on *Question Time* (Read 2019c). See Jem's warning (Bendell 2019a). Cf. 'Why Deep Adaptation Needs Relocalization' (Bendell 2019b) for an outline of a possible way forward. Cf. also Tim Lang's work.

[13] I expand below on the hopeful synergy that readers may have spotted lurking here: that TrAd and DA overlap to a considerable extent. And that overlap grows to the extent that DA unweds itself from collapse certainty. If DA is inflected by TrAd, if it is not heard as insisting that collapse is certainly coming but regards it rather as bearing down upon us unless something phenomenal (that we cannot fully control) shifts it and our course; if our adaptational path is systemic, even if mostly bottom-up; then it is probably our best shot *at* collapse mitigation. (Transformative-and-)deep-adaptation might, even yet, help prevent the very col-lapse it appears to forecast. (This point connects with John Michael Greer's wry aphorism, 'Collapse now, and avoid the rush.' The more we act as if collapse is coming and move in a resonant way to pre-empt it overtaking us unawares, the more it might morph into a non-mega-lethal relocalization, energy descent, etc.). On this, see my and Rughani's (2020) review of Michael Moore's *Planet of the Humans* that we published in *Byline Times*.

for what is probably coming. (Some of our collective unpreparedness has been fairly starkly visible in the sudden coronavirus crisis.) In particular, if collapse *takes* us and we are unprepared, then this will make less likely a subsequent renaissance.[14] One important possibility to try to prepare for, as we prepare for possible collapse, is for a successor civilization to emerge from the wreckage of this one. The better prepared we are for that – whether through making safe those elements of our current society that could take out or weaken any successor, or through preparing resilient seedbanks and biobanks, or through creating resilient multi-form libraries, or through learning relevant skills, or through preparing ourselves collectively mentally for a crash – the more likely we are to be able to build something meaningful, *after* a collapse event.

These things should therefore start to be present in our politics. How very far we are from that point – how far we are instead still denominated and dominated by narratives of endless 'growth', endless 'progress', endless 'development', and so on – is obvious.

My argument is that it is high time for this to change. The two 'conventional' horses, of an utterly dominant hegemony of industrial-growthist materialism and of an utterly marginal doomerism or drop-out culture that is a kind of shadow to it, are not those I recommend we ride. I recommend instead staying with the trouble; living and acting in the uncomfortable but fertile realm of unknowing, represented by the slight hope of civilizational transformation and the deep need for deep adaptation in the face of (in my judgement, very likely) eco-driven civilizational collapse.

These two horses are not so far from each other as they seem, for much of what transformative adaptation *amounts* to overlaps with most of what deep adaptation amounts to.

Thus we might perhaps start to talk of transformative-and-deep-adaptation as a kind of programme, an alliance inhabiting the land that we need to settle. Metaphorically – and literally. It is a programme that is as novel as it is necessary. For even

---

[14] See 'Some Thoughts on "Civilisational Succession"' (Read 2018c) for discussion of the possibility and importance of (preparing for) a new civilization to emerge after a collapse. Cf. on this also David Fleming's life work.

conventional 'de-growthism', brilliant and necessary though much of it is, fails (at least publicly) to recognize the need for the horse of deep adaptation. I focus in the remainder of this chapter upon what the effects of bringing DA into politics can reasonably be hoped to be. What will happen if we manage to make the (real) 'progress' we need by way of injecting the kinds of concerns and hopes outlined above into the discourse of our nations?

A key likely effect is creating a further, more general wake-up call. In other words, having some of us (including radical climate activists: see below) starting to act as if the risk of collapse is real will actually start to make that risk more believable more widely. Many people are being held back from believing in the truth of the crisis of our civilization by the slightly naive notion that if the crisis was as bad as XR et al. say it is, then the government would be acting more strongly. (We saw this on a shorter timescale during the earlyish stages of the corona crisis: in my country, the United Kingdom, many people took a lead from the complacent UK government in assuming until late March 2020 that basically nothing much needed to change.) Until *government* declares a state of long climate and ecological emergency, until there is a national live address on the matter from the prime minister, until there is a public information leaflet put through every door, then there is a ceiling to how wide and deep eco-concern about potential vulnerability and collapse can go.

We also need other pillars of society to do the same. Scientists need to get franker about the threat of collapse.[15] More challengingly, the media too, and 'think tanks' (not just our own), need to become truth-tellers (Cain and Murray 2020; Extinction Rebellion UK 2020). Without better media, the prospects for much worthwhile adaptation to occur, prior to a situation of something like catabolic collapse,[16] are slim. Thus the importance of (for instance) systemic challenges to complacent 'balanced'

[15] This is starting to happen (Moses 2020; *Guardian* 2020). It needs to proceed much further. Until scientists are breaking down and crying on live television, little will change relative to the scale of the challenge.
[16] *How Civilizations Fall: A Theory of Catabolic Collapse* (Greer 2005); this is an important piece of work by John Michael Greer, a proposed corrective to Tainter that needs to be better known.

state-owned media[17] and to the murderously climate-denying or -delaying Murdoch empire, though it must be admitted that the chances of success in this enterprise are slim.[18]

This all mirrors a central motivation for the concrete form that XR's first and pivotal demand, 'Tell the truth', takes. And this is a reason why that demand should continue to be pressed hard everywhere, especially upon the state and the media.

But in the absence of a truth-telling government (or media), there is still much that can – and must – be done. As I say, we need continuously and cleverly to counter the nostrum that if there really were a crisis the government would be acting as if there is: and taking DA seriously *helps to do so*. Every time we converse about our fears with others (the personal certainly is political, when it comes to collapse conversations), every time we manage to get collapse taken seriously in the media, every time we place our vulnerability to (e.g.) food-supply shocks onto the agenda, we chip away at the popular soft-denialistic hope that everything is and is going to be fine. And every time we are seen to be actively preparing for possible/likely hard times ahead, for example by taking local food growing seriously, then once more we *are* changing the agenda slightly, we are making it possible for people and politics to start to really face climate reality. For we are speaking through deeds, not just words.

Having some people who have been looking hard at the issue actually start to live as if collapse is possible/probable changes the salience of collapse more widely. It makes it more believable in a way that cascades across society. To say it again: the personal (and especially the interpersonal, the community) is political here. It is a political act to act as if collapse is possible.

(The same is true for taking geoengineering seriously. Geoengineering, including many 'negative emissions

---

[17] A happy example is to be found here (Sinclair 2018).

[18] As demonstrated by the crude response to XR's direct challenge to the Murdoch empire in September 2020, when XR UK blocked the Murdoch printing presses for a day; too many people who should have known better simply hollered 'Free speech!' in response, forgetting that a printing press is supposed to be merely a medium, not a message.

To the extent that the media are not transformed in the next few years, deep adaptation appears an ever more salient insurance policy. Thus my stance in Read (2020g) of upping the ante against the climate-denialist Rupert Murdoch.

technologies' – the attempt to control the earth's climate top-down through engineering-style 'solutions' – raises a massive, obvious moral hazard issue, and the hope invested in it is already having dangerous effects, i.e. in encouraging people to think of substantial rapid climate-deadly-emissions-reduction as less crucial than it in fact is (Paul and Read 2019). But: *debating* geo-engineering – very much including setting out why (in my view) it would be utterly reckless, should not be done, etc.[19] – *itself* helps people to believe in the depth of the crisis, and this prob-abilifies freedom from capture by the status quo, i.e. from the widespread inability even now to comprehend our real vulner-ability to climate-driven decline and fall. The thought process is roughly this: 'If scientists and those who understand are contem-plating crazy shit such as mirrors in space, then we must really be in trouble.')

Let me explore in a little more depth now what all this means especially for what has so far been the most effective movement more or less willing to try to face the likelihood of collapse head on: Extinction Rebellion. I write as someone who has been inti-mately involved with XR since before its launch, but who has now taken a step back to concentrate on other projects (including, crucially, transformative – and deep! – adaptation). This gives me, I trust, a useful perspective: very well informed not only as an insider[20] but also now as a critical friend and fellow traveller.

Now that it seems clear that there is very unlikely to be a sig-nificant course change from government (at least in the United Kingdom, where I write from) before 2025, it seems time for XR's actions and platform to start to morph into accomplishing what we can more directly of the necessary agenda for change, in the face of the crisis, and into being franker still about the stakes.

This could mean:

- probably altering Demand 2, the demand for government to 'act now', *to explicitly include transformative and deep adaptations*;
- initiating the *creation* of people's assemblies/citizens'

---

[19] See 'Apollo-Earth: A Wake Up Call in Our Race against Time' (Read and Rughani 2017), however, for some suggestions as to what *can* usefully be done.
[20] For my perspective as an insider, as I was until recently, see my book *Extinction Rebellion: Insights from the Inside* (Read 2020a).

assemblies (CAs) (including *on* deep adaptation), rather than waiting for government to create them (for they are not going to).[21] This can include working with local authorities to create genuine CAs. It may also include the visionary idea of creating a global citizens' assembly. It should not include CAs directly sponsored by XR, any more than the Deep Adaptation Forum should seek to create a CA: this would not be trusted. Rather, it should be about initiating and supporting processes whereby independent CAs (independent of XR/ of the DAF, etc.) get created. A partial model here is available in the UK 'High Pay Commission'. Commissioned by Compass, this body came to have perceived legitimacy partly because of its high-profile chair (Helena Kennedy). CAs chaired by (say) someone like Jonathan Dimbleby (or indeed Helena Kennedy) or someone similar might well be at an advantage in a similar fashion. But, as I say, they should at minimum be fully arm's-length bodies;

- probably seeking alliance with permaculture and the Transition Towns movement (including through seeking to politicize their activities somewhat more: e.g. creating pop-up allotments on council/government/NGO-owned/private land and being serious about using any non-violent means necessary to defend them);
- and, I should think, starting to see movements such as XR as potentially embodying/prefiguring the forms of society that could survive what is coming. This last is the real, deep meaning of the regenerative culture that XR speaks about and starts to instantiate. (In this connection, obviously, there is room potentially for XR to cooperate directly with the DAF.)

---

[21] The citizens' assembly (https://www.climateassembly.uk) which reported to the UK *Parliament* (not government) in September 2020 was agreed in 2019 as a de facto concession to Extinction Rebellion (Horton 2019), but it falls far short of what is needed if XR's demands are to be met. Most crucially, it was merely advisory, and one can be certain that much of its advice will not be taken by the current government. Furthermore, it did not aim at a rapid carbon-zero target (such as 2025 or 2030). What XR is actually calling for is embodied in the bill it is now (in 2020–1) bringing to Parliament: https://www.ceebill.uk. The work of Trust the People is also important in this context of *bringing about* sufficiently bold citizens' assemblies, from the bottom up. This can be considered *part of* the vision I term 'transformative adaptation'.

As anyone who has participated in XR actions and (particularly) in XR rebellions is likely to attest, the experience is itself transformational. A powerful experience of acting as an organism to get something done; of a noble intent for which people are willing to 'sacrifice'; of its being no *sacrifice* because the whole experience is saturated with existential meaning; and of the whole often being saturated with love, joy, fellowship, authenticity and power.

I do not know how many of these suggestions XR will want or be able to implement. All four of them are clearly potentially important from the perspective of DA. The third and fourth suggestions at least (and maybe also the second) should be enacted by advocates of transformative and of deep adaptation, regardless of what government does or does not do. This is part of what I am now seeking to do in my work both outside of and in cooperation with XR. As is implicit in the way I have outlined these suggestions, the probability, unfortunately, is that most of this work will *have* to be done/led from the bottom up.

For while it is clear that we are in for a long, probably permanent, period of climate decline, political parties, even to a large extent the Green Party (my own), have barely begun to even contemplate this psychologically wrenching fact (Read 2019d). It will be incredibly hard to integrate it into politics as we know it, for politics has for so long been founded on the concept and assumption of progress or of promises for a better tomorrow.

Might this assumption be able to be radically[22] refigured; might we be able to start to see 'a better tomorrow' as being one that is more honest, less insanely materialistic, more satisfied with humble pleasures, more spiritually rich? Might a political philosophy drawing on the best of Gandhi, Thoreau, Rousseau and so forth, and bathed in an ecologistic world view,[23] now become more feasible or popular?

---

[22] By employing this overused word, I mean to index Jonathan Lear's book, *Radical Hope* (2006). His book seeks to outline how one can refashion ideas for a tomorrow by way of a radical abandonment of yesterday's assumptions about what even makes sense, culturally.

[23] I am thinking here of ecologism as argued for by Andrew Dobson (2000) but also to some extent of the philosophy of deep ecology.

One slim but real ground for hope might be found in the effects of the eco-driven pandemic[24] that has of course gripped our world in a shared crisis of potential/parental mortality, a shared crisis of vulnerability (Read 2020c) and of refigured priorities (Read 2020d). There are features of the human response to Covid-19 that point intriguingly in the direction of the kind of relocalized,[25] more caring, more nature-attuned world that could stand as an alternative aim to the ubiquitous growthist hegemony in politics-as-usual. Covid may well turn out to be the moment at which not just neoliberalism but the entire broadly hegemonic political philosophy of liberal individualism (including globalism and growthism) passes its zenith and begins to decline. For, once more, we can be certain that nothing very like the globalist capitalist paradigm, which until 2020 was still almost unchallenged, will survive the coming shocks. The only question is whether it finishes by way of collapse (as Jem supposes inevitable) or by way of transformative change (as I continue to hope; just). What I think could unite every one of us who is behind the DA project is the aspiration to stand up for a vision of the future in which the insanely unequal world we inhabit will not be prolonged. For it is of crucial importance, if the future, however hard, is going to be *human*, that we look to rebuild and re-root community in ways that are not atavistic/racist and that are not grossly elitist/classist.

And yet the recent/current coronavirus emergency has offered interesting lessons, too, concerning how far the status quo in politics is from the kind of conception that has been outlined in this short chapter. There has been a widespread tendency – visible from Wuhan to London, with only certain partial exceptions (e.g. South Korea, which is seeking to create a Green New Deal to emerge from the corona recession, just as it did in 2008–9) – to seek to adapt *shallowly* to the corona crisis. I mean: most of the economic moves made have been either envisaged as purely short term (e.g. moves towards a *temporary* universal basic income) or

---

[24] Salient discussion of Jem's view that the drivers of the coronavirus may well include more specifically climatic drivers can be found here (Kishan 2020).

[25] On which, see John Gray's 'Why This Crisis is a Turning Point in History' (2020) and Maurice Glasman's 'The Coronavirus Crisis has Sounded the Death Knell for Liberal Globalisation' (2020). See also the chapter which follows by Slater and Rathor (chapter 12).

as a way of hastening a return to business as usual (BAU) (e.g. most of the bailouts, 'stimulus' packages, etc.; and these packages are by and large destroying our potential capacity to reset in a genuinely different and greener way, in real time: McCarthy 2020 and Read 2020e). Astonishingly little attention appears to be going, for instance, to the question of how to redesign a world which is in suspension so as to make it less fragile to future shocks. The airline industry is at the leading edge of destroying our common climate, and at the leading edge of fragilizing us to unprecedented global pandemics. (The Spanish flu a century ago travelled at the speed of ships, not of jets; that is a key, staringly obvious reason why the world was brought to a standstill by Covid-19.) Yet across most of the world there is hardly any talk of deliberately permanently reducing our collective reliance (a reliance skewed massively of course towards the rich and privileged) upon air travel (Read 2020f).

So there has been very little effort to transformatively adapt the world in the light of Covid-19. Moreover, while it is true that governments around the world demonstrated (in response to the sudden Covid emergency) that there is a magic money tree, that heaven and earth can be moved within weeks when there is a will, we should not take too much comfort from that. Some of this marvellous effort was carried out to save lives (in response to a *short*-term emergency, which the eco-emergency is not), but most, again, seems to have been carried out to save 'the economy'.

In working to start to think and do adaptation, in a way that is not merely incremental and shallow, in working to achieve transformative adaptation and deep adaptation,[26] long lead times are required. Rebuilding our paradigm, either psycho-culturally or in terms of economic model and of heavy infrastructure (such as that needed to safeguard nuclear installations, etc., in case of possible societal collapse), doesn't happen overnight. The coronavirus emergency showed that certain kinds of government are unable, even when it is so badly needed, to think a few weeks ahead, let alone years (or decades) ahead, if doing so challenges paradigmatic assumptions. Governments such as the US and UK governments chronically failed, in the early stages of the crisis

---

[26] Jem and I are now working on a paper to bring these two explicitly together.

in 2020, to comprehend the newness of the situation, the dire urgency of strong precautionary action running ahead of both the evidence and the virus itself, the scale of the threat posed by the exponentiality of the virus's contagiousness and the real risk of health-service breakdown. Insofar as they did dimly perceive these things, they considered them outweighed by the effort to keep economic BAU on the road a little longer. Weeks longer only: their failure to sew a stitch in time cost ninety-nine, necessitating mass lockdowns that could have been pre-empted by swifter targeted action.

The lessons for climate and ecology are, as I say, on balance somewhat grim-looking. If we can't take for granted that governments will be intelligent enough to plan just weeks ahead, if we can't expect them to take a precautionary approach to something which they have seen playing out viciously elsewhere in the world (as in for instance the UK failure to learn adequately from what was happening in north Italy in early 2020), how can we expect them to be convinced by activism to plan years ahead? Thus the national policy-action agenda of DA – which as I see it would crucially include making nuclear and toxic chemicals safe, as well as pulling back ahead of time from investment in infrastructure that will likely be overwhelmed by sea-level rise and so on – seems stymied at birth. Perhaps the rational thing to do is to 'go local' from the get-go.

However, there are two reasons (which we can deduce from the corona crisis) for thinking that such despair about high-level DA policy activism may be premature, even in those countries whose political cultures seem ill equipped to engage in emergency thinking and precautious planning:

1. What was encouraging in countries such as the United Kingdom was the extent to which citizen action pre-empted government mandating. In particular, March 2020 saw a huge wave of citizen action on physical distancing, self-isolation, community aid for those going into self-isolation, cancellation or alteration of events, etc. – all leading where government failed to. (Even the widespread home stockpiling and sometimes anti-social hoarding behaviour that was observed during that period has, in my way of seeing it, a positive aspect: it showed people taking the crisis seriously

and has inculcated a far wider awareness of the sense of a good modicum of 'prepping'. What we need to do now is to follow through on that by way of encouraging *community-friendly* prepping, including through local councils, pro-active mayors, etc. Building resilience. Getting people who have now, usefully, experienced a sense of vulnerability and of emergency to carry that sense across to preparedness together for likely eco-driven breakdowns. That *is* a key element in the basic DA agenda.) So there may be more popular desire than is usually supposed to change policy in the way that is necessary.[27] Citizens may press government to do the right thing in preparing for disaster.

2. Perhaps governments (and nations which choose their governments) might *learn* from their failure. Perhaps they will finally start to take on board the precautionary principle in the wake of corona (Eyres 2020). Perhaps they will listen more henceforth to those of us who spoke out strongly against the complacent modellers of death who created the absurd doctrine of herd-immunity-by-way-of-deadly-infection. Perhaps, just as East Asian states learned from SARS (and this is a key reason why, democracies and dictatorships alike, they were better prepared for corona than western states were), we will all learn from Covid-19. (Perhaps this will even bleed into a 'corona dividend' for the climate struggle; perhaps we can get somewhere in encouraging chastened governments subject now to public inquiries, etc., not just to revert to their BAU backing for fossil-fuelled airlines and airport expansion, etc.)

All these 'perhapses' may seem unlikely. But they cannot yet be judged to be impossible. And they can be probabilified somewhat by smart activism and thought-leadership. So it is too soon to write off the potential of DA to enter into not only the personal as politics and community politics but also conventional national politics. The DA agenda ought to be grafted onto discussions of energy systems, of food systems, of infrastructure build, and much more. The post-corona reset may provide an opportunity

---

[27] And the evidence suggests that there is: that, for example, there is a popular will to build back greener: see, for example, 'Just 6% of UK public "want a return to pre-pandemic economy"' (Proctor 2020).

for that, having provided a lived shared experience of vulnerability and of emergency across the globe for the first time since the Cold War, an experience centred, moreover, upon love: our love especially for our parents and for the medically vulnerable.

Moreover, corona has inadvertently provided many of us collectively with something else that, following Paul Kingsnorth, I've been arguing for over the last few years: a chance to pause (Read 2020c). To stop. Many of us virtually never have the luxury of experiencing what many of us were forced to experience while we were locked down, with at times half the world being 'alone together' in this way. That chance to stop built a chance to reassess. To think whether we want to go back to the same frenetic life that is driving us collectively off the cliff. Even though much of that momentum – a very special kind of momentum, the momentum of stasis – has been wasted, nevertheless people still *had* that time. (And moreover, as I write, there are new lockdowns; maybe the time of pause is coming again . . .) Many of us have at last definitively had the experience of pausing, of not commuting, of gardening, of clapping together for NHS staff who were caring for us, or whatever it was. That experience can never be removed. It may have a part to play in the different world we could rebuild, a world less likely to collapse perhaps, or at least a world less likely to collapse terminally, and/or because it is more likely to be deeply adapted.

Finally, let me note that what I have written in this piece implies a partial redefinition of 'activist' – from taking action for political change towards taking action to deeply (or at least transformatively!) adapt locally. In other words, I'm saying that, as well as informing conventional politics, DA calls for something genuinely new.

At least new in our time, in countries in the global North. It wouldn't seem that new to (say) the landless movement in Brazil, nor to the Diggers in Civil War times in the United Kingdom. There is nothing more political, and more positive, than people who have been deprived of the means of provisioning themselves looking to take back that power. And nothing is more important in a time when (multi-)breadbasket failure is gradually being probabilified.

Our times call for a dialectical integration between what has traditionally been thought of as activism on the one hand and local 'direct' action on the ground to protect ourselves against what may be coming on the other. This is perhaps the most subtle fruit that a transformative-and-deep-adaptation perspective can bring to bear on politics: a *unification* potentially of movements like XR, on the one hand, with movements like Transition Towns and permaculture, on the other. This could create a new power in the land that would give us the kind of strength and harmony we need as we move into evermore uncharted waters – a power based *on* the land.

We need to be humble about what we know. We cannot know in any detail whatsoever the fate of something as infinitely complex as contemporary globalized civilization. But we can, I argue (see Read and Alexander 2019), know that it will not continue in anything remotely resembling its current form for much longer. It seems overwhelmingly likely that the way in which our civilization will come to an end is via a collapse, slow (as many previous collapses have been)[28] or fast (we are, after all, a desperately interconnected complex of leviathans, and we have badly breached the limits to growth). For it seems almost inconceivable that most people – still less, the powerful – are going to accept the vast, necessary changes to lifestyle that are required in the short time we have available, partly because climate and ecological breakdown can always be driven out of the headlines, including by more immediate crises, such as civil conflict or large-scale refugee-seeking or indeed pandemics *that are driven by it*.

These points together form the simple, central reason why deep adaptation as a practice and a policy is now so necessary. So the more it can start to find an intelligent and humane way into politics, the better.

References

Bendell, J. (2019a) 'Notes on Hunger and Collapse'. Jembendell.com. Available at: https://jembendell.com/2019/03/28/notes-on-hunger-and-collapse/

Bendell, J. (2019b) 'Why Deep Adaptation Needs Re-localisation'. Jembendell.com. Available at: https://jembendell.com/2019/11/02/deep-adaptation-relocalisation/

---

[28] On this somewhat encouraging point, see John Michael Greer's work (2005).

Cain, S. and Murray, J. (2020) '"Culture of Misinformation": Artists Protest against London Thinktanks'. *Guardian*. Available at: https://www.theguardian.com/environment/2020/sep/02/ground-zero-of-lies-on-climate-artists-protest-at-london-thinktanks

Dobson, A. (2000) *Green Political Thought*, 3rd edn. Abingdon: Routledge.

Dolley, S. (2020) *Dozens of US Nuclear Power Plants at Risk Due to Climate Change: Moody's*. S&P Global. Available at: https://www.spglobal.com/platts/en/market-insights/latest-news/electric-power/081820-dozens-of-us-nuclear-power-plants-at-risk-due-to-climate-change-moodys

Energyskeptic. (2014) 'David Fleming. 2007. "The Lean Guide to Nuclear Energy. A Life-Cycle in Trouble"'. Available at: http://energyskeptic.com/2014/david-fleming-2007-the-lean-guide-to-nuclear-energy-a-life-cycle-in-trouble/

Extinction Rebellion UK (2020) 'Keep Speaking Truth to Power – Here Comes Week 2'. Available at: https://extinctionrebellion.uk/2020/09/06/keep-speaking-truth-to-power-here-comes-week-2/

Eyres, H. (2020) 'How Coronavirus Has Led to a Return of the Precautionary Principle'. *New Statesman*. Available at: https://www.newstatesman.com/international/2020/04/how-coronavirus-has-led-return-precautionary-principle .

Foster, J. (2015) *After Sustainability: Denial, Hope, Retrieval*. Abingdon, UK: Routledge.

Foster, J. (ed.) (2019) *Facing Up to Climate Reality: Honesty, Disaster and Hope*. London: London Publishing Partnership/Green House.

The Glacier Trust (2020) 'Framing Adaptation'. The Glacier Trust. Available at: http://theglaciertrust.org/blog/2020/8/26/framing-adaptation

Glasman, M. (2020) 'The Coronavirus Crisis Has Sounded the Death Knell for Liberal Globalisation'. *New Statesman*. Available at: https://www.newstatesman.com/politics/economy/2020/04/coronavirus-crisis-has-sounded-death-knell-liberal-globalisation

Gray, J. (2020) 'Why This Crisis is a Turning Point in History'. *New Statesman*. Available at: https://www.newstatesman.com/international/2020/04/why-crisis-turning-point-history

Greer, J. M. (2005) *How Civilizations Fall: A Theory of Catabolic Collapse*. Ecoshock. Available at: https://www.ecoshock.org/transcripts/greer_on_collapse.pdf

Guardian (2020) 'After Coronavirus, Focus on the Climate Emergency'. [Letter from W. Knorr et al.] Available at: https://www.theguardian.com/world/2020/may/10/after-coronavirus-focus-on-the-climate-emergency

Hester, K. (2018) 'This Civilisation is Finished. Rupert Read, Paul Ehrlich and Jem Bendell'. Kevinhester.live. Available at: https://

kevinhester.live/2018/12/28/this-civilisation-is-finished-ruppert-reid-paul-ehrlich-and-jem-bendell/

Horton, H. (2019) 'MPs Bow to Extinction Rebellion Demand, as They Send Out Invitations to Climate Change Citizens' Assembly'. *The Telegraph*. Available at: https://www.telegraph.co.uk/climate/2019/11/01/mps-bow-extinction-rebellion-demand-send-invitations-climate/

Kishan, S. (2020) 'Professor Sees Climate Mayhem Lurking Behind Covid-19 Outbreak'. Bloomberg. Available at: https://www.bloomberg.com/news/articles/2020-03-28/professor-sees-climate-mayhem-lurking-behind-covid-19-outbreak

Lang, T. M. and Heasman, M. (2015) *Food Wars: The Global Battle for Mouths, Minds and Markets*, 2nd edn. Abingdon: Routledge.

Lear, J. (2006) *Radical Hope: Ethics in the Face of Cultural Devastation*. Cambridge, MA: Harvard University Press.

McCarthy, D. (2020) 'The Bank of England's Coronavirus "Recovery" Plan is Pushing Us Deeper into a Climate Emergency'. *Independent*. Available at: https://www.independent.co.uk/voices/coronavirus-bank-england-economic-recovery-plan-climate-change-rishi-sunak-a9548396.html

Moses, A. (2020) '"Collapse of Civilisation is the Most Likely Outcome": Top Climate Scientists'. Voice of Action. Available at: https://voiceofaction.org/collapse-of-civilisation-is-the-most-likely-outcome-top-climate-scientists/

Norberg-Hodge, H. (1991) *Ancient Futures: Lessons from Ladakh for a Globalizing World*. San Francisco: Sierra Club Books.

Paul, H. and Read, R. (2019) 'Geoengineering as a Response to the Climate Crisis: Right Road or Disastrous Diversion?', in J. Foster (ed.), *Facing Up to Climate Reality: Honesty, Disaster and Hope*, 1st edn. London: London Publishing Partnership.

Phillips, M., Bridewell, A. and Richards, C. (2019) 'We Need to Talk about Adaptation'. The Glacier Trust. Available at: https://static1.squarespace.com/static/54b52dbde4b09c18186752fd/t/5e3d99797ffea47838bb08c0/1581095295885/WeNeedToTalkAboutAdaptation_TheGlacierTrustUK_FinalReport_Feb5th2019.pdf

Proctor, K. (2020) 'Just 6% of UK Public "Want a Return to Pre-Pandemic Economy"'. *Guardian*. Available at: https://www.theguardian.com/world/2020/jun/28/just-6-of-uk-public-want-a-return-to-pre-pandemic-economy

Read, R. (2018a) 'This Civilisation is Finished: So What Is to Be Done?' Available at: https://www.youtube.com/watch?v=uzCxFPzdO0Y

Read, R. (2018b) 'After the IPCC Report, #climatereality'. Medium. Available at: https://medium.com/@rupertread_80924/after-the-ipcc-report-climatereality-5b3e2ae43697

Read, R. (2018c) 'Some Thoughts on "Civilisational Succession"'. Truth and Power. Available at: http://www.truthandpower. com/ rupert-read-some-thoughts-on-civilisational-succession/

Read, R. (2019a) *The End of Globalisation and the Return of Localisation: How Climate Breakdown Terminates Developmentality*. HDCA Plenary Mahbub-ul-Haq Lecture, London, Sept. Available at: https://media central.ucl.ac.uk/Play/18827

Read, R. (2019b) 'Climate Catastrophe: The Case for Rebellion'. Available at: https://www.youtube.com/watch?v=RnonKverhOg

Read, R. (2019c) 'BBC Question Time, 10-Oct-2019'. [video] Available at: https://www.youtube.com/watch?v=QK7DKiKh9_Q

Read, R. (2019d) 'We Must Adapt to Climate Decline'. Green World. Available at: https://greenworld.org.uk/article/we-must-ada pt-climate-decline

Read, R. (2020a) *Extinction Rebellion: Insights from the Inside*. Melbourne: Simplicity Institute.

Read, R. (2020b) 'A Discussion of Transformative Adaptation: A Way Forward for the 2020s'. Available at: https://www.youtube.com/ watch?v=msvHevicz24

Read, R. (2020c) '24 Theses on Corona'. Medium. Available at: https:// medium.com/@rupertjread/24-theses-on-corona-748689919859

Read, R. (2020d) 'Smell the Roses'. The Idler. Available at: https://www. idler.co.uk/article/smell-the-roses/

Read, R. (2020e) 'The Coronavirus Gives Humanity One Last Chance – but for What Exactly?' Compass. Available at: https://www.compas sonline.org.uk/the-coronavirus-gives-humanity-one-last-chance-but-f or-what-exactly/

Read, R. (2020f) 'Imagining the World after COVID-19'. ABC Religion and Ethics. Available at: https://www.abc.net.au/religion/ rupert-read-imagining-a-world-after-coronavirus/

Read, R. (2020g) 'I'll No Longer Be a Source for Murdoch's Empire of Lies'. Open Democracy. Available at: https://www.opendemocracy. net/en/opendemocracyuk/ill-no-longer-be-a-source-for-murdochs-em pire-of-lies/

Read, R. (2021) *Parents for a Future*. Norwich: UEA Publishing Project.

Read, R. (unpublished(a)) 'Transformative Adaptation: A Declaration'. Available at: https://docs.google.com/document/d/1yJbpvCi651_E 1tsTtYuuaSTJ1dByfAhjMET8X7Yqs-Q/

Read, R. (unpublished(b)) 'An Introduction to Transformative Adaptation'. Available at: https://docs.google.com/document/d/1lAW JxPFbV7IuShx2ShSIzN1yORL-v5_BgAbUtcAqTNI

Read, R. and Alexander, S. (2019) *This Civilisation is Finished: Conversations on the End of Empire – and What Lies Beyond*. Melbourne: Simplicity Institute.

Read, R. and Rughani, D. (2017) *Apollo-Earth: A Wake Up Call in Our Race against Time*. *Ecologist*. Available at: https://theecologist.org/2017/mar/09/apollo-earth-wake-call-our-race-against-time

Read, R. and Rughani, D. (2020) 'Heartbreaking Genius of Staggering Over-Simplification'. *Byline Times*. Available at: https://bylinetimes.com/2020/05/14/review-michael-moores-planet-of-the-humans-heart breaking-genius-of-staggering-over-simplification/

Sinclair, I. (2018) 'No More Climate Cranks on Our Screens'. *Morning Star*. Available at: https://morningstaronline.co.uk/article/no-more-climate-cranks-our-screens

Todd, M. (2019) 'Extinction Rebellion's Tactics Are Working. It Has Pierced the Bubble of Denial'. *Guardian*. Available at: https://www.theguardian.com/commentisfree/2019/jun/10/extinction-rebellion-bu bble-denial-climate-crisis

12

Relocalization as Deep Adaptation

Matthew Slater and Skeena Rathor

This chapter aims to be very broad, touching on many aspects of the idea of localization or, as some prefer, relocalization. There are myriad different ways to take action towards deep adaptation, across all aspects of life and society; anyone living anywhere can work with their neighbours to create more resilient life-support systems. That involves physical factors such as food, water, shelter, energy and suchlike. But it also includes the social and psychological factors that comprise not only our resilience but also our joy at being alive. In this chapter, we will describe how relocalization could be an important pathway for deep adaptation if pursued with a mindset of solidarity with all people being made vulnerable from climate disruption, no matter their location, race, gender, economic class or belief.

There is a vast assortment of wishful, intellectual and utopian explorations of the merits of a more localized society. *Small is Beautiful* (Schumacher 1973) is an elegant treatise in favour of a simpler world with smaller, more local economic systems, written in the early 1970s. In academia, there is a small bioregionalist school of thought (McGinnis 1999) premised on the idea that water catchment areas (and other geographical features) provide a natural basis for shared cooperation and responsibility, more so than race and history. In fiction, there are the 'World Made by Hand' novels describing a post-peak oil America.[1]

[1] https://kunstler.com/writings/books

None of these expressions particularly serve people who feel responsible, if not for building a better world, then at least for disengaging ourselves from an economic machine hurling itself towards the maelstrom; a machine which, nonetheless, meets most of our physical needs. Where does one begin trying to meet these needs in other ways? And where do we begin to meet our social needs that are not being met or that are being made worse through interaction with this economic machine?

Resilience

Many theories of collapse, particularly those emphasizing complexity, suggest that the social order will be simplified and decentralized because that very complexity consumes resources which will become unavailable (Homer-Dixon 2006: 221). That would indicate less control from distant centres of power, less regulation, weaker law and its enforcement, less taxing and redistribution, less access to technology, a smaller military and, owing to infrastructure decay and security concerns, reduced freedom of movement. If nation-states themselves are weakened, self-sufficiency on a regional or local scale becomes important.

This principle of local self-sufficiency in the face of global economic disruption seems advisable, although the nature of the threats and shocks we face as individuals, families and communities is different. Over the previous decade, before climate change had had much direct impact on their countries, western governments pursued austerity policies domestically, slashing funds to police, hospitals and schools, allowing homelessness to rise and cutting back on emergency services and disaster response. In so doing, these governments are increasing rather than reducing vulnerability to future climate-induced or climate-exacerbated shocks.

Resilience is discussed as a branch of system theory about how complex systems prevent, minimize and recover from the consequences of outside shocks (Haimes 2009: 1). It can be specific to particular kinds of shock, but there are also general principles of resilience in circumstances defined by unpredictability.

Generally, more diverse systems are characterized by greater 'redundancy' and more linkages between components, and more uses for each component, which enables them to 'work around' many types of shock, attack, damage or environmental change. One of the most recognized aspects of resilient systems is the absence of single points of failure, which means, in other words, that functions are not performed centrally but in a more distributed way. Centralized systems tend to be efficient at the expense of being fragile. For example, a town could get all its water through one pipe, but the supply could stop completely if a bomb should damage the pipe, or it could make everyone sick if it became contaminated. Conversely, if every house stored its own rainwater in an underground tank, the system would cost more to build and maintain but it would be much harder to disrupt, not only because the water tanks are in many places, separate from each other, but also because the water is stored closer to where it is needed.

The near-ubiquity of globalized neoliberalism has resulted in a very complex economic system which takes the 'law' of comparative advantage to its logical extreme, in which all countries are encouraged to specialize their production for the global market. This tendency is embedded in the international development paradigm and community, which pushes countries towards greater complexity, growth and specialization.

This has the effect of making all countries heavily dependent on the market (i.e. on other countries), as well as making it easier and more likely that many countries become subjugated by debt. These and other critiques have been discussed, along with alternative approaches, under the banner of 'post-development' (Bawtree and Rahnema 1997), and even 'counter-development' (Norberg-Hodge 1991).

Although they don't usually use the language of resilience, some governments have envisioned a different path of development, not through opening up their markets but through protecting them from predatory capital and cheaper imports. Protectionist policies can increase economic resilience by nurturing that country's productive sector. However, they are more usually framed in terms like 'self-determination'. Such concepts have not been the preserve of either the left or the right in the history of politics. For instance, the popular Swadeshi movement demonstrated that India could be self-sufficient, not 'needing' British trade, while the government of Mussolini, despite its destructive failings, navigated Italy through the difficult interwar period by making the country largely self-sufficient.

The political principle of subsidiarity brings principles of decentralization to European Union law (EU 2014: 23) and to the Christian Democratic movement (Grabow 2011: 17). This notion that authority should be devolved towards the most affected and to the nearest to the situation is not usually invoked with resilience in mind; rather, it is for social and practical and even moral reasons, as emphasized in the papal encyclical which introduced the notion to modern politics:

> Just as it is gravely wrong to take from individuals what they can accomplish by their own initiative and industry and give it to the community, so also it is an injustice and at the same time a grave evil and disturbance of right order to assign to a greater and higher association what lesser and subordinate organizations can do. For every social activity ought of its very nature to furnish help to the members of the body social, and never destroy and absorb them. (Pius XI 1931: §79)

Though some issues do need large-scale management, like high technology or the global commons, proper application of subsidiarity would greatly strengthen politics at the local level and could increase general societal resilience.

But in practice, subsidiarity has done little to prevent the aggregation of political and economic power in ever-greater centres. In the United Kingdom, 'localism' is an agenda to give more political and budgetary power to local authorities. It has had limited cross-party support, though it is prominent in Green Party policy and some hard-right movements. Tony Blair's government took some steps in that direction, notably creating a parliament for Scotland and an assembly for Wales. The 2011 Localism Act was less well received. The *Guardian* noted that: 'Services have been devolved to boroughs, yet it is often simply a cost-shunting exercise rather than a true devolution of power and fiscal autonomy – that is, the responsibility is devolved, but not the money to fulfil it' (Pipe 2013). To the cynically inclined, the Act was the opposite of local empowerment: having bailed out the banks, central government devolved much of that cost and the consequences of making cuts to local government. Today, local authorities across Europe are spending more and more on debt servicing, having to take on risky entrepreneurial activities and sell off assets (Doward 2017).

Although our focus in the chapter is mostly on matters of material resilience, we wish to take a moment to recognize that the concept is not an objective one outside of either culture or personal psychology. Rather, the resilience of any community includes the way that people relate to each other within their community and between communities. As disruptions to normal life increase, and people become more anxious about those changes, so their emotional resilience will be increasingly important (chapter 4). In particular, the resilience of our capacity for reflection, our empathy for each other's situations and our capacity for joy are all important. We believe that a relocalization agenda can help with such psycho-social resilience if it includes an intention to avoid parochialism and be part of a wider multi-local movement. These aspects of resilience are central to deep adaptation (chapter 7), and the potential for them to be sustained through localization needs to be a key focus for any localism movement or initiative. It is something we will return to in concluding this chapter, which primarily focuses on the material aspects of relocalization.

Aspects of relocalization

A few rugged survivalists do attempt to take matters into their own hands and retreat from the city, solarize their houses, grow vegetables, learn first aid and maybe even keep a small stash of weapons. This is certainly a form of resilience to certain types of shock, but it is simply not an option for many people and not attractive to many others, nor can it compare with the efficiency of a more coordinated response.

Instead of that 'prepper' or survivalist approach, the relocalization movement is about working with their neighbours to co-create new local infrastructure and new lifestyles. The projects are also small enough to allow inclusive decision making and participation by amateurs and enthusiasts, but large enough to pool mutual encouragement, support, learning and affirmation. Skills and knowledge of every kind are needed, for institution building, activism and lobbying, business and technological problem solving (Giangrande 2018). Many of these activities are hard to finance and to license because their small scale, or their values, make them appear less viable by the standards of a hyper-financialized economy. However, surprises abound because economists rarely model humans who care about anything other than themselves.

Although the following examples are very UK-focused, we try to present them in a way useful for readers everywhere. It is worth noting the predominance of cooperatives in the projects we will mention. The cooperative movement, with its focus on worker ownership and control of the means of production, chimes with the 'taking back the power' ethic of relocalization.

Food

Food is usually the first concern of localists, not only because of the quantity of it that is needed for our day-to-day survival but also because it is what fuels our very bodies, and most of us do not control it. Growing food and working with the soil brings many people a deep sense of satisfaction, of purpose or of connection to ancient traditions. Before the Industrial Revolution, peasants and villages had a high degree of self-sufficiency because they produced their own food, often on their own land. With the forced or economic migration to the cities, ordinary people became dependent on complex socio-economic systems, including money and politics, for sustenance.

These larger systems can be very hard to opt out of and do not necessarily improve the lives of all their participants. The industrial food system is extremely vulnerable in an insecure future: it depends on massive inputs of fossil fuels, both to power machinery and for fertilizer; it results in high waste, pollution and wholesale animal abuse and torture; the food itself often has impaired nutritional value and is contaminated, contributing to long-term health problems.

In that light, working towards self-sufficiency in food can be seen as the ultimate political or rebellious act. The literature in this field often quotes a nineteenth-century English radical MP: 'If I write grammars; if I write on agriculture; if I sow, plant, or deal in seeds; whatever I do has first in view the destruction of those infamous tyrants' (Cobbett 1819: 8). The relevance of this view is all the more striking today if companies like Monsanto are striving to create a seed monopoly, ultimately to control the price and availability of the world's food. The regulatory system tends to create hurdles much more easily cleared by the largest corporations than by sole traders and family businesses. In the United Kingdom, even the organic certification issued by the Soil Association is prohibitively expensive for the smallest producers. Since the 2001 foot-and-mouth outbreak in the United Kingdom, which was a problem caused by industrial agriculture, even the smallest cheese producers are now required to be equipped with stainless steel facilities before they can put their produce on the market. Feeding pigs and chickens with waste food was also banned, requiring pork producers to buy industrial animal feed (Harrison 2018). If animals are not slaughtered in an industrial abattoir, it is illegal even to give away the meat or feed it to guests (Jarman 2016). Raw milk is subject to strict laws in the United Kingdom, being banned in Scotland and prevented from sale in shops in England (Akehurst 2015). These kinds of difficulties riddle every attempt at small-scale and organic food production, leading one micro-dairy producer to propose that it is the inorganic food which should require certification (Fairlie 2016).

The obstacles are not just regulatory, though, as government subsidies also stack the market in favour of larger producers. Farms smaller than five hectares (e.g. 200m x 250m) are not eligible for agricultural subsidies (Global Justice Now 2017: 1). All of that financial stress also leads lenders to look unfavourably on small enterprises.

So local food production is sometimes possible but is usually a struggle. Most of those trying to make a difference instead of making a living adopt other strategies like:

- encouraging the development of allotments;
- guerrilla gardening and planting vegetables on public land, like Incredible Edible;
- community-supported agriculture, in which consumers pay farmers directly and operate a distribution network, sometimes also paying in advance.[2]

---

[2] Many use free logistics software provided by Open Food Network. https://www.openfoodnetwork.org

- focusing on changing the law – Vermont's Farm to Plate initiative, for example, began with state legislation;[3]
- community-financed (see below) bakeries, breweries or cafes;
- changing the culture by making documentaries.[4]

Electricity

Most of our electricity production, including much of what passes for 'green', consumes huge amounts of non-renewable resources and emits CO_2. Finance aside, larger centres are more efficient because of the need for load balancing. Failures can therefore also be large, as happened in the 2003 blackout that struck much of the northeast United States (Minkel 2008).

The mega-energy companies and their financiers constantly talk about renewable energy but do very little and stand accused of backtracking on commitments (Macalister 2015), buying out their opponents, and obscuring their main activities behind greenwash campaigns (Watson 2017). Projects which do materialize are 'sustainable' only by the narrowest possible definition, with limited lifespans and non-renewable components, and are neither resilient nor localized: 'The dominant model for renewable energy today is large-scale, centralized generating systems such as big solar plantations and large wind farms. It is an extension of the legacy model of centralized, fossil-fuel-based electrical energy production, a product of concentrated financial and economic power' (Fairchild and Weinrub 2017). From a localization perspective, energy would be more secure, cheaper, cleaner (chemically and ethically) and locally appropriate if managed and owned by the community, with its own long-term interest at heart.

> Energy democracy is a way to frame the international struggle of working people, low-income communities, and communities of colour [and culture] to take control of energy resources from the energy establishment – the large corporate energy producers, utility monopolies, and federal and state government agencies that

---

[3] https://www.vtfarmtoplate.com/plan/chapter/appendix-a-enabling-legislation
[4] A good one is https://www.biggestlittlefarmmovie.com

serve their interests, and use those resources to empower their communities: literally (by providing energy), economically, and politically. (Fairchild and Weinrub 2017)

However, in most countries it is forbidden, or at least very difficult, having generated electricity by whatever means, to legally supply it to one's neighbours. Providing energy directly to the public is often illegal; in the United Kingdom, it requires a fixed-fee licence, without which producers must sell to the national grid at only 22 per cent of the retail rate. Beyond installing a solar panel on the roof, generating energy for others to consume requires a considerable amount of knowledge, commitment and money. It is not just about investing in electricity-generating capacity but working with the national grid and customers to ensure that what is generated is consumed and paid for, and at a predictable rate. Some who have navigated this territory offer consultation to those who follow or set up companies specializing in regulatory 'hacks' or other functions. For example:

- Sharenergy nurtures new projects and publishes live share offers.[5]
- Energy Local uses smart meters to prove that local energy consumed correlates to local energy produced and so gets better prices for local energy going through the grid.[6]
- Big Solar Coop aims to bring community solar producers together to share skills and resources to increase their organizational efficiency.[7]

Government

Despite devastating cuts, some local governments have still been capable of forward-thinking policy making. Following an example set in Cleveland, Ohio, Preston council in the United Kingdom pledged, along with various 'anchor institutions' which they identified, to prefer local suppliers and later also cooperatives where

[5] https://www.sharenergy.coop/live
[6] https://energylocal.org.uk
[7] https://bigsolar.coop

possible. Aside from creating local jobs, there is also a multi-plier effect as more money stays local for longer. As momentum grows, they are exploring a number of other economic and finan-cial ideas (Preston City Council 2020). But all this is only possible for those in power. One UK group worked together to win control of a small town council and published their strategy in a book called *Flatpack Democracy*,[8] inspiring many others, some of whom have succeeded.[9]

It is not only government that needs to improve but the way that we ourselves engage in groups, establish legitimacy, build trust and participate in and abide by decisions. We will also need to improve our ways of transforming conflict, especially in situations of increased anxieties. Social technologies like soci-ocracy have been developed within progressive businesses and self-organized groups and projects which do not have a clear hierarchy established by money. That is one important approach amongst many that are enabling people to engage in ways that do not reproduce the ideologies which created our ecological and climate crisis (as described in chapters 5, 6 and 7). There are also many software tools supporting various deliberative and democratic processes.[10]

Finance

Being driven by social values more than by profit and growth, small and community enterprises are unattractive prospects to banks and traditional investors, so they lack ways to raise small and medium amounts of capital. That's why UK millionaire Dave Fishwick tried to open his own high-street bank in his hometown of Burnley, where banks, reeling from the financial crisis of 2008, were refusing to finance local businesses. His Kafkaesque experi-ence was captured in the 2012 documentary *Bank of Dave*.[11] The regulatory hurdles to issuing new money proved too great, but he

---

[8] https://www.flatpackdemocracy.co.uk
[9] The movement's news is reported on http://www.indie-town.uk
[10] One example is https://decidim.org
[11] https://youtu.be/0fIGZOe-Oa0

was able in the end to support local businesses with his own and other people's savings via a savings and loans institution. Capital can be raised not only from borrowing from people or banks but also from selling equity (shares) in the enterprise. However, even when such money might be obtainable from customers, neighbours and relatives, the legal vehicles are few and far between for investing in a local business or infrastructure project in a responsible and accountable way.

One UK initiative, the Community Shares Unit,[12] offers some support for community projects (350 projects in the first decade of its existence) to raise risk capital by issuing shares. Since these projects are too small to be publicly tradable, Community Shares guarantees some 'liquidity' to shareholders by requiring that the enterprise retain some money in case a shareholder needs to sell. This reassures the shareholder that their money won't be locked up potentially for ever and, if they need to sell, they won't be responsible for finding a buyer; rather, the enterprise must find replacement buyers by continuously demonstrating viability.

These share issuances commonly facilitate the purchase of cafes, pubs and village halls. This is the result of a UK law giving local groups a 'right to bid' when these kinds of assets are put onto the market – usually to prevent them being snapped up by chain stores. The Plunkett Foundation[13] helps local groups through the process, including organizing the finance. This kind of organizing can be an empowering experience for any community. It can help to forge relationships in trust and shared purpose, accelerating recognition and empathy – vital forces for local resilience.

Money

Most recent local currency projects have focused on driving spending to local businesses in order to keep businesses and jobs under more local control and prevent wealth 'leaking' out of the community into offshore tax havens. The most prominent of these projects have been the Bristol Pound in the United Kingdom, Berkshares in New York State and Cheimgaur, one

[12] https://communityshares.org.uk
[13] https://plunkett.co.uk

of several RegioGeld projects in Germany. However, even these showcase projects have little to show for the resources poured into them. Bendell and Greco further point out that, 'Such systems are not appealing to communities and businesses with cash flow problems, and their potential for scaling up is limited. In essence, these local currencies are not local at all, as the source of credit is the international banking system that issues the national money that is required to buy the local notes' (Bendell and Greco 2013).

The resilience issues around localizing money are much greater than the struggle between small businesses and supermarkets. One study drawing on biology to look at financial resilience questioned the homogeneity of our money system, stressing the need for a diversity of currencies and types of currencies. 'Economics seems in pursuit of monistic goals and all too willing to sacrifice everything for the betterment of market efficiency . . . Preoccupation with efficiency could propel into disaster' (Lietaer and Ulanovicz 2010).

Diversity in money should mean much more than trying to keep 'hard currency' on the same high street. It could mean different units of account or separate 'spheres of exchange'.[14] The greatest homogeneity of modern money, though, is its basis of issuance: almost all modern money is issued as bank credit to the enterprises that banks judge most profitable, and it is backstopped by government bailouts pending austerity programmes. The whole economy is shaped by the way that banks maximize their profits through financing some projects and not others (Bendell and Greco 2013).

The growth in popularity of Bitcoin has provided a lot of fuel for discussion, drawing on Hayek's ideas about 'concurrent' currencies (Hayek 1976). Cryptocurrencies are branded tokens – they have no debt obligation behind them, no institutional weight, and consequently have had no 'value' beyond the power of speculation and expectation of resale. The system of cryptocurrencies which has emerged in the last decade therefore bears little resemblance to Hayek's model. The interest in 'stable coins' of some people in this field of currency innovation will bring the

---

[14] An idea in anthropology that not anything can be exchanged for anything.

movement full circle because stable coins, like the Bristol Pound, for example, depend entirely on legal money backing and consequently do nothing to challenge the diversity of its issuance.

To really challenge the hegemony of money means finding ways for *parties other than banks to issue credit* trustworthy enough to circulate. The ability to issue credit is a huge responsibility and a boon because the issuer is effectively borrowing something for free. Different approaches grant that privilege to different parties; one movement encouraging the government to issue more credit is that of modern monetary theory; another idea is that established businesses could issue voucher-like credit; but the idea of relocalization is that small businesses could associate and issue credit on a mutual basis, which is the undertaking of business barter networks. (The same thing happens between neighbours in local exchange trading systems, though more as a way of accounting for favours than replacing money.)

All of these approaches have been deployed to good effect in the past when mainstream money has failed. The most local of those options, business barter networks, number a few thousand around the world and, with a few exceptions, such as Sardinia's Sardex and the Swiss WIR, are mostly small businesses with no transformative agenda. Overheads are quite high and their having to pay tax in the very currency they exist to sidestep seriously undermines their efficacy. Many barter-infrastructure providers compete to ensure that every network stays small, and all of this means that business barter only works for certain types of businesses.

Few heterodox economists pay business barter any attention, although the potential benefits are obvious: 'The rapidly growing body of evidence . . . indicates that their popularity is counter-cyclical, that is to say that they flourish in times of liquidity crisis, when there is not enough conventional money to support necessary economic activity' (Scott Cato 2012).

One of the authors, Matthew Slater, has published a software inter-operability protocol that would enable such networks to collaborate rather than compete.[15] The Credit Commons is a way of saying that any group of peers can determine an exchange

---

[15] http://creditcommons.net/

rate and issue and accept credit to exchange amongst themselves. It also involves an accounting protocol which works between members *and groups* (Jenkin and Slater 2016).

The localizing of credit builds on a feeling of trust within the community, and it is likely to further feelings of mutuality and interdependence which then support a stronger relationship and trust. It is why it can be such a central focus for relocalization initiatives. If a community is able to issue its own credit-based currency, rather than relying on either national currencies or non-local entrepreneurs for issuance, then it can tap into its own abundance (by bettering access to its own unused and often unrecognized assets). As such, it can challenge the scarcity story of our debt-based economy, which has enabled domination and hierarchy (chapter 5).

Space does not permit discussion of myriad other projects like the relocalization of construction, biodiesel production, preventive health and herbal medicine to reduce reliance on hi-tech medicine, or displacing globalized Uber with local platform cooperatives, and/or growing mutual aid and time banking. Instead, we have given you a few examples of the way localization can be pursued and the barriers it currently faces. We have seen that the viability of businesses and projects is very much about the regulatory and cultural environment in which they exist. In western culture, small and medium enterprises (SMEs) are treated as an economic niche, despite employing more people than large corporations. From a deep adaptation perspective, it is possible to hope that as societal collapse unfolds, simplification of the regulatory environment could result in projects which do not seem viable now becoming much more so. In any case, innumerable projects continue undaunted, hoping to cross the regulatory barriers if and when they appear.

Localization movements

Notions of localization, political decentralization and resilience have appeared from time to time in history. One example is the Tanzanian Ujamaa ideology, by which the country was governed for a decade and resulted in extensive villagization and self-reliance. Among the reasons for its decline are its incompatibility with a strengthening neoliberal order, and the lack of foreign investment in what was viewed as a socialist project. Another example is the system instituted and financed by the government of Hugo Chavez of more than 30,000 communal councils (*colectivos*) across Venezuela to strengthen democracy in the country.

Truly anarchist thinking is the most extreme form of political decentralization, putting the individual at the centre of political life to ensure justice and freedom. It is organized at the level of small communities first and then federates into larger structures, all of which help to ensure the political power is held at the local level (Bookchin 2015). This structure implies economic decentralization also and hence resilience. Functioning anarchist-like societies include the Zapatistas in Chiapas since 1994 (Ramírez 2008), the Federation of Northern Syria, a Kurdish area from which the state withdrew to focus on other battles,[16] and more informally, Cooperativa Integral Catalana, a federation of producers in Catalunya that uses the anarchist framing of that region's brief independence during the Spanish civil war.[17]

In the modern industrial society, which is complex, and which contributors to this book believe is probably or inevitably doomed, localization is an answer to a felt malaise, the alienation people feel from their economic participation: a sense of wasted time and money spent on commuting, isolation from their neighbours, despair at what is happening in their high street and, increasingly, concern about societal collapse. Sectoral actions like those described above satisfy the urges of some, but others try to actually live as locally as possible as whole communities.

Intentional communities

An advanced form of communal relocalization is that of intentional communities, many of which call themselves ecovillages.[18] The latter are 'created by self-selected groups of people who deliberately come together to create an intentional living

---

[16] https://mesopotamia.coop/david-graeber-syria-anarchism-and-visiting-rojava/
[17] http://cooperativa.cat (Catalan)
[18] For directories of intentional communities see http://ic.org, http://ecovillage. org and https://www.diggersanddreamers.org.uk

environment centred on values of sustainability and cooperation'
(Peters, Fudge and Jackson 2010). Some are focused on spirituality, such as following a common teacher or set of practices. These
groups co-create a more communal way of life by sharing land,
decision making, livelihoods and often money. Logistic, social,
legal, regulatory and economic hurdles in simply doing things
differently make life quite difficult for many such communities
and lead to a high failure rate. Nonetheless, some have made
wonderful progress, designing, building and honing physical and
social technologies which surely deserve wider application. These
include social technologies, such as the ZEGG Forum, a methodology for exploring personal and interpersonal conflict.[19] They
also include many locally appropriate physical technologies, such
as urban energy[20] and a solar 'bowl' which powers a whole community kitchen.[21]

But it is hard to see ecovillages as a template for a world population of nine billion by 2050 without massive land reform. One
common criticism of the movement is that it offers little in the
way of urban solutions when over half of the world's population
now live in cities. The cost of acquiring land and building communal structures on it is not only prohibitive for many people but
also a much riskier investment than normal property development, which is why almost all ecovillages in developed countries
are populated by the middle classes. Be that as it may, it is to the
credit of the philanthropically funded Global Ecovillage Network
that it has sought to include communities and build links even in
the poorest countries.

The anticipation of societal collapse in the last few years has
led to some people launching intentional communities that uti-
lize the concept of deep adaptation, from the United Kingdom,
to Hungary, to South Africa. Although such initiatives are useful
practical responses to anticipated collapse, they will need to be
part of a wider political movement in order to have a significant
impact as industrial consumer societies are increasingly disrupted
– an issue we return to below.

---

[19] https://www.zegg.de/en/community/social-and-communication-skills.html
[20] https://www.theguardian.com/sustainable-business/2016/jul/12/eco-village-hi-
tech-off-grid-communities-netherlands-circular-housing-regen-effekt
[21] https://auroville.org/contents/3294

Transition network (TN)

It is easy to see now that the fear that oil prices would spike as supply 'peaked' was based on the simple oversight that rising prices would finance extraction of harder-to-reach oil, but many serious people believed that a decade ago and can still anticipate the economics of oil extraction becoming problematic. The first Transition Towns were a response to that threat of 'peak oil' but have relevance far beyond that anticipation. Western populations depend on finite and irreplaceable oil for so much of everyday consumption, from energy to food, clothes and electronics, and therefore face a serious decline as it becomes increasingly scarce.

Transitioners have spawned or participated in a great many projects of the types listed above, and the movement has effectively been the face of relocalization in the United Kingdom and many other countries. The network comprises many hundreds of local projects around the world, close enough to build a common language but independent enough to have their own destiny and identity (Giangrande 2018). The movement seems to have stopped growing, and, in the spirit of wanting to do better next time, it is worth looking at some of these critiques.

TN and deep adaptation have a strong common narrative about likely or inevitable decline, although the emphases are different. The latter starts with the climate crisis, and emotional responses to it, while the former starts with the oil dependence and the need to skill up on local food production.

The TN is sometimes accused of being politically ineffective: 'It is on the issues of power and sociocultural change that many questions about the promise of the Transition movement's pursuit of community resilience and relocalization must be raised' (Yanarella and Levine 2017). Though there are doubtless political sentiments within the movement, it has always been about something other than changing the world by grasping the levers of power. Similarly, the deep adaptation agenda encompasses many issues of policy and therefore politics, but at the time of writing we have not seen within the movement an appetite for embarking on what would be a multi-decade strategy to gain power. This is something that Rupert Read invites the movement to consider further (chapter 11), and which we return to below.

Political power is important, but it often follows social change as much as driving it. Meanwhile many acts of relocalization can provide mutual security when security at the national and international levels is lacking. Even if certain existential threats such as war cannot be tackled, and even if it means working without monetary support, relocalization is a much more achievable goal than a political revolution.

Another explanation offered for the limited success of TN and, latterly, Extinction Rebellion (XR) is that they predominantly involve middle-class people of European descent, thus creating an atmosphere which does not resonate or is not welcoming to working-class and minority groups (Bardos 2016). Much of TN has been characterized by private citizens meeting together to bring change to their communities, so focusing on their lack of diversity and unconscious biases can seem a little harsh; but if middle-class Caucasians recognize the necessity of building a mass movement, then it is surely necessary to actively engage other sectors of society (Anantharaman et al. 2019; Zinn 1980). That will not only increase participation, but other people might have better ideas and should have a significant influence. For XR, therefore, many support the view, 'People of colour and working people need to be integrated directly into XR strategy and decision-making processes, not just permitted to get involved in a tokenistic fashion incapable of acting "upwards" on how XR as a whole defines itself, understands the crisis, and formulates change actions' (Ahmed 2019).

This concern has led to decolonization initiatives (chapter 6) within XR and now an effort towards co-liberation, which appreciates how we are all differentially oppressed by the dominance of cultures of patriarchy and coloniality. The issue is recognized also by the Deep Adaptation Forum (DAF), with volunteer-led initiatives on diversity, decolonization and co-liberation (chapter 7). The challenge for DA is complicated by how a concern about future existential threats to the planet and society can seem beyond the horizon of those struggling to pay bills already overdue. The economic justice agenda seems essential for the DA movement to engage in if it is not to be irrelevant to people suffering increasingly from the everyday precarity of a capitalist economy under the stress of ecological and sociological disruption.

Global justice and organizing for relocalization

If relocalization initiatives are to be more useful in deeply adapting to our climate tragedy, they will need to grow, proliferate and sustain themselves, while contributing to a shift in national and global systems and policies. Co-liberation is therefore a useful principle and framework to include in relocalization efforts. On the one hand, it may help reduce any parochialism that could emerge during the championing of local identity and self-reliance. The past and ongoing undermining of local initiative and identity can be understood within the context of wider systemic oppression by the monetary system and the ideology of e-s-c-a-p-e, which it co-maintains. As such, mutually addressing how we uphold those oppressions in our own habits of thought is part of the same co-liberation (chapter 5). On the other hand, co-liberation invites us to consider how we can live in solidarity with people suffering from the impacts of climate change elsewhere in the world. That means working together to push back against both global neoliberalism and xenophobic authoritarianism. It means organizing across borders to promote national and international institutions and rules that support localization globally (Norberg-Hodge and Read 2016). A co-liberatory movement towards relocalization in the West needs also to recognize the implications of current and historic economic injustice. Local communities could consider how to contribute to other communities in poorer and more impacted parts of the world as part of reparations for the exploitation which has underpinned western privilege and power. If there is not this global movement for fair and just relocalization, as part of deep adaptation to our climate predicament, then local initiatives may be fragile in practice yet ideologically unhelpful in reducing othering and prejudice, which are the conditions for future conflict.

Conclusion

The future will surely surprise us, and organizing ourselves more locally is no guarantee of surviving it. A political power centre in its dying throes might 'redistribute' any and all wealth

Figure 13.1 Government propaganda in support of emergency localized food production

Source: https://commons.wikimedia.org/wiki/File:PLANT_A_VICTORY_
GARDEN._OUR_FOOD_IS_FIGHTING_-_NARA_-_513818.jpg
'Government propaganda in support of emergency localised food production'

towards itself, just as the Roman Empire did during its precipitous decline in the third century AD (Homer-Dixon 2006: 248). But the reasons for building resilience in this way are not only about playing the odds. A relocalized lifestyle, as Helena

Norberg-Hodge (2019) pointed out with her book title *Local is Our Future: Steps to an Economics of Happiness*, is likely to be happier and healthier.

One approach which encapsulates a great deal of this chapter about systems thinking, the importance of food and being practical, grounded and self-sufficient, and which has repeatedly demonstrated its efficacy, is permaculture. Permaculture is the philosophical soil in which the Transition Network germinated; it is a whole-systems approach, usually applied to small-scale agriculture, which stresses diversity, interactions between species, long-term soil health and regeneration, natural (non-toxic) strategies for pest control and respect for local climate, soil type, native species, and so on. Through paying greater attention to the complexities, cycles and subtleties of natural systems, permaculture can invite us into a fuller sense of our co-being with nature. As such, it aligns with reducing our sense of separation from the natural world and therefore the restoration of our sense of inter-being that is a part of the deep adaptation agenda (see chapters 5 and 7). With that, we return to the start of our discussion, where we recognized the importance of relocalization not only for a more resilient means of meeting material needs but for the transformation of those needs through a shift in a sense of selfhood to one more connected to the people and natural environment around us. The original wealth of those connections is something that we may find helps to sustain us emotionally in the difficult periods ahead as industrial consumer societies further destabilize.

References

Ahmed, N. (2019) 'The Flawed Social Science Behind Extinction Rebellion's Change Strategy'. *Medium*. Available at: https://medium.com/insurge-intelligence/the-flawed-science-behind-extinction-rebellions-change-strategy-af077b9abb4d

Akehurst, William (2015) 'Where Do You Stand on Raw Milk? Interview with "Raw" Dairy Farmer *Low Impact*'. Available at: https://www.lowimpact.org/where-do-you-stand-on-raw-milk-interview-with-raw-dairy-farmer

Anantharaman, M., Huddart Kennedy, E., Middlemiss, L. and Bradbury, S. (2019) 'Who Participates in Community-Based Sustainable Consumption Projects and Why Does It Matter? A Constructively

Critical Approach', in C. Isenhour, M. Martiskainen and L. Middlemiss (eds), *Power and Politics in Sustainable Consumption Research and Practice*. Abingdon, UK: Routledge.

Bardos, L. (2016) 'Is Sustainability Only for the Privileged?'. *Degrowth*. Available at: https://www.degrowth.info/en/2016/05/is-sustainability-only-for-the-privileged/

Bawtree, V. and Rahnema, M. (1997) *The Post-Development Reader*. London: Zed Books.

Bendell, J. and Greco, T. H. (2013) 'Currencies of Transition: Transforming Money to Unleash Sustainability', in M. McIntosh (ed.), *The Necessary Transition: The Journey Towards the Sustainable Enterprise Economy*. Sheffield: Greenleaf, ch. 14.

Bookchin, M. (2015) *The Next Revolution: Popular Assemblies and the Promise of Direct Democracy*. Edinburgh: Blair Taylor.

Cobbett, W. (1819) *Political Register*, Vol. 35. Available at: https://babel.hathitrust.org/cgi/pt?id=chi.22519144&view=1up&seq=12

Doward, J. (2017) 'Bankruptcy Risk as "Desperate" Councils Play the Property Market'. *Guardian*. Available at: https://www.theguardian.com/society/2017/apr/29/vince-cable-cash-strapped-councils-at-risk-credit-bubble

EU (2014) *How the EU Works*. Available at: https://europa.rs/images/publikacije/HTEUW_How_the_EU_Works.pdf

Fairchild, D. and Weinrub, A. (2017) 'Energy Democracy', in D. Lerch (ed.), *The Community Resilience Reader*. Post Carbon Institute, ch. 11. Washington, DC: Island Press.

Fairlie, S. (2016) 'Why Do Organic Farmers Have to Pay for Certification Rather than Farmers Who Use Toxic Chemicals?' *Low Impact*. Available at: https://www.lowimpact.org/organic-farmers-pay-certification-rather-farmers-use-toxic-chemicals

Giangrande, N. (2018) 'Seven Lessons on Starting a Worldwide Movement for Change'. *Transition Network*. Available at: https://transitionnetwork.org/news-and-blog/seven-lessons-starting-worldwide-movement-change

Global Justice Now (2017) 'Policy Briefing: From Handouts to the Super-Rich to a Hand-Up for Small-Scale Farmers'. *Global Justice Now*. Available at: https://www.globaljustice.org.uk/sites/default/files/files/resources/postbrexitagsubsidies_briefing_3.pdf

Grabow, K. (2011) *Christian Democracy, Principles and Policy-Making*. Berlin: Konrad-adenauer-stiftung.

Haimes, Y. (2009) 'On the Definition of Resilience in Systems'. *Risk Analysis* 29: 498–501. Available at: https://onlinelibrary.wiley.com/doi/abs/10.1111/j.1539-6924.2009.01216.x

Harrison, J. (2018) 'On a Small Scale, Why Is It Illegal to Give Food

Waste to Chickens and Other Animals?' *Low Impact*. Available at: https://www.lowimpact.org/whats-wrong-with-feeding-food-waste-to-chickens-and-other-livestock

Hayek, F. (1976) *Denationalisation of Money*. London: Institute of Economic Affairs.

Homer-Dixon, T. (2006) *The Upside of Down: Catastrophe, Creativity, and the Renewal of Civilization*. Toronto, Canada: Knopf.

Jarman, N. (2016) 'Home Slaughter, Part 1'. *Country Smallholding*. Available at: https://www.countrysmallholding.com/livestock/home-slaughter-part-1-1-4368809

Jenkin, T. and Slater, M. (2016) *The Credit Commons: A Money for the Solidarity Economy*. Available at: http://creditcommons.net

Lietaer, B. and Ulanovicz, B. (2010) *Is Our Monetary Structure a Systemic Cause for Financial Instability? Evidence and Remedies from Nature*. Available at: http://www.lietaer.com/images/Journal_Future_Studies_final.pdf

Macalister, T. (2015) 'BP Dropped Green Energy Projects Worth Billions to Focus on Fossil Fuels'. *Guardian*. Available at: https://www.theguardian.com/environment/2015/apr/16/bp-dropped-green-energy-projects-worth-billions-to-focus-on-fossil-fuels

McGinnis, M. V. (1999) *Bioregionalism*. Abingdon, UK: Routledge.

Minkel, J. R. (2008) 'The 2003 Northeast Blackout – Five Years Later'. *Scientific American* Available at: https://www.scientificamerican.com/article/2003-blackout-five-years-later

Norberg-Hodge, H. (1991) *Ancient Futures*. San Francisco, CA: Sierra Club.

Norberg-Hodge, H. (2019) *Local is Our Future: Steps to an Economics of Happiness*. Totnes: Local Futures.

Norberg-Hodge, H. and Read, R. (2016) *Post-Growth Localisation*. Weymouth: Green House.

Peters, M., Fudge, S. and Jackson, T. (2010) 'Low Carbon Communities: Imaginative Approaches to Combating Climate Change Locally'. Elgar. Available at: https://pdfs.semanticscholar.org/1c3b/89197efae2e29ddc1a8e0ace2597ea9388e4.pdf

Pipe, J. (2013) 'Two Years On, What Has the Localism Act Achieved?' *Guardian*. Available at: https://www.theguardian.com/local-government-network/2013/nov/02/localism-act-devolution-uk-local-authorities

Pius XI (1931) *Quadragesimo Anno*. Available at: http://www.vatican.va/content/pius-xi/en/encyclicals/documents/hf_p-xi_enc_19310515_quaragesimo-anno.html

Preston City Council (2020) 'What is Preston Model?' Preston City Council. Available at: https://www.preston.gov.uk/article/1339/What-is-Preston-Model-

Ramírez, G. M. (2008) *The Fire and the Word: A History of the Zapatista Movement*. San Francisco, CA: City Lights.

Schumacher, E. F. (1973) *Small Is Beautiful: A Study of Economics as if People Mattered*. New York: Routledge.

Scott Cato, M. (2012) 'Local Liquidity: From Ineffective Demand to Community Currencies'. Greenhouse Think Tank. Available at: https://greenhousethinktank.org/uploads/4/8/3/2/48324387/local-liquidity-inside.pdf

Watson, B. (2017) 'The Troubling Evolution of Corporate Greenwashing'. *Chain Reaction* 129: 38–40. Available at: https://search.informit.com.au/documentSummary;dn=766428450523476;res=I ELAPA

Yanarella, E. J. and Levine, R. S. (2017) 'Power, Democracy, and the Commons: Community Resilience Activism and the Problem of Governance'. Bonus chapter. *Community Resilience Reader*. Post Carbon Institute. Washington, DC: Island Press. Available at: https://reader.resilience.org/bonus-chapter

Zinn, H. (1980) *A People's History of the United States*. Harper: New York.

Concluding the Beginning of Deep Adaptation

Jem Bendell and Rupert Read

Facing up to climate reality and considering the need for collapse readiness is initially something one almost certainly doesn't want to do.[1] This book is therefore not just an intellectual exploration. By reading it, you have allowed yourself to consider an emotionally challenging topic. If you are on broadly the same page as us, then the pain of anticipating collapse is likely to be with you for the rest of your life, as it is with the contributors to this book. Hopefully, the more people who have the courage of staying with the trouble, and not finding a simple way out, the more we will all generate ideas and initiatives for humanity to reduce harm and create more possibilities for the future.

Deep adaptation (DA) is a 'broad church'. This book has made that fact evident. There is a fundamental reason why DA is a broad church. That is because it is an emergency response, and, moreover, one to a novel, unprecedented threat. It is a way – rather, a panoply of ways – in which human beings are trying to respond to a desperate, incomputable situation: an existential threat to our world. Emergency responses, especially to a categorically new, 'slow-burning' and long (potentially endless) 'emergency', are bound to be diverse, and they ought to be so: we are called to a real rethinking, to experimentation and to a deep honesty. Moreover, in an emergency it is literally vital to

---

[1] A recent attempt to explore this widely shared reluctance can be found in Green House think tank's book, *Facing up to Climate Reality* (Foster 2019).

pull together, to find some kind of consensus from within very different but overlapping perspectives. In other words, the narcissism of small differences is an unaffordable luxury in a true emergency. Rather, there is a need to find ways of sharing the burden, even when there are differences of experience, ideology, analysis or indeed moral outlook. In short: there is a need for a broadness of church – for finding common cause within a sea of difference.

Consider this analogue, another sometimes aligned emergency response: Extinction Rebellion (XR). When ordinary, attitudinal, semi-passive, non-radical hope dies, action begins; and those taking action together because they can do no other, on the side of life, may have deeply discrepant ideologies, experiential horizons, spiritual traditions, and so forth. What it means to say that XR is broad-based – beyond party politics, beyond ideology – is that XR has brought together people committed to non-violent direct action for system change who might not be on the same side in a non-emergency setting. It is the emergency, the threat of collapse, which brings us together. An overlapping consensus forms, because it must, out of that initial sea of difference (Bradbrook and Bendell 2020).[2]

We two decided to put this book together in part to explicate that deep adaptation itself is and ought to be a broad church, so broad that the 'church' metaphor itself starts to wear thin. Jem sees societal collapse as inevitable (and fairly 'near-term', so must be responded to now). Rupert sees it as likely (but not inevitable, as we do not know for sure what is coming). Both of these are widely held views within the DA movement. Nor are they the most 'extreme' views. A few participants in the DA field are inclined to think that human extinction within the lifetimes of some born today is likely, or even inevitable. At the other end of the spectrum are some people engaged in the Deep Adaptation Forum (DAF) who think that eco-driven societal collapse is 'merely' possible. Even that latter stance is perfectly compatible with a belief in the profound importance of DA by reason of the precautionary principle: if collapse is

---

[2] On 'overlapping consensus', see John Rawls's book *Political Liberalism* (2005), and on its relevance to this specific context, see Vlad Vexler's interview with Rupert Read (Vexler 2020).

so much as possible, then it is necessary to prepare for it, as a collapse without any real practical or psychological preparedness would be far worse than one in relation to which we had sought to soften the blow.

It is crucial therefore that in considering DA one does not make the reductionist move of equating all its founders' views and its founding paper (chapter 2) with the concept of DA itself. This point has been a motivation for and, we trust, a product of this book of many voices. As you have made it thus far, it should now be clear that DA is a broad 'more-than-church'. We see that process as likely to continue, as more sectors of society, particularly perhaps academics, wake up and start to respond, as our life-support systems degrade to the (at minimum) unavoidable *possibility* of eco-driven societal collapse. And to the necessity of facing up to that dire (and, as some chapters in this book have intimated, possibly hopeful) possibility.

We are entering uncharted territory for humanity, where we will have as much unlearning as learning to do (chapter 10). Therefore, in this conclusion, we wish to open up topics, rather than narrow them down. We will do this by summarizing what we consider to be some of the most interesting points of discussion within the emerging field of collapse anticipation. If we can explore such topics with compassion, curiosity and respect, then that will be as important as any conclusions that are reached (chapter 7). Once again, that is the spirit in which the two of us have sought to conceive and design the book, one of open co-sympathetic dialogue. Thus we'll occasionally develop a little further, in what follows, interesting and salient points of difference between the two of us.

Communicating deep adaptation

The first topic of discussion and of some disagreement in the DA field is the matter of a responsible communication strategy. Is it best that people who believe societal collapse is likely, inevitable or occurring avoid promoting their knowledge and opinions to the general public? Most people involved in the DA field are focused on processing what their collapse anticipation means for their own lives and then seek to create resources for other people who come to the same realization. Until now, very few people in the DA field have focused on how to promote the anticipation of collapse amongst the general public. Rupert has been more open to such public engagement. It is easier for him to take this path than it is for Jem as Rupert does not close off the (slim) possibility of this civilization ending by way of deliberate transformation rather than by way of collapse.

There are many reasons for that somewhat deliberate paucity of mass public presentation of DA, including the belief that the mass media will not address the matter seriously and give the relevant psychological advice. Without the ability for people to talk with others and find a community of support, such information might just shock and alienate people. It might also make them unconsciously more susceptible to duplicitous messaging supported by vested interests. But there is another reason for the reticence. It is emotionally very tough to bring this news to other people. It will inevitably lead to difficult emotions and so needs to be done sensitively while recognizing the emotional toll it can exert on oneself when doing so (chapter 4).

In many cases, people have decided to keep their collapse anticipation to themselves and instead focus their public communication on the need for bold mitigation and drawdown. Many of us have therefore contributed to the protest movement XR. The rationale is that it is worth trying to achieve bold mitigation and drawdown measures from policy makers and the general public while working on developing inner and outer resilience to future collapse through the person-to-person conversations that occur amongst activists. However, as the initial excitement about sometimes strikingly successful new tactics for generating a growing climate awareness begins to wane, some activists are looking again at this choice of focus. XR had extraordinary success, especially in the United Kingdom, in turning the dial and opening the 'Overton Window' on the importance of climate. But XR may have contributed to the risk of burnout by sometimes not staying true to its founding insight of the desperateness of our predicament (Knorr et al. 2020; Moses 2020). It has been tempting for some people within XR to make it sound as if its demands could be achieved within something resembling our current system, as if we had 'twelve years' (now nine) to 'save the world' (Read 2020a). As the XR founders and their earliest rebels know, the situation is worse than that, especially now that three precious years have passed (Read 2020b; Read and Scavelli 2020).

A lack of mainstream outreach on DA, on the risks of societal collapse and the most kind, wise and accountable ways of responding to it, does not come without drawbacks. It has meant that people who are antagonistic to such an outlook misrepresent it and criticize it in the public domain. Does that mean people who anticipate collapse should do more proactive outreach? To ensure that at least there is some accurate information about this topic in the mainstream media? Perhaps there is an even more important reason. If this is our truth, then should we look for more ways to share it? By doing so, might we help more people to prepare themselves and their communities?

In the original deep adaptation paper, some data suggested that over the last ten years people are intuiting the end of the story of economic progress. Environmental degradation may be part of that. New research finds that half of British and French people believe that society will soon collapse (Cassely and Fourquet 2020); and that finding was before Covid-19. Therefore, could it be a narcissistic delusion that those of us who consider collapse to be likely, inevitable or already unfolding should hesitate before speaking to the masses about that? By not speaking about it and inviting generative dialogue about what it means, then we lose time. In particular, an intuition of future malaise could be leading people to engage with hard-right and authoritarian messages that offer a counterproductive means of restoring a sense of psychological safety. If people without such politics do not engage in the conversation about safety and purpose in the face of turbulence, then that could become a massive political blunder (Bendell 2020; chapter 9).

This relates to another argument for why it may be time to reach out to the general public on matters of collapse. There is evidence that the militaries of many countries have anticipated how climate change will disrupt societies and the global economy. The Pentagon and the US Navy are well known examples (Ahmed 2019). If they have known this situation is coming, then what other departments of what other governments have also known? What might they have been discussing and deciding away from the gaze of the mass media and the normal process of discussion in civil society? How might that be affecting current political trends, in ways that we do not understand? Instead of moving into the realm of conspiracy theories, there is a simpler and pragmatic answer: normalize discussions of collapse readiness in the public domain.

One argument against more outreach is that it will invite more criticism from people who have adopted a public role in environmental communications and do that from within an ideology of modernity and control, which means they are averse to collapse anticipation (as explained in chapters 5 and 6). The reason why that could be a problem is it means that people engaged in deep adaptation might spend much time engaged in the ideas and modes of communication of people existing within that paradigm, rather than embodying and expressing something altogether new.

Yet are they mutually exclusive? Could we engage critics and general publics in a way that maintains our ethos and does not distract from the core work of deep adaptation? If we turn away from public communication, would we be prioritizing an easier life over that of remaining with the full difficulty of our time, which will include more moments of panicked and aggressive criticism?

When doing new outreach, it will be important to maintain a gentleness, even when under fire. It would also best be done with the advice and feedback of mental health professionals and with requests for media outlets to provide means for audiences to connect with people to express and explore reactions together. In addition, all DA volunteer groups could be ready to point people to mental health support services in any emergency situations. Anxieties in societies are likely to increase, whether or not anyone chooses to do outreach about climate or not, and so deep adaptation groups could provide a supplement to how societies support mental health (chapter 4; Bendell 2019).

Our conclusion is that it *is* time to seek a broader audience for DA, which is one reason why we have put together this book. Rupert's experience of going public with his thought that 'This civilization is finished', and that the only way it potentially gets to end without collapse is via a transformation so deep that what emerges the other side would in no meaningful sense be *this* civilization, has been on balance a positive one. Rupert at first didn't want to make his thesis public at all, fearing that the reaction would be one of hostility and of demoralization. In fact, the reaction turned out to be more vibrant than for anything he had ever said before. Rupert believes that DA will experience less pushback if it is communicated without an insistence on collapse being inevitable – so the broad-church approach is maintained and deepened. However, it can be recognized that the original DA paper concluded collapse is inevitable and that appears to have been part of its impact – which was very big (ergo the present book). Jem believes that, for communications concerns, people should not be dissuaded from concluding that societal collapse is inevitable, especially when millions of people are experiencing forms of collapse already. He notes that for many people who conclude that societal collapse is near certain or inevitable, it means the matter becomes unavoidable in their daily experience, and thus they stop postponing exploring the implications for their lives, beliefs, politics and suchlike. However, like Rupert, he promotes the utility of the DA framework and community for people with any level of collapse anticipation. This is critically important: the point we share is facing up to the reality of collapse as more than simply a thought-stopper. Taking collapse seriously is the game changer.

Seek more justice?

Some people have asked whether the people engaged in collapse anticipation in general are focused more on their own vulnerability and survival in the future than on the experience of others' suffering at present (chapter 6). It does appear that many of the stories that reach the media about previous collapse-anticipating households and communities suggest they are focused on hyperlocal resilience, whether off-grid living or concerns about personal security. This is the image of the 'prepper' who learns to grow food and shoot. Whether or not this is an accurate portrayal of the diversity of people who anticipate collapse is, to say the least, unclear to us. For decades, the Transition Towns movement has involved people who are preparing for a breakdown in society, and their vegetable allotments and knitting clubs are probably less 'media friendly' than the gun-toting prepper (chapter 12). So what of the concept and people involved in deep adaptation? The concept and growing movement is explicitly about enabling and embodying loving responses to our predicament. It is therefore a peace-movement alternative to the image of preppers readying themselves for crime and civil conflict (chapter 8).

In outlining DA in this way, we do not mean to denigrate all efforts at 'prepping' which anticipate increased crime. Nor do we dismiss the practice of acquiring more supplies of food, medicines and other essentials. In our experience, though, one of the chief beneficial effects is that doing these things and their ilk tends to make evident how relatively futile many possible efforts to 'prepare' for a possible collapse are, especially insofar as those efforts are mainly individual. It shows one viscerally the importance of being able to survive a shock *along with*, at minimum, the other people whom one lives near, for starters. So, if one brings in extra food, one ought to encourage others to do so too, bring in some *for* them, and recognize that such activities are not a replacement for more collective action to help whole communities (at least) to be more resilient. In Rupert's case, he has found that doing a little prepping in these ways also helped people to understand how serious he is about trying to start readying for potential collapse. Deeds speak louder than words alone.

These kinds of considerations already encourage an elementary awareness of issues of justice, as a pragmatic necessity as well as a moral or political desideratum. Most of us had some experiences relevant to this matter in the initial stage of the Covid-19 pandemic. In the United Kingdom, there was much panic-buying (famously of toilet roll, but more saliently of pasta, rice, etc.); food-sellers moved to begin an elementary form of rationing, and there were public appeals, some heeded, for fairness of access to food. Unfortunately, the desirability in this context of some genuine form of food rationing, along with increased availability of foods that are not imported, never quite reached the public debate; but we think that the experience of vulnerability that was shared in spring 2020 could potentially have lasting positive consequences for beginning processes of both collapse awareness and collapse readiness (Read 2020c). Whether it does or not may depend upon whether deep adaptation can become understood as a wise and needful 'insurance policy' in the troubled era into which we are moving.

It is clear how this discussion is related to the previous one, that of public outreach. If 'collapse' is not merely in the realm of concept but a label for some difficult experiences (present, imminent or potential) in the real world, then arguing whether it is good for people to communicate about it could be a form of solipsism. Instead, our task can be how we make sense of our situation in ways that discourage violent or exclusionary approaches and encourage more kind, wise and accountable responses. There is an interesting question as to whether the conversations and initiatives of deep adaptation can be more relevant to the understandable desire of people to protect themselves against uncertain futures. If it can, then that increases the prospects of the DA agenda for turning purely defensive approaches to potential societal breakdown into smarter and kinder approaches. The huge upsurge of care on both macro and micro levels was an encouraging aspect of the 2020 Covid-19 tragedy, and can be learned from and built upon. Without this development – without a potential nexus between DA and individual/neighbourhood practical resilience – there is a risk that DA may be restricted to a particular middle-class 'ghetto', and that it may be rendered irrelevant to most minds in the hard times to come. Frowning upon people looking to grow their own food and even protect their land and food against violent expropriation by state or non-state actors might restrict the potential appeal and relevance of the deep adaptation agenda.

Clearly, questions not just of prudence but of justice thread through all of this dialogue. It is going to be very important to keep those questions alive, to prevent a fear-based fixation on survival from shoving everything else aside, as society inevitably plans more for the existential risks it faces, as the climate and ecological crisis inevitably worsens in the 2020s. We hope that the difficult issues being aired here are pursued in both research and in real life in the coming months and years.

We nurse this hope partly because, with all these intentions and values in mind, one can question whether the present discussions and initiatives in the field of DA are too focused on the anticipation of future collapse rather than on people's current experience of collapse and the ongoing harm caused by our current systems (chapter 6). When looking at our current system's production of inequality, poverty, poor mental health, animal suffering, toxic pollution and habitat destruction, there is, some might argue, enough to criticize and challenge without focusing on future trends and probabilities. For many people and other forms of life, collapse is a current experience directly resulting from the continuance of the societies that most of you reading this book benefit from. *They* are experiencing high-intensity disruptions and struggles for justice and healing. It is important to note that some people in DA networks have been badly affected by forest fires, storm damage, rising costs of living and the impacts of a pandemic made more likely by environmental degradation; in some cases, that is even why they have got involved. However, most people are not yet experiencing the extreme impacts of climate disruption. That brings us to the matter of whether their engagement in DA is enabling people to change in ways that reduce intense suffering, either by reducing their complicity, challenging systems or supporting humanitarian action. Some people who have roles within the DA field are promoting such responses. But it is probably not the main focus for people who engage in this discussion, who tend to be middle-class people in modern consumer societies. Nevertheless, it is possible to reduce daily suffering and injustice from our current lifestyles, while also preparing for a coming or potential societal collapse. As the last chapter made clear, this issue is one of emphasis, rather than an insurmountable barrier.

A related issue is the limited diversity of people engaged in DA at present. The concept was published in the English language in the United Kingdom and the main networks are in English, so a preponderance of white people might be expected. However, that means the communities emerging around DA may operate in ways that feel unwelcoming to black, indigenous and people of colour (BIPOC). For instance, some of the emphasis on grief, love and wisdom may seem somewhat self-soothing, and may downplay matters of complicity, accountability, justice, reparations and healing. They may see this as a means of depoliticizing a topic to make it attractive for people who are less oppressed or less concerned with oppression (as discussed in chapter 6).

Another – in our view, crucial – aspect of diversity is economic class, both in and between countries. Many people find it difficult to earn their living and have little spare time for engaging in discussions on public matters, or to volunteer. That situation is becoming worse with declining pay and working conditions in many countries, including in the post-coronavirus recession. Should engaging in the anticipation of collapse become helpful to these people, and if so how? Whether DA initiatives and people should seek more actively to engage people who are not well represented at present, or seek to complement other frameworks and initiatives, is open to discussion. Different countries and cultures will have their own concepts, phrases and places for discussion. For instance, in the French-speaking world, *collapsologie* has been developed as an academic field, albeit with a built-in openness to a non-academic 'audience' (chapter 3).

These issues all relate to a broader question of the extent to which DA could or should become a new social movement that seeks to secure changes to power relations in societies. Some criticize participants in DA for not being explicit about such an agenda. Part of the reason for not doing that is because of the previous reticence about mass public outreach, described above. But perhaps that reason is, as we have implied, becoming less salient or valid. Another reason is much of the early focus has been on inner changes and developing support systems for people who anticipate collapse; and that is likely to need to continue. A third reason is much of the impetus for political action on climate has been channelled towards and through XR, which launched at a similar time. But XR, despite its remarkable successes in changing the climate of public opinion, has not made big inroads on the more vital matter of stopping the actual climate changing for the worse. Our view is that it makes sense for XR now to embrace an agenda focused on transformative and deep adaptation, not just on 'mitigation' (i.e. greenhouse gas reduction). The converse applies too: that adaptational movements need to recognize the long period of struggle and remaking that we are entering into, and not be shy of power. In other words: if XR should move towards adaptation, so should adaptation think about moving towards XR and the like, and indeed towards conventional politics where appropriate (chapter 11).

Given that collective action through local, national and international government will be essential to reduce harm from climate disruption, the lack of a political agenda emerging from deep adaptation would be a cause of future criticism, discussion and new initiatives. Though, as Rupert indicated in chapter 11, saying that something is 'essential' does not mean, in our profoundly imperfect political world, that it is going to happen (Read 2020d). Perhaps the need is to articulate and work for – as part of DA – what a more just world, one that is energy-descending and differentiating between survival emissions and luxury emissions, would look like, but without assuming that it will actually be feasible to achieve such a world.

If collapse anticipation does give rise to political agendas and campaigns, then serious attention will need to be given to where influential and legitimate allies might be found. Although DA has arisen from the environmental movement, as illustrated by our own careers and interests, it is uncertain whether the environmental movement will be the best source of constituents for driving the revolutionary changes now required to our entire system, both to give humanity a chance of a less bad climate and to adapt to growing disruption. Wider conversations with all kinds of people and organizations will be important to see where political alliances might emerge.

Integrate more clearly?

A third important topic of discussion is that many people involved in DA have been treating it as a separate field from mainstream climate change adaptation (CCA) and its sub-field of 'transformative adaptation'. For some decades, there has been research and policy making to enable changes in practices so they are less disrupted by human-triggered climate change.[3] These changes include irrigation for agriculture, new sea defences, storm proofing buildings and suchlike (Few et al. 2017). There is also growing attention to, though little implementation of, transformative adaptation, which considers how to adapt in ways that are low carbon and adjusted to more severe impacts, for instance, and crucially, the restoration of 'mobile' natural sea and flood defences (such as wetlands or mangrove swamps), which simultaneously draw down carbon. Some people involved in this area

---

[3] See e.g. the Transformative Adaptation Research Alliance https://research.csiro.au/tara/core-concepts/ and https://research.csiro.au/tara/people/. See also Foster (2019).

suggest that the collapse-readiness aspects of DA could find an audience within the international and national policy processes on these relatively mainstream approaches to adaptation. There could be connections in the areas of disaster-risk reduction and preparedness for delivering humanitarian relief. If DA ideas and initiatives were able to be connected with these existing fields, then there might be more opportunity to mainstream the ideas in sectors such as education (chapter 10).

A contrary view is that the concept of DA is defined as distinct from, and as a criticism of, mainstream adaptation approaches insofar as those are superficial or shallow. The mainstream adaptation field can be regarded as counterproductive in assuming the aim of maintaining industrial consumer societies, despite their contribution to dangerous climate change and forthcoming severe disruption from its direct and indirect influences. If the people, ideas and initiatives in the DA movement begin to be incorporated into mainstream adaptation contexts, then they may lose what is making them vibrant and imaginative. Worse, it might lead to a compromise with the eco-centrist ideology of most mainstream environmentalism and thus the marginalization of a radical political agenda.

It appears that some mixing of ideas and approaches may happen in future, and the implications will depend on how much time we have before more societies become severely disrupted. The view that the two of us are converging upon is that there are good grounds for convergence between DA and what is termed 'transformative adaptation'. Rupert has previously made clear the aspects of transformative adaptation that can make it worthy of the term 'transformation'.[4] It must be understood as adaptation that simultaneously mitigates, that works with nature rather than against it (e.g. restoring wetlands and mangroves *rather than* building hard flood defences). It must be adaptation that seeks to co-create the transformed society that we need and want anyway. It can also be a way of self-organizing rather than just something that we call on governments to deliver if they are failing

---

[4] Transformative adaptation is a concept with a background in the academy and the UN; see e.g. Fedele et al. (2019) for an overview. It has been developed further and 'radicalized' somewhat by Rupert and by Green House so that it lives up to its name. See also Read 2021.

so to deliver, as they mostly are. It is then/therefore something that we *do* ourselves (including potentially, where necessary, via non-violent direct action/civil disobedience); which helps make its overlap with DA clear, and deeply helpful. Transformative adaptation, for Rupert, comes from a sense that collapse is likely but not certain; deep adaptation, for Jem, comes from a sense that collapse is now certain. This disagreement need not get in the way of the productive confluence that is feasible here. Part of our joint future research agenda, continuing from this book, will explore how exactly transformative and deep adaptation may be framed and developed.

Map collapse better?

Some readers might be wanting more clarity still about what precisely we mean by 'collapse'. A fourth topic of discussion for some people involved in the DA field therefore is that the myriad drivers of societal collapse, additional to climate decline and the mechanisms or stages of that collapse, have not been sufficiently mapped out. One part of this argument is that collapse needs to be better understood so that people can more confidently engage in implications and be listened to by others. Another part of the argument is that, with more detailed mapping of collapse pressures and processes, people and policy makers will be more able to decide how to slow the process, reduce harm and prepare for what happens next.

It appears that people would be helped with more information on the processes of collapse, and so bringing more 'collapsology' to the DA movement appears important to do (chapter 3). That would mean that more specific policy debates will emerge, such as what should be the best approach to nuclear power (and weapons), which are a potentially debilitating legacy for a declining society to cope with; what to do with industrial agriculture (including but not restricted to most animal agriculture); how to develop, govern or prevent forms of geoengineering (Paul and Read 2019); how to change banking and finance (Bendell and Greco 2013); and what the future of foreign policy could be. It would also mean the general public and policy makers will have more knowledge to understand what the hedge funds, insurance companies and other financial institutions may be planning to do with their superior assessments of risk (Aronoff 2020), and therefore respond better to any unhelpful pressures from those institutions. This enhanced expertise will also better inform any initiatives to develop DA as a social movement that seeks political influence.

Work on mapping collapse better may help respond to the criticism some people have aired that using the term 'collapse' might be unhelpful. They point out that many people regard 'collapse' as something which must be complete and sudden, so do not consider how to moderate it in a more granular way or how forms of collapse may be underway already. Therefore, some people argue that the term 'breakdown' may be more suitable as it conveys less of a total and permanent situation. However, the term 'breakdown' can imply that the situation can be resolved whereby the previous systems are restored. Neither of us see a future with systems of finance, industry and government operating as they do now, and so the terms 'collapse' and 'transformation' seem more appropriate for our discussions.

Probably, more mapping of the ways in which climate amplifies other stressors and the way these are then felt in societies – including through the development of scenarios (including both very dire and more 'hopeful' scenarios) – will be helpful for that. This issue relates to the nature of sense-making about the various disruptions that are happening already within societies around the world. Outbreaks of coronaviruses and other epidemics/pandemics are caused or made worse by capitalist-driven habitat destruction, by animal mistreatment and by anthropogenic climate change (Kishan 2020) (then vectored by key super-spreaders: jet planes), and it is clear that the pandemic of Covid-19 has led to a momentary semi-collapse of some communities and the livelihoods of millions of families. However, this is not yet understood widely enough as an eco-driven disruption (Read 2020e). That is something we all need to work more on changing. That kind of broadening of understanding will be literally vital to softening the blows that will fall on humanity in the coming decades (chapters 5 and 7).

Avoid safety of frameworks?

A fifth topic of discussion and disagreement is quite the contrary to the previous two. It arises from the idea that there are extremely deep causes for our destruction of the biosphere that involve our psychological and emotional attachment to a problematic culture of possessive modernity (chapters 5, 6 and 7). We have become a species that experiences life as separate from the natural world and each other, which generates a deep and suppressed fear that then informs a range of assumptions and behaviours. This perspective on the deeper psychological processes that lead us to uphold a range of problematic aspects of modernity, coloniality, patriarchy and economic exploitation is not something widely understood but is sensed in some way by many people who are able to let despair melt away their previous unquestioning allegiance to current systems and cultures. This perspective suggests that any shortcut to the path of personal identity disintegration and reconfiguration could impair the process for people. Therefore, giving collapse anticipation a terminology and framework for discussion (with the 4Rs) might give people a false sense of tangibility in a way that means they might not let themselves dissolve and reconstitute their own knowing and identity. That is because we have been schooled in a culture that invites us to feel better for knowing the 'right answer' in terms of correct facts, models, values and beliefs. That desire is related to the insecure ego that arises from a world view of separation (chapter 7).

On the other hand, there is a benefit to there being a name for this field, like a kite in the sky that people can spot and orient towards so as to then meet other people, support each other and discuss ideas. The framework is deliberately just a set of four questions without answers, in order to keep the space fluid and emergent. However, the problem of a name and framework that has 'gone viral' is that some people are thinking of deep adaptation as a brand that has emotional resonance and might therefore be attracted for the wrong reasons – popularity! Some people might be engaging partly for wanting to be involved in the latest ideas and discussions about society and the environment. As such, they might bring an unhelpful energy and attention to how to grow, maintain or adjust the 'brand' so that more people can be engaged and fewer people upset by this conversation spreading around the world. On this point, we simply urge vigilance. So long as there is a broadly philosophical attitude, rather than any imposition of dogma, we feel fairly confident that some framework hereabouts is better than none.

Be more positive?

The sixth and final topic of disagreement and discussion that we would like to describe to you here is quite widespread: it is that some people suggest that DA concepts and participants could and should be 'more positive'. The way discussions about DA occur at present is with an agnosticism on what comes during and after any societal collapse. Perhaps there will be a chance for a new ecological civilization, but perhaps there will not. The ethos of the DA concept and spaces at present is not to colonize people's own explorations of the topic and to welcome 'unknowing' (and in *this* way we are in sympathy with the wariness concerning frameworks, which was explored just above). That is partly because a key aspect of the DA ethos is to find a motivation for enabling and embodying loving responses to our predicament without the expectation of a specific outcome (chapter 9).

We've mentioned already the difference between the two of us relevant to this: that Rupert does not rule out a non-collapse, non-multiple-megadeaths way of ending our toxic civilization (Read and Alexander 2019). He emphasizes not *knowing* whether collapse is coming at all. However, just *because* his starting point is more within a space of epistemic uncertainty than Jem's, it is worth stressing that the two of us strongly *agree* that, while it is very much worth exploring and developing possible future scenarios (including enabling us to imagine viable sequences of steps towards possible non-catastrophic futures), we cannot afford, at a potential cost of inauthenticity – or of setting people up for a crushing disappointment and burnout – to *attach* to any specific future scenario, negative *or* positive. Moreover, we are convinced that the widespread nostrum that a vision that is not resolutely 'positive' cannot gain adherence and traction has been disproven – by the resonance that our own outputs have achieved in the last few years, and, on a larger scale, by the phenomenon of Extinction Rebellion, an organization whose very name is an affront to those who used to claim that if one's dream included a nightmare, then it was bound to fail.

So we are unconvinced that promulgating a *specific* vision of a 'better' world is necessary, or even authentically possible, or even helpful. However, many people disagree with not having a specific vision of a hopeful future. Some people believe they must have a material hope for the future because of their religious perspective. For instance, some Christians assume that the hope they are invited to have by their faith is a physical one, rather than a metaphysical or spiritual hope. 'Positive thinking' has also become central to modernity and the assumption of 'progress' (chapter 5). Some views on quantum mechanics have spread in popular culture in ways that are misleading about the implications. In particular, our individualist culture (including in 'New Age' versions) means that some people believe that each individual's perspectives and intentions will shape what is manifested, no matter what anyone else is thinking or doing. Some other people think we all have to think a certain way for something to be manifested. This is not the place for us to explain the fallacies of such magical thinking. Suffice to say, we all are co-creating our realities with the rest of the cosmos at all times, and any desires for physical manifestations are more likely to arise from separation than unity consciousness and thus will not have any welcome effect. We realize that sentence might need rereading a few times and some discussion. But we would like to add that it corresponds with the mystic traditions of many mainstream religions that invite alignment with divine will, rather than petitioning it for our own ends (chapter 8).

Despite the various concerns that we've intimated, some critics still assert the 'necessity' and 'power' of being clear about what it is that a person, group or organization wants to see in the world. We agree that having an intention can sometimes be helpful for having an effect. But recall: in the case of the Deep Adaptation Forum, the expressed aim is to promote more loving responses to our predicament and to embody that in the way we go about our efforts. For the two of us, that very much includes building a culture that is less dominated by exploitative colonial patriarchal modernity and more welcoming of the wisdom from Buddhism and the mystic strands of most religions. There is increasing potential for an eco-spirituality to grow (Read 2020f), and to make an enormous difference, in this time of trial (Read 2018; Studley 2018). The key, though, will be to be serious about not 'end-gaining' through that contemplative-activist formulation. In other words: not to *use* spirituality, materialistically, as just another tool to attain desperately elusive goals of individual or collective survival, but rather to be serious about acceptance, about relinquishment, about despair. The broader saving power of such experiences will come, if it does come, from their very authenticity. To experience and process despair, rather than to suppress or short-circuit it, can be transformational for self and society. Provided one does not become stuck within it, *and* provided one does not pretend that despair, any more than hope, can guarantee a desirable outcome (Bradbrook and Bendell 2020).

Conclusion: an end to the beginning

Some people's resistance to the deep adaptation agenda is extremely understandable, as it challenges assumptions of personal identity and purpose, and invites us to contemplate the virtually uncontemplatable: the feasible death not just of oneself and of those one loves, but of the very taken-for-granted framework of civilizational continuity or 'growth' within which life and death have been made sense of for centuries.

As the climate worsens and societies become more challenging, so the ideas, initiatives, confusions and backlashes will all grow. Given the increasing stresses in society and on individuals, the way we show up in those conversations is key. Enabling open-hearted and open-minded dialogue on various topics will be important.

If you have considered the anticipation of societal collapse to be wrong or unhelpful, then we will still be here for when you are ready. As we hope you will have gathered from this book, there is no one right way to respond to an anticipation or experience of societal disruption, with much to unlearn and learn as we go.

The cultural commentator John Michael Greer once quipped to an audience, 'Collapse now, and avoid the rush.' This is black humour of the most relevant kind. Transformative and deep adaptation is an agenda for the whole world, and for the whole person. Who knows – perhaps we can turn eco-driven collapse from something terrifying into something tolerable or, possibly, even positive for some people. Or, as the collapsologists imply, perhaps collectively facing collapse as an inevitable reality might, paradoxically, be the one thing that can still slow or transform it (chapter 3). One thing we are united in certainty on is that willed ignorance is no longer an option. That facing up to collapse reality is a good and necessary step. We thank you for being willing to walk with us on this difficult imaginal and practical journey, a journey that the more shared it is, the more bearable and even brighter it becomes.

References

Ahmed, N. (2019) 'US Military Could Collapse Within 20 Years Due to Climate Change, Report Commissioned by Pentagon Says'. Vice. Available at: https://www.vice.com/en/article/mbmkz8/us-military-could-collapse-within-20-years-due-to-climate-change-report-commissioned-by-pentagon-says

Aronoff, K. (2020) 'The Planet Is Screwed, Says Bank that Screwed the Planet'. New Republic. Available at: https://newrepublic.com/article/156657/planet-screwed-says-bank-screwed-planet

Bendell, J. (2019) 'Glocalising DA – Launching Deep Adaptation Groups Network'. Jembendell.com. Available at: https://jembendell.com/2019/09/09/glocalising-deep-adaptation-launching-the-deep-adaptation-groups-network/

Bendell, J. (2020) 'What Activism Next? Ideas for Climate Campaigners'. Jembendell.com. Available at: https://jembendell.com/2020/02/06/what-activism-next-ideas-for-climate-campaigners/

Bendell, J. and Greco, T. (2013) 'Currencies of Transition', in M. McIntosh (ed.), The Necessary Transition, 1st edn. Sheffield: Greenleaf Publishing.

Bradbrook, G. and Bendell, J. (2020) 'Our Power Comes from Acting without Escape from our Pain'. Resilience. Available at: https://www.resilience.org/stories/2020-07-30/our-power-comes-from-acting-without-escape-from-our-pain/

Cassely, J.-L. and Fourquet, J. (2020) 'La France: Patrie de la collapsologie?' Fondation Jean-Jaurès and IFOP. Available at: https://jean-jaures.org/nos-productions/la-france-patrie-de-la-collapsologie

Fedele, G. et al. (2019) 'Transformative Adaptation to Climate Change for Sustainable Social-Ecological Systems'. *Environmental Science and Policy* 101: 116–25.

Few, R. et al. (2017) 'Transformation, Adaptation and Development: Relating Concepts to Practice'. *Palgrave Communications* 3. Available at: https://www.nature.com/articles/palcomms201792

Foster, J. (ed.) (2019) *Facing Up to Climate Reality: Honesty, Disaster and Hope*. London: London Publishing Partnership.

Kishan, S. (2020) 'Professor Sees Climate Mayhem Lurking behind Covid-19 Outbreak'. Bloomburg. Available at: https://www.bloomb erg.com/news/articles/2020-03-28/professor-sees-climate-mayhem-lu rking-behind-covid-19-outbreak

Knorr, W. et al. (2020) 'Letters'. *Guardian*. Available at: https://www. theguardian.com/world/2020/may/10/after-coronavirus-focus-on-the climate-emergency

Moses, A. (2020) '"Collapse of Civilisation is the Most Likely Outcome": Top Climate Scientists'. Voice of Action. Available at: https:// voiceofaction.org/collapse-of-civilisation-is-the-most-likely-outcome- top-climate-scientists/

Paul, H. and Read, R. (2019) 'Geoengineering as a Response to the Climate Crisis: Right Road or Disastrous Diversion?', in J. Foster (ed.), *Facing Up to Climate Reality: Honesty, Disaster and Hope*, 1st edn. London: London Publishing Partnership.

Rawls, J. (2005) Political Liberalism, 2nd edn. New York: Columbia University Press.

Read, R. (2018) 'Religion After the Death of God? The Rise of Pantheism and the Return to the Source'. Medium. Available at: https://medium. com/@GreenRupertRead/religion-after-the-death-of-god-the-rise-of -pantheism-and-the-return-to-the-source-54453788bbaa

Read, R. (2020a) *Our Last Chance to Save a World that Won't Be Saved*. Available at: https://www.youtube.com/watch?v=LZtRv58OeCM

Read, R. (2020b) '24 Theses on Corona'. Medium. Available at: https://medium.com/@rupertjread/24-theses-on-corona-7486899198 59

Read, R. (2020c) 'Negotiating the Space between Apocalypse and Victory'. *Byline Times*. Available at: https://bylinetimes.com/2020/06/12/neg otiating-the-space-between-apocalypse-and-victory/

Read, R. (2020d) 'The Coronavirus Gives Humanity One Last Chance – but for What Exactly?' Compass. Available at: https://www.compa ssonline.org.uk/the-coronavirus-gives-humanity-one-last-chance-but- for-what-exactly/

Read, R. (2020e) 'Imagining the World after COVID-19'. ABC. Available at: https://www.abc.net.au/religion/rupert-read-imaginin g-a-world-after-coronavirus/12380676

Read, R. (2020f) *Eco-Spirituality at the Moment of Last Chance*. Available at: https://www.youtube.com/watch?v=4kbzI_jTGIk

Read, R. (2021) 'Transformative Adaptation: A New Framework for Responding to Our Predicament'. *Permaculture Magazine* 107.

Read, R. and Alexander, S. (2019) *This Civilisation Is Finished: Conversations on the End of Empire – and What Lies Beyond*. Melbourne: Simplicity Institute.

Read, R. and Scavelli, F. (2020) '2025 No More? The Tory Victory, XR, and the Coming Storms'. Open Democracy. Available at: https://www.opendemocracy.net/en/opendemocracyuk/2025-no-more-tory-victory-xr-and-coming-storms/

Studley, J. (2018) *Indigenous Sacred Natural Sites and Spiritual Governance: The Legal Case for Juristic Personhood*. London: Routledge.

Vexler, V. (2020) *The Future of the Climate Crisis and Extinction Rebellion?* Available at: https://www.youtube.com/watch?v=hctKL9R2eUE